Log of a

TWENTIETH
CENTURY
COWBOY

Daniel G. Moore

Log of a TWENTIETH CENTURY COWBOY

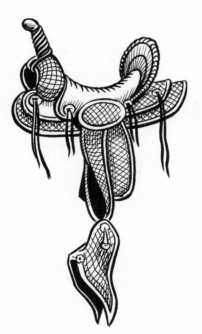

THE UNIVERSITY OF ARIZONA PRESS
TUCSON   ARIZONA

JH RP

Copyright © 1965

CONTENTS

c,1

Old Man Mills was an early day lawyer around the little cow town of Springer, New Mexico. The story I heard had it that he once fought a big suit for the Santa Fe Railroad and won, and had collected part of his fee in railroad land. This put him in a good position, in that grassy country, to operate a ranch. The story also had it that he railroaded a small rancher into the Pen at Santa Fe and had then taken over *his* spread, which lay in the Hell's Canyon of the Canadian River. So, when I went to work for him in the spring of 1915, a lively sixteen-year-old, he had this double-barreled ranch which he called the Diamond M.

Ranch headquarters were at the one-time Springer Hotel—a great, rambling two-story frame building with porches clear around both floors. It was covered with scrollwork and gingerbread, which made it quite a fancy hotel in its day. It was on the prairie east of the railroad tracks and had several outbuildings consisting of a barn, a blacksmith shop, a small printing office, a store, and a number of corrals.

Every day, for about a month, another young button and I had been herding some forty head of saddle horses out on the prairie. We ate in the dining room of the old hotel with several Mexican cowboys employed by the ranch, and were waited on by the Mexican women.

Old Lady Mills was a big old woman who always wore long, black dresses and a leather belt to which was attached a key-ring about the size of a dinner plate, holding all the keys to every door on the ranch. Lawyer Mills, as he was called around Springer, was away most of that first month, and I only got to see him a couple of days before he sent me down to his lower ranch in Hell's Canyon. He was a tall, bony old codger who wore a black hat, a black frock-tailed coat with a sort of green patina to it, and a celluloid collar with a gambler's black string tie. Under the right side tail of his coat was the bulge of an old six-shooter he always carried. The day he sent me to the lower ranch, he called me into his office and drew me a map showing how to find the place.

"Just stay on the wagon tracks that look the least traveled," he said, "and stay with the ones that bear to the right. About fifteen miles out you'll go around some sand hills, and about four miles past them you will come to the head of the road leading into the canyon. You'll have a heavy load, so ease down the canyon sort of slow. Once you get there, you take your orders from Les Wagoner, my foreman in the canyon, and tell him to go to the town of Mills (on the E.P. & S.W.) about the tenth, to pick up the mail. I'll have some instructions for him then."

The big Winona freight wagon, with six-inch wide tires, was loaded with supplies from the store; sacks of grain for the horses, blocks of cattle salt, kegs of horseshoe nails, horseshoes, and a general assortment of ranch gear. The Mexicans had hooked up the four-horse team, so all I had to do was climb up on the load, pick up the lines, kick off the brake, and be on my way.

The air was cool and crisp, the teams fresh, the beckoning mountains blue in the far distance, and life was good as I rode off across the prairies of Northern New Mexico on my way to new horizons and fresh adventure. The day went well until we reached the sand hills. Where the road skirted the dunes, the teams had to lean into their collars hard to pull through the soft yellow sand that was felly deep. Pulling around one bad dune, I let my lead team cut in too far, and before I realized it the wagon was stuck fast. The horses began seesawing and I let them blow awhile as I looked over the situation. On the next try they all hit the collar in unison, but the old Winona was still stuck, hard and fast.

"Well, here is where we start unloading," said I to the teams. In about an hour I had thrown off enough weight to enable the teams to drag the cramped right front wheel free of the sand dune and pull around on to harder ground.

Then came the hard part, carrying every sack of grain, every block of salt, and whatever else I had thrown off to where the wagon was now, and reloading it. My breakfast was long since gone and I was so hungry that I was weak as a sick cat. I pawed through the grocery supplies trying to find something to eat, but all I could find were four one-gallon cans of Karo syrup. With my knife I pried the lid from one can and drank the contents straight. After several swigs at the can I perked up enough to resume my trip.

At the beginning of Hell's Canyon road we bounced around over malapai boulders until we came to a man-made cut, barely wide enough for the wagon to pass through. The walls were solid rock, about ten feet high. Once through that, we were on a narrow track which sloped down pretty steeply along the canyon wall for another half mile. Then it crossed over at the bottom to the other side, where it squirmed and wiggled like a crippled snake along the rocky side of the canyon, always dropping downward past pine and pinon trees, and brushy ledges of shale, and malapai rock slides. I was riding the brakeblocks with all the weight I had to hold the wagon off the wheel team. In two or three places the road went around ridges of the mountainside that were so sloping on the outer edges that it seemed impossible that Old Winona could keep her balance without tipping over. But we *did* make it. About seven miles from the top we finally rolled to a stop at the Hell's Canyon Diamond M.

Les Wagoner's dog had been barking long before we came in sight of the ranch, so he was waiting to see who was coming, with interest. I was so tired and hungry I scarcely looked at anything that evening. All I wanted was to get the teams unharnessed, eat and go to bed. Les helped me with the horses, and after wolfing down a bait of beans and cold biscuits and coffee I rolled out my bed on a cot in a room next to the kitchen and promptly fell asleep. I don't think that I even turned over during that first night in the Canyon.

When Les awoke me the next morning, he already had our breakfast cooked. The sun was climbing down the red and yellow walls of the canyon, and I figured that he had stayed on the bed ground a lot longer than usual to let me catch up on rest a bit. While we were having breakfast, I gave him the Old Man's message about going to Mills for mail on the tenth.

After we had eaten and washed the dishes, Les showed me where to store the grain and salt blocks and where to stow the foodstuff in the cellar. He saddled a horse and took a boot-top of staples and his wire cutters, saying that he had a bit of rimrock fence to fix up the Canyon and would probably be back late in the afternoon.

After he rode off, I wandered about the house and outside to see what the spread looked like. The house was unusual for a ranch house. It was built of rough stone and was two stories high, with four rooms to each floor and a huge cellar underneath. The rooms had all been plastered at one time, but age and neglect had taken their toll of the plaster until only a few slabs of it were left on any of the ceilings. Most of the walls showed big spaces of bare lath. There were fireplace chimneys on both ends of the house and fireplaces in most of the rooms. Every room was large enough to hold a square dance in. I had never before seen such a house.

The cellar had piles of tin dishes and cups and old bone-handled knives, forks and spoons; enough to feed about forty people at once.

Les told me later that the place had been built as a rest station on the Santa Fe Trail in the early days. It had been abandoned after a great section of the west canyon wall had collapsed and buried the road forever, causing a new stage route to be laid out. This route passed far to the west, near the town of Wagon Mound.

North of the house was a big apple orchard. Many of the old trees were dead, yet quite a few were still bearing apples. Sitting out in the orchard was the cooker part of a copper still, a real big one. The belly part of it must have been seven feet across, and it stood about six feet high. It was all shot full of holes, and I wondered what drunken cowboy had emptied his .45 six shooter into it. Les couldn't tell me, as the holes had been made long before he came to the ranch. A couple of sows with a bunch of quarter-grown pigs, about twenty chickens, and Les's yellow mongrel dog seemed to size up the domestic livestock.

I got busy storing away the load I'd brought from Springer, and the shadows had begun climbing up the east wall of the canyon in the afternoon by the time I had finished. I was betting that Les would ride in hungry pretty soon, and if I had a meal cooked for us my stock would rise high with him.

Cooking was one thing I sure knew little about, but I figured that I would never learn any younger and got busy looking through the high old wooden cupboard in the kitchen for the makings of a feed. Why, I'll never know, but I settled on boiling some rice. I guess because I figured that it wouldn't take long. I picked the smallest of the roundup-size pots and pans that I could find and began my disaster. I figured that I might as well cook up a little extra so that we could fry some rice cakes for breakfast, and maybe have some rice and raisins (Bear Sign, the cowboys call it) the next day. However, I got a little generous with the rice. When it began boiling and expanding, I saw that there was going to be a little more than I had figured on, so I dipped out a slather of it into another pot. And still it continued to increase like the locust hordes of Egypt I'd read about when I was a little boy on the farm. Every dang pot and pan in the place was full of rice, and by the time it finished cooking it looked as though I would have to open the door for the overflow. I packed enough outside to fill the hog trough and the chicken pen tub, scattered some in a weed patch outside the orchard, and still had enough left to feed a Georgia camp meeting.

The biscuit-making project came next, and it wasn't any howling success either. I'd seen biscuits made lots of times, but my powers of observation must not have been in gear. Either I put in something I shouldn't have or I left out something that should have been added. They looked pretty fair when I put them into the oven, but somehow they squatted to rise but forgot to jump. They looked a *little* like biscuits. but that's about as far as the resemblance went. Flat doorknobs would have been about their nearest kinfolk. I carried the pan outside and threw them, one by one, down the hillside, hoping that they wouldn't hit a pig or a chicken and cripple it.

There were about five of Les's cold, day-before biscuits left in the cupboard. I popped them in the oven and sprinkled a little water over them, sort of like christening a baby.

"Nothing had better happen to these," I thought, "or my stay at the Diamond M may be short."

When Les rode in, unsaddled and turned his horse into the corral, I kept as quiet as a thief in a chicken house, wondering what he was going to say about my culinary "delights." After he had washed up and sat down at the table, I brought out my endeavors, poured his tin cup full of coffee (the only passable part of the feast), and sat down. Inwardly, I was quaking right down to my runover boot heels; but I need not have been because that cowboy was a true son of the West, a gent from where the clear water flows out from the head of the creek. He ate that conglomorate, which would have insulted a wolf's stomach, and smacked his lips like it was ambrosia. I'd never known a happier moment in my life. I wasn't fooling myself, and his act wasn't fooling me either; but after that, if he had asked me to eat a cow chip, I would have done it or died a-trying.

During the days that followed I rode with Les, learning the country, the cattle and horses, what needed doing, and how to do it. He took special pains to enlarge on my cooking education, and I sure soaked in everything he showed me.

The day came when he was to go to Mills for the mail. He had a married sister living there, and said that he would stay over a day or so with her. While he was in the Canyon with me I hadn't even thought about being lonesome; but once he was out of sight the solitude hit me hard. He had taken his dog with him, and the silence of that deep canyon where the sun only touched the bottom about three hours a day, was giving me a real shaky feeling.

That first day passed awfully slowly and I went to bed soon after dark. I had just dozed off to sleep when a loose slab of plaster fell smack dab on top of me. It was about four feet wide by seven feet long, and dropping from that high ceiling, it hit me quite a wallop. I wasn't hurt, but it sure scared hell out of me. At first I thought that the whole house had fallen down.

While I was having breakfast the next morning, I came up with one of my locoed ideas. Guess all kids have 'em. Les had a half-broken bronc in the pasture which he had been playing with whenever he had a little spare time. Yes, that's right I wrangled the trap and corralled the bronc along with some saddle horses. I cut them back outside, and hung my twine on that old mustang as he sashayed in a fog of dust around the corral fence. Taking a couple of dallies around the snubbing post in the center, I began easing up closer to him. He circled and set back on the rope, walling the whites of his eyes at me and whistling through his nose.

I didn't have much sense, but I was sure long on confidence. It never entered my head that the time to sap out a bronc was when someone else was with me, or at least in the same canyon, not alone with the nearest human being probably at least twenty-five miles away. But, as the Mexicans say, "El Senior Dios" was with me that day, or I wouldn't be here this day to tell about it. I got him saddled, got on, got bucked off, got on again, got bucked off again, and around and around again Willy. I lost count of how many times I mounted him and how many times he bucked me off. It must have been about a standoff between us when I finally quit playing bronc stomper, pulled off the saddle, and let him out the gate to go tell the other horses in the pasture what sort of "Johnny-Come-Lately" Hell's Canyon had come up with this time.

The next morning when I got out of bed, I had more aches and pains and sore places than old Job ever thought of having. Most of the day passed before I could make a sudden move without hollering "Ouch!" The day Les returned from Mills, most of the soreness had gone except across my stomach muscles. I was careful not to move too quickly and give myself away by groaning.

The letter Les received from Lawyer Mills instructed him to box up a load of apples and top off the load with all the dead tree wood he could haul out of the canyon. He was to drive it out to the top of the canyon road, and then let me bring it on to the ranch at Springer while he (Les) returned to the canyon ranch. I boxed apples while Les chopped down dead apple trees and trimmed off the branches.

When we were ready to start out, we found that one of the teams had gotten out of the river pasture and was long gone. Rather than waste a day or two hunting the lost team, Les decided that we could make do with a couple of the saddle horses that had been worked a few times in harness. We hooked up the old team as wheel horses, and the saddle horses as leaders. He put his saddle over the harness of the nigh lead horse, while I saddled the wheel horse behind his in like manner. Then we tied a spare horse behind the wagon for him to use on the ride back from the head of the canyon.

On the trip out, everything went along fine until we were about halfway to the top. There, one wheel slipped off a big boulder and dropped the rear axle on it, hanging us up. Les got the axe, climbed up the mountainside and cut a pry pole. We piled rocks under the axle and endeavored to pry Old Winona off that big rock which was solidly embedded in the road. However, just as we had the axle raised above the boulder, our pry rocks tipped over, and the whole rear end of the wagon dropped back to the ground on the very outer edge of the road, with one wheel practically hanging in space. It was impossible to back up because of the high boulder on which we had hung up; and if we tried to go ahead, the whole rearend of the wagon would slide off the road on the canyon side. Les thought that perhaps we could build up with rocks the crumbling outer edge of the road, thus bringing that hanging wheel back on solid ground. So, for an hour, we carried rocks and build a false outer edge to the road.

Then came the moment to try out our engineering experiment. Les climbed on the wagon with the wheel team lines, and I mounted the nigh leader with their set of lines in my hands. When Les gave the word, we squalled at the horses and they hit their collars. The wagon rolled forward, and just as we thought that we had won out, our rockwork slid out from under, the whole rearend of the wagon slewed sideways down the mountainside, and the wreck was on. The teams were clawing for a foothold, trying to regain the road as the wagon tipped over completely. The reach pole snapped, leaving the teams hooked only to the front wheels and axle. Les had fallen off the wagon as it turned over, and was scrambling to regain his footing on the steep hillside. The teams, with a frantic effort, were making some headway toward regaining the road. As they dragged the front half of the running gears along, one wheel ran over Les, breaking his arm. Just as the four horses finally made it to the top in a mad tangle of lines and traces, I jumped off my horse, grabbed all of the trailing lines, and stopped them in a sweating, frightened group on the road. Les's extra horse had broken loose and had run away earlier when the wagon turned over. Old Winona had hit a large jagged outcrop of rock about five hundred feet down and split into kindling wood. Apples and wood were scattered everywhere all down the mountainside.

Les, his face white and drawn with pain and holding his broken arm, staggered back to the roadway. While he sat on a rock all bent over, I got the teams untangled, then tied each horse separately to brush and trees nearby. Taking the harness off the leaders, I saddled them both, helped Les onto one, mounted the other and headed for Mills (the nearest town) leading Les's horse by the reins.

Poor old Les sure suffered during that ride. Even after we reached the top and hit good travelling country, he was groaning with pain. His arm hurt so that he couldn't stand a trot, so we just had to keep our horses in a fast running walk.

At Mills, I took Les to his sister's house, and after she had sent one of her kids for the doctor, headed back alone for the Canyon, where I drove the remaining team ahead of me to the ranch.

Now I had the entire Canyon to myself. What to do? I guessed that Lawyer Mills was going to throw a running fit when he found out that we had lost both his wagon and his apples. Being just a button of a kid, I'd never had to face up to any real responsibility alone before. There had always been someone older to tell me what to do, but this time I was really on my own. I sat by the fireplace late that night, trying to think out the best way to go about what I had to do. I guessed that Les would get word to the headquarters ranch within a few days. At least I hoped so, because I sure didn't want to be the one to break the news to Lawyer Mills.

I had plenty of chuck, and enough horse feed to last for months, but what I really needed was a "boss." As it happened, Lady Luck was with me for a change. About noon a couple of days later, a preacher and his son from some little settlement on top rode in, hunting for a mare and colt of theirs that had strayed. They ate a meal with me and I told them of my predicament. The preacher assured me that he would get word to Lawyer Mills just as soon as he got home. I slept better that night; and three days later Francisco Amayas, one of the Mexican cowboys from the Springer ranch, rode in leading his bed horse.

Was I glad to see him! He'd taught me a whole passel of roping throws on the Springer remuda, and I considered him pretty "big potatoes." He was a square-built, bow-legged Mexican about fifty years old. His face was pockmarked and he sported a black handle-bar mustache. However, he sure looked handsome to me that day.

Francisco and I grew to be good friends during the next few months in the Canyon. I learned a lot of cow sense from him and, I hope, some horse sense too. He had worked for the Diamond M for about seven years, and he told me lots of yarns about that particular outfit and others for which he had punched cattle. I gathered that he wasn't any admirer of Lawyer Mills. He called him Old *Culebra Ojos* (Snake Eyes); but as long as he hadn't had any serious run-ins and his wages came in regular each month, he was satisfied to stay on.

He told me his version of how Lawyer Mills had added his Canyon Ranch to his holdings. According to him, the lawyer had planted one of his own cows and calves in the Canyon, with the brands worked over. Then some of his cowboys "found" them there. A jury of cow-men, who considered the former owner a nester, wasted no time in finding him guilty, and a hard-nosed Judge sent the poor gazebo up to Santa Fe for a ten-year stretch, to ponder on the sins of being a nester in cow country. Francisco said that, just before he was led from the court-room, the nester shouted at Old Snake Eyes, "I'll be back to hang your rind on the fence some day!"

From that day on, Old Snake Eyes carried an old Colt .45 under his coat tail.

After his arm had healed some, Les came back to the ranch one day to collect his gear and a private horse he had left behind. He had decided to settle in Mills, and was getting married to the school teacher there. Then he was going to work for the E.P. & S.W. railroad. He asked me to come and see them some day, but I never did.

One day when Francisco and I had been working up the Canyon, I started back to the ranch early to do the chores and cook supper. Trotting along on a dusty cow trail, I just happened to notice a fairly fresh man's track in the dust. The man had crossed the Canyon and had gone into some brush on the other side. I trailed him for a little way, but soon lost the track in a rocky place. Later when Francisco came in I told him about the tracks, and we cogitated on who the man might be, and what he would be doing afoot in a country where everyone traveled horseback.

We forgot about him for a couple of days until we came into camp one evening and found that someone had been in the kitchen. Our visitor had taken some cold biscuits from the cupboard and packed off some canned milk, and a few other edible things. The next morning we cut sign around the house and found footprints in the wash back of the place. After that Francisco began carrying his short 30-30 on his saddle whenever he rode out.

We never got to see the hombre who laid down those tracks, but it wasn't long until we heard about him. Seems it was the nester again, but he didn't use very good judgment. He had escaped from the Pen at Santa Fe, worked his way back to his old stomping ground in the Canyon, having stolen a gun from some line camp on the way. When he discovered that we were camped at the old ranch, he had hidden out in the brush and watched us ride off, then worked the camp for enough chuck to keep him going for a few days. When he figured it safe, he quit the Canyon and made tracks for Springer, figuring, I guess, to salivate Old Snake Eyes for dealing him that ten-year stretch off the bottom of the deck.

When he reached the headquarters ranch, he found out from a Mexican kid that Old Snake Eyes was at Maxwell (another little town) and would be back next morning. So this nester hid himself in the hayloft of the barn, where he could watch the door of the ranch office, and waited. During the night he must have come up with the idea that it wouldn't do to kill Old Snake Eyes unless that gentleman realized *who* had done the job, and why. So he scribbled a note addressed to Melvin Mills saying:

"FOR VALUE RECEIVED, (FIVE YEARS, TWENTY-ONE DAYS AND THE LOSS OF MY RANCH), I GUARANTEE PAYMENT OF ONE 45-70 LEAD SLUG AND THE STINKING RIND OF THE BLACKEST-HEARTED SON-OF-A-BITCH IN NEW MEXICO."

He signed his full name at the bottom. When the ranch was asleep, he crawled over and fastened his note to the doorknob of the office with a piece of bailing wire, then returned to his hideout in the hayloft across the road.

About nine the next morning, Old Snake Eyes drove up in his buckboard, got out and walked over to unlock his office door. He spotted the note, read it, and dropped dead on the wooden doorstep. The Mexican stable boy who was taking the team and buckboard to the corrals saw him crumple and yelled for help. In no time the scene was swarming with Mexicans, but during the excitement the nester slipped out of the loft and made deep tracks away from there. However, that note he had left on the door cooked his goose. A posse ran him down in short order, and back to the penitentiary he went. The poor bastard didn't get to pull the trigger, although the results were just as good. Perhaps they were even better for him, because now he wouldn't hang for murder even though his note did scare Old Snake Eyes so bad that he had dropped dead of a heart attack.

Soon afterwards the will was probated and the Old Lady sold the ranches and moved to California. The new owners let most of the cowboys working on the ranches go, and I was among them.

Thus ended my youthful adventures on the Diamond M. Excitement, danger, new experiences, and responsibilities—I'd had them all. I wasn't being treated like a kid any more, whatever the future held for me. I had learned a lot among the cowboys of Northern New Mexico about "making a hand." That was the highest praise those taciturn, quiet men of the saddle could bestow on anyone, be he Governor or saddle tramp. It was no idle honor, lightly handed out. It had to be earned the hard way, by doing (or trying hard to do). Mistakes they could condone, but a quitter, never. I didn't leave with a great deal more money in my levis than I had arrived with, but something went with me that I had not brought to Springer: a little something that made me stand straighter and feel a warm spot beneath the second button of my jumper.

I was no longer a tenderfoot.

Late in the Fall of the following year, I was riding fence for the Pitchfork Ranch in the Texas Panhandle country. The Pitchfork was a big outfit in those days, and the barbed wire drift fences stretched for miles and miles across the open plains of Texas, sometimes crossing several county lines. For us line riders, life was real monotonous. One day was pretty much like another, except that some days the wind would blow harder than others. I can't recall any day that it didn't blow at all.

Like a number of English-owned outfits in Texas, the wages were low and the chuck poor. Good cowboys could be hired for twenty-five to thirty dollars a month and board, and the board wasn't anything to write home about. Old John Spain, the foreman, wasn't a bad *Tehana* himself, but if one of us line riders gave him a list of chuck we needed for our camp he had to have it O.K.'d by the ranch manager. Now this manager was a Company man and an Englishman himself, down to the last cup of tea. So, if we sent for a can of peaches to satisfy a craving for sweets, caused by a steady diet of beans, corn, salt pork and biscuits, the best we could hope to get was maybe a half-gallon can of dark Karo corn syrup. And many times we had to settle for a few cans of tomatoes instead.

There were a few little whistle-stop cow towns strung along the railroad like beads on an Indian necklace, none of them large enough to raise Hell with a barrel of whiskey, and so, as I said, life was thoroughly monotonous.

One day when the round-up crews were combing the breaks, gathering the fall shipment, Old John Spain came by my line camp to ask me if I would like to go through on the railroad with a shipment of a trainload of Pitchfork steers destined for Strong City, Kansas. I hemmed and hawed a minute, not wanting to seem too eager in case they'd think that maybe they ought to cut my pay a little. Finally I agreed to go. John said that he would be back in a couple of days with another line rider to take my place. Right away the days grew longer, the wind blew harder, and that stretch of fence I was responsible for seemed to stretch clear to Timbuktu.

When John came for me I felt sorry for the old boy we left standing in the doorway watching us drive off in the old T-Model Ford. That evening about dusk, at the cattle pens on the rail siding, the cowboys finished loading the last car of steers, put in the bull board, slid the car door shut, and fastened the door latch with its steel pin.

John and I had already been to the depot where he signed me onto the contract with the railroad to go through with the steers to Strong City. Carrying my wooden prod pole and a flour sack containing Bull Durham, a couple of pairs of socks and a few other belongings, I walked back to the caboose and climbed aboard. In a little while the engineer gave the highball sign with his whistle. After a few tooth-jarring jerks, and a couple of false starts, we began rolling out onto the main line.

"That God-damned grease ball son-of-a-bitching hog head couldn't run his aunt's sewing machine without tearing it to pieces!" swore the head brakeman with his head out the caboose window.

Once clear of the switch at the end of the siding, the rear brakeman swung his lantern, got an answering highball from the engineer, and we were on our way.

Rattling along over the rail joints, the caboose lights lit, and a coal fire giving out a cheerful glow through the sides of the pot-bellied stove, I felt on top of the world once more. After a little while the conductor checked my contract, entered the data in his road and division books, signed the contract, and handed it back to me.

"About a two-hour run now before we stop long enough for you to look at your cattle," he informed me. "Stretch out on this bunk if you want to. We'll wake you as we come into the yards at Wichita Falls."

I stretched out on the bunk all right, but was much too excited to fall asleep — yet.

Division by division we progressed on northward, and the weather got colder by degrees. We reached Strong City around three o'clock one cold, frosty morning several days later. Leaving the cattle cars on the siding by the pens, a switch engine took the caboose away, and the road engine went to the round house. Not a soul was in sight, and I was about frozen, so when a switch engine came by I rode it up into the main freight yards. The town was dark, but nearby at the roundhouse two big road engines were standing outside, fired up for their run. I climbed up in the cab of one to get warm. Leaning against the boiler, I managed to keep fairly warm until daylight. When the hostler came out to move the engine, I climbed down stiff and hungry, and began looking for a place to get some coffee. Across the tracks I found a small restaurant patronized by the railroad men, and got outside of a big plate of ham and eggs and coffee. I was told that my cattle would be unloaded about seven.

I stayed inside where it was warm as long as I could, then began walking back toward the cattle pens. This country seemed even colder than Texas, if that was possible. Soon some railroad men began unloading the cattle, and three or four old yarn sock farmers rode up on plow horses, all bundled up in overcoats and caps with ear flaps tied under their chins. Most of the steers were to stay at Strong City for other buyers, and the mounted farmers had come to get four carloads to deliver to a farm somewhere off south. The old farmer in charge wanted me to help them drive the cattle to his place. I agreed, and he rustled up a work horse from somewhere for me to ride.

Four miles south we passed through the little town of Cotton-wood Falls, and on to another named Banner. A few miles outside of Banner we reached the farm where the steers were to be fed out before being shipped to Kansas City, their final destination on this earth. The owner hired me to feed, and showed me what to do. For the next two months I ground corn, mixed silage, molasses and bran, and fed the steers.

Around Christmas the cattle went to Kansas City, and once more I was at loose ends. I hadn't seen my mother in years, so I purchased a ticket to Minneapolis, Minnesota, where she now lived, and paid her a visit. My stepfather worked in the passenger ticket office of the Great Northern Railroad, and they lived in an apartment house.

It only took me a little over a week of loafing there to get the itch to move on. I hung around the stockyards of South St. Paul across the river until I got a chance to ship out with a load of feeder cattle, to Lemon, South Dakota. Old man Lemon (for whom the town was named) was a banker, and as soon as we arrived he resold the cattle to a Mr. Delaney, owner of a ranch thirty miles south, across the Bad Lands. I helped drive the cattle that thirty miles, and went to work for Delaney.

His family—a wife, two boys and two girls—were real nice folks and I got along fine with them all. But their way of working stock was sure different from any I had ever seen before. They had a lot of big husky old calves to brand out and their only corral was a big lot, the north and west sides a snow shed, and the other two sides solid board fence about seven feet high.

We corralled the calves and their mothers in the lot, and the boys built a branding fire outside the gate and put their irons in to heat. Mr. Delaney rode his horse into the corral and handed his rope to one of his sons, who spread out a great big sort of a Mother Hubbard loop on the ground, then brought one part of it up against the board fence and draped it over a big spike nail driven into the wood. Then Mr. Delaney began milling the cattle around, and when a big calf stepped into the loop one of the boys jerked up the slack. Wherever it caught seemed to be all right; around the neck, belly, foot, or any old place. Then the boy ran over and handed his dad the end of the rope. With a wrap or two around the saddle horn he would head for the gate, with the calf bucking and bawling. One of us opened the gate to let him out, and then we had to flank the calf down, hold and brand him, then turn him loose. Many times the cattle would knock the rope off the nail without getting caught, or else a cow would get in the loop instead of a calf. I stood it as long as I could without saying anything, but at last I had to pop off.

"Seems to me it would go a lot quicker just to rope them old calves and drag 'em out to the fire and forget about trying to snare 'em with that nail."

"We've tried that before," Mr. Delaney said, "and we didn't make much headway."

"I'm not trying to brag, but I know we can beat this if you'll lend me your horse," I told him. I thought maybe he'd get mad, but he was agreeable and stepped down and handed me the reins. I just sat still in the center of the lot and dabbed a small loop on any old calf that showed his head, and went to the fire with him on a lope. It was a cold day, but I had those old boys sweating mighty quick, and I'd be there on my horse with a calf ready while they were still working on the one I had brought in just before.

We went through that bunch of calves in short order, and the Delaneys acted like they'd never seen anything like that before, unless it was in a circus.

One of the girls was about seventeen, and every once in a while a half breed Mexican cowboy working on a ranch south of theirs would ride over to see her. He was sort of a Fancy Dan, with a silver-mounted saddle, concho-decorated leather vest, and brocaded neckerchief. He claimed his father owned a big horse ranch some place in Wyoming. On my birthday in early March the whole family went off to town for the day, leaving me at the ranch. This breed,

Ortiga, rode in that day to see the girl, found her gone, so stayed to chew the rag with me for a while. I didn't have anything that needed doing right away, so hit on an idea to celebrate my birthday while I had some help.

During the winter before, it seems, a little travelling Wild West Show had found itself broke and stranded in Lemon. The owners had auctioned off their bucking horses and Delaney had bid in three or four of them. After they got them back to the ranch, they found none of the boys could ride them, so the horses had been running loose in a pasture ever since. My idea was to corral them and top off a few for some excitement and fun. Birthdays only come once a year, after all. Ortiga helped me saddle and mount and get the horses headed down a long open draw. When they went to bucking, he kept them headed away from the fences for me. Whenever one quit bucking, I'd ride him back to the corral and change to another one. The third one, a big blue roan, almost "slipped his pack" once. He practically had me bucked off and I was away off on one side of him trying to get straightened up in the saddle when Ortiga ran into him with his horse and knocked his head up, saving my bacon. When the Delaneys came home I never told them what had happened, and if any of the boys noticed the sweat marks on the horses in the pasture, they never mentioned it.

April came and the urge to travel, so I drew my wages and went into Lemon. There I ran into Ortiga on a spree. He'd been in town a couple of days and was pretty well organized. We patronized many of the bars and by night began to regard ourselves as a couple of real "curly wolves". Nothing would have changed our opinion of ourselves if Ortiga hadn't decided it would be great fun to shoot out all the lights in the Lemon Hotel bar. He did, and wound up *in durance vile* in Lemon's chicken-coop-sized jail.

Since Lemon took such a dim view of celebrating cow servants, I shook the dust of their fair city off my boots and took the train to Miles City, Montana. It was April, but the weather was colder than a pawn broker's smile. After fortifying myself against the cold a little, I began looking for a job. A bartender suggested I try Fort Keough, west of town. He said they were always looking for bronc riders at the Army remount station. I took a taxi out and made my bid, and danged if they didn't hire me right off.

That part of Montana was full of big horse ranches, and the

French and English governments had buyers in Miles City, purchasing horses for their armies and shipping them overseas as fast as they could. At Fort Keough our government had thousands of horses out on the reservation, and buyers were out picking up more throughout the Northwestern states. Both cavalry and artillery types were being brought in. Keough was an old cavalry post in the days when our troops were trying to make hash out of the Sioux and other plains tribes, and the Indians considered very "chic" a bridle or saddle decorated with white man scalps. Now, the Fort was used to take the rough edges off a lot of big horses that had other ideas in the matter.

There was a bunch of pretty salty bronc stompers there, like Yakima Canutt, Denver Sherman, Yellowstone Kid, Sharky the Bull Rider, Onay (a flathead Indian), Lee Caldwell, and too many others to mention. I was away out of my class in such company, but before I left Keough I had had many a workout on the hurricane deck of a lot of rough horses. Sunday wasn't a real working day, so a bunch of us would usually saddle up one of our roughest mounts and head for the Miles City Fair Grounds. We would draw lots and then buck our horses out of the chutes there to see who could make the wildest ride and still qualify without pulling leather. We always had a good audience of townspeople who came out every Sunday to see our free show.

I rode in the Number Two stable at Keough, where the raw cavalry horses were started off, for quite a while. Then Sergeant Griffin, in charge of the artillery stables, talked me into coming over to him. Those were big horses and rough to ride. I've had them pop my head like a coffee pot lid flying open; and when one of those big broncs hit the ground bucking, he'd shake the earth and jar your eye teeth. After we had them under saddle for a while we put them on caissons in harness — artillery style —, with a man riding each nigh horse and driving the other one, and one man riding the caisson to set brakes. Some of the wrecks we had would make a western movie look tame. I figured myself lucky to get off with only a broken nose and two broken collar bones when I parted company with Fort Keough.

I turned down a couple of bids, one to go up on the reservation with a flathead Indian, the other to go to Elko, Nevada, to put up hay. Instead I bogied off down to Nebraska and then over to Wyoming to the town of Guernsey. I heard of a construction job on a dam and reclamation project at Fort Laramie, so thought I'd give that a try.

When I stepped from the train at Fort Laramie, it had all the appearance of a movie set depicting a gold strike boom town. The streets were lined with tents and newly erected tar paper shacks, with big signs across the front advertising which was what. Hungry, I entered one big tent with a sign proclaiming "Wyoming Cafe." It contained a table of pine boards laid across sawhorses with rough pine benches on either side to sit on, a wood cook stove with the stovepipe stuck up through a hole in the tent, boxes and pots and pans scattered on the floor real fancy. A couple of greasy boiled potatoes, fried salt pork, bread, and flour gravy on a tin plate, and a tin cup full of weak coffee cost two dollars. Supper was the same, except for the fact that a couple of spoonsfull of cooked dried peaches to top off the meal brought the price up to two fifty.

Down the dirt street was about the largest building in the town, the sign proclaiming it to be "The Hotel De-Bill," in bold lettering. Thrown together of black tar paper and two-by-four lumber, it was just one big, dark enclosure with no floor but the mother earth. Crowded as close together as possible were several old iron bedsteads, (no two alike), a few wooden boxes on which were dirty wash bowls and a pitcher of water. The bedding was foul, and three men slept together on each double bed. The price, two dollars per head. Since the construction work went on around the clock, the beds were occupied steadily. When one man got up to go on night shift, another coming off would climb in bed to take his place. None of the beds had a chance to cool off. The snores and snorts from the sleepers in that room were real musical.

About every fifth tent on the street contained a saloon, and in the alleys behind were a lot of crib tents and gambling tents. There were sure a lot of ways of separating a worker from his money, and they used them all. I lasted out three pay days, skinning a mule team on a fresno, before I left that gentle den of thieves.

Three   The Wild West Division

Along about that time, Uncle Sam and a stiff-necked squarehead in Europe called Kaiser Wilhelm had been thumbing their noses at one another too long for either one to back down without looking as though he had a yellow streak down his back. A real set-to pretty soon seemed inevitable, and recruiting stations were beating the bushes for volunteers "honin'" to let a little fresh air through some of the Kaiser's bully boys. I got sort of swept up with the idea myself, and before I got around to changing my mind a real fast-talking sergeant had my signature on the dotted line. I was prodded, punched and examined like a prize show-bull, sworn into Uncle Sam's Army as a "Lodge Member in Good Standing," and was on my way to the recruit barracks at Fort Logan, Colorado.

During my ranching days I had helped dip a lot of scaly cattle and lousy horses, but I never thought then I'd be the "dipee" some day. At Logan they fumigated us, sheared us, shot us full of bug killers, and vaccinated us for everything they could think of. My arms and butt had so many punctures I looked like I had come out second best with a horde of Arkansas mosquitos. I washed enough dishes on K.P. the first two weeks at Logan to feed a circus with, including the elephants. We drilled, learned our general orders, and special orders, backwards and forwards, did calisthenics, ran until our tongues hung out like a red necktie, and had our pictures taken, holding our rifles real fierce-like, to send home to the folks to be Ohed and Ahed over, and "don't Johnny look handsome in his uniform, Aunt Mary?"

Came the day we were *real* soldiers, (all of two months' worth). Rumors (the old Army grapevine) worked overtime as to where and when we were to be sent out. One day we were to be shipped to California, the next to New York State. Not until we were on the troop train and somewhere in New Mexico were we enlightened that we were headed for Yuma, Arizona, assigned to the third battalion of the 14th U.S. Infantry stationed there to keep Pancho Villa and his Yaquis on their own side of the fence awhile.

One boy who had enlisted with me and passed through Logan's gentle ministrations alongside of me got sick on the train. The farther we went the worse he became, and long before we got across Arizona he was past knowing or caring where he was. At Yuma they put him in the hospital tent right away, dying of spinal meningitis. I went around to see him a couple of times and sat by his cot fanning flies from his face, but that poor cowboy never even knew I was there. He crossed the Great Divide one night, and the company bugles blew taps over a grave on the banks of the muddy Colorado River in a land he never even got to see. Poor lad, so young, strong and full of hopes and plans a week ago.

I was assigned to Company K, commanded by Captain Little, a West Point graduate. Our Colonel (soon to retire) looked like an older brother of General Robert E. Lee with his white goatee and long hair. This outfit, being regular Army, still had men who had fought in the Boxer Rebellion before the gates of Peking, and in the Philippines against Aquinaldo's head hunters.

At ten-day intervals one company of us would take over at Andrade, on the border of Mexico, for guard duty. Villa had no troops stationed permanently across from us, but about once a week a mounted patrol of his would ride east, or west, and wave at us or stop to banter insults a moment. His patrol consisted of about forty men, and they were a rag-tag Army if ever I saw one. Their arms were carbines, Winchesters, shot guns, twenty-two single shots, pistols, and swords. Most of the men carried riatas on their saddles. Their mounts were mostly scrubby mustangs, mules, and even burros. Hats, caps, and even sailor blouses were worn as uniforms, and about thirty out of the forty were captains or lieutenants — more chiefs than Indians.

Villa didn't have any of our men, but we had several of his in our barbed-wire guard house at the Yuma Camp. I stood guard duty on them several times, and they were convinced Pancho would make a raid across the line to liberate them, but he never tried it. Once or twice some jittery recruit sentry would shoot a couple of holes through a saguaro cactus at night, sure that it was a Mexican slipping up on him, and cause an alarm in camp until the guard found out the source.

When not on guard duty at Andrade the battalion made many practice marches with full packs. Colonel Wilson (old Robert E. Lee) led the march, mounted. Those were about the toughest slog-fests I ever made, even to the mud of France in 1918. Carrying a seventy-pound pack through the desert under a sun that could cook the soles of your feet through G.I. shoes was no picnic.

One evening at Guard Mount, while changing guards in front of the camp's barbed wire stockade, a recruit dropped his rifle as he slung it up to the port position. Colonel Wilson, it so happened, was watching. As the red-faced recruit stepped out of ranks to pick up his rifle, Colonel Wilson descended on him like a buzzard on a dead rabbit. His white goatee fairly snapped with indignation as he roared:

"Young man if I *ever* see you do that again I'll have you put in captivity. By God I will, Sir."

That scared the recruit so he almost dropped his rifle again.

The old territorial prison was located on a bluff on the bank of the Colorado River, across town from our camp. Solid adobe walls surrounded it and the cells were caves dug out of the hillside, with crossed flat steel bars on the doors. A Mexican family was living in one of the cells. It was some home. The old wooden guard towers still stood around the walls. Out back near the riverbank was the graveyard. Many of the old wooden headboards had fallen, and rotted away with time. Others stood at crazy angles, soon to go like the others. The names and numbers of the convicts buried there were painted on the boards, and the sun and sandstorms had cut some of the wood away from the paint, leaving the names and numbers raised from the wood. Many of the names were Chinese, Indian, and Mexican, with a smattering of white men's names among them. Serving a sentence inside those adobe walls must have been pure hell in the summer, with the sun beating down at around one hundred and twenty degrees day after day, and hordes of mosquitos from the river banks at night. No wonder the prison graveyard was well populated!

Yuma Indians came to our camp every few days selling baskets and horsehair trinkets they had made. The men wore their hair long, hanging down their backs in a multitude of slender braids. They walked around on the burning-hot ground barefooted, never seeming to feel the heat through the soles of their feet. One morning one of them squatted down on the bank of the river, drinking water from his cupped hands. All he wore was his pants. A soldier standing by a chest that had just been filled by the ice wagon from town was sucking on a piece of ice. Temptation got the better of him and he touched that Indian on his bare back with it. That Yuman bullfrogged right into the river headfirst. When he climbed out, mad as a hornet, all he saw was a few innocent looking soldiers in a crap game for milk tickets. He stalked off, his back more expressive than words. I never saw him in our camp again.

About then the old grapevine began working overtime once more. This time the outfit was to be sent to Schofield Barracks at Honolulu, T. H., according to one rumor. Another said we were headed for Fort George Wright at Spokane, Washington. As usual, none were correct. Entrained one night, our troop train carried us west into California, then northward up the coast to Vancouver, Washington, just across the Columbia River from Portland, Oregon. After camp life at Yuma, Vancouver barracks looked mighty good to us. No sand storms, mosquitos, or one hundred twenty degree heat. The barracks were nice and clean, with real iron cots, and even sheets to sleep between. There were dress blue uniforms for parades and guard mounts, and a whole big town full of pretty girls to flirt with. This was the life. The fly in the ointment for me was that it didn't last very long.

Shortly came an order from the War Department with instructions to divide our company. One battalion of the 14th infantry had been stationed in Alaska for years. In small detachments they were scattered from Point Barrow and Tanana in· the Arctic Circle to Valdez and Nome on the coast. Now, through losses of personnel by deaths and expiration of enlistments, they were down to only skeleton strength; hence the replacement orders from the War Department. Another detachment from our company was to go to the Orient to take over legation guard duty from a marine unit long overdue to return to the states.

On the bulletin board one morning I found my name as a supernumerary on the Alaskan detail. If anyone dropped out because of sickness I would be sent in his place. I kept my fingers crossed the three days remaining before they left, hoping they'd all stay healthy, for I didn't want any part of Alaska. Once they were away I volunteered for the Orient assignment and was accepted. By then I had made buck sergeant, three grades above my rank of Yuma days. After a whole new set of vaccinations and innoculations of various types, twenty-eight of us were ready to leave the States.

At San Francisco we boarded the transport ship "General Sherman," a tub about as old as its namesake. She wallowed along through the Pacific just about as fast as I could have walked. She was an old coal burner, and at Guam, Wake, and Honolulu she had to lay over to be coaled up. From there on we hit bad weather and it was a Mexican standoff which of us were the most seasick. It would have been a *pleasure* to have died and been buried at sea. We scraped by the side of one big typhoon and once saw seven waterspouts at one time off the port side. After we got over our *mal de mer* a little everyone was afflicted with the appetite of a horse. And through some fluke, that was when the ship's stores were practically depleted. Bread from the ship's bakery and oranges were all we ate until we hit the coaling station at Nagasaki, Japan. We watched the little Japanese women trotting up the gangplanks each with a big sack of coal on her back as the bunkers were being filled.

We had two days shore leave there to look over the town. Right away some of us hit a tattoo parlor and had some fancy work embossed on our skins as mementos of Japan.

At Hong Kong, China, we left the transport and took the Mukden railroad about six hundred miles north to Tientsin, our destination. Everything about this country was alien to our eyes: the people, the houses, and even the horses. They were little, shaggy animals about the size of a big Shetland, carrying great loads or pulling big wooden-wheeled carts piled high with various assortments of cargo. Sometimes two or three people pushed the carts from behind. Long caravans of hairy camels passed, each with a woven wicker basket hung from a harness beneath his tail to catch its manure for fertilizer. These people didn't believe in wasting anything, even if they did *do* everything the hard way. This was cold country, where every yellow silt hillside was honeycombed with man-made caves, used as homes, and villages of mud houses, each with a big mud oven to cook in. The whole family slept on the oven tops. Baggy cotton quilted clothes and caps with ear flaps were the usual dress. There was no variety or color such as we were used to seeing.

The French and English also maintained legations at Tientsin and each had its representative guards. Some enterprising Eurasian had set up a bowling alley not far from our quarters, with three alleys, — two regular, one duck pins. I never saw any Chinese playing the game. They preferred to play the lotteries and fantan games that ran night and day in big gambling houses. However, the Frogs, Limeys and ourselves gave the alleys a big play most of the time. One drunk Frenchman stabbed a British guard with a bayonet in a hot argument at the duck pin alley one night. So the whole joint was put out of bounds for us all. After that, poker, blackjack (the old Army game), and craps comprised most of our recreation.

We were just getting settled in when another order came through to replace us with marines once more. About two weeks later we were again on our way back to the states, this time travelling in better style on the S.S. President McKinley, a Dollar Line passenger ship returning to San Francisco from a world tour. From the City of the Golden Gate we transferred to a coastwise vessel that delivered us at Tacoma, Washington, where we were assigned to the Ninety-First Division at Camp Lewis.

Camp Lewis was a sprawling cantonment, seventeen miles south of Tacoma. By now, the Selective Service Act had been in effect for some time, and Camp Lewis was a beehive of activity. A nucleus of regular army personnel had the responsibility of whipping a whole wartime strength division into shape as a fighting unit in a damn short time.

Although the Ninety-First was a Western outfit, first formed with men from Washington, Oregon, Montana, Idaho, Wyoming, and Utah, by the time I arrived it had begun to fill up with draftees shipped in daily from Wisconsin, Michigan, and New York. The contrast was something to behold. Among the earlier group were loggers, miners, and a lot of cowboys, mostly big strapping men — real Westerners who fit right in with the Ninety-First Division's name, "Wild West Division." Among the midwest draftees were a lot of dairy farmers and factory workers, many of whom were Bohemian and who spoke broken English. But the cream of the crop was the New York contingent — East Side Italians and every nationality imaginable, most of whom spoke a language even their drill sergeants couldn't decipher. They were, on the whole, little, short, flat-chested specimens who had never known a lung full of fresh air before in their lives. It was a man-sized job to teach them the art of soldiering. Actually I had to teach a lot of them the wigwag semaphore system first, before I could get over to them what they were to do. Night schools in English were conducted, and were a *must* for that group. I'll bet the teachers had a worse time than we drill sergeants did, if that was possible. G.I. issue clothing and uniforms were never known for any degree of fit, but on those little runty guys they fit like a tent. The baggy clothes I had seen the Chinese wear at Tientsin looked like a Brooks Brothers ad compared to my company when it turned out for drill. The coat tails came down behind their knees, and there was room enough in the seat of the pants to hold a Sunday school picnic in. And the English Enfield rifles (now issue in our army) were about as high as the soldiers. It was sure amusing to see those little duck-legged guys trying to take long enough strides to wheel into line along with the rest of the platoon or company when they were on the outer end of same. They practically had to run to catch up. It sure looked like Uncle Sam had already scraped the bottom of the barrel when he gathered in that lot of men. I drilled the hell out of them by day and worried about them at night, wondering how long we had before entering the donnybrook over there. I sure hoped they'd learn to shoot straight and not have to face any big tough "Boche" in hand-to-hand bayonet combat.

When he thought the signs were right, the commanding general of the Division ordered the whole kaboodle on a two-day bivouac. Infantry men, artillery men, engineers, signal corps men, medical men, military policemen, transports, bandsmen, mounted headquarters companies, ordnance, and quartermaster corpsmen — all were ordered out. Field rations were issued even though the field kitchens of each outfit took part in the maneuvers. This was a good precaution too, as it turned out. Scouts led the route under a grey leaden sky, at daybreak. There were thousands of foot soldiers with full field packs. The old timers, with corks in the muzzles of their rifles to keep the rain out, slogged through the mud and rain through forests of fir, spruce and pine, wet as a sponge.

I guess as a whole it could have been worse, as communications seemed fouled up most of the time, and several outfits got themselves lost in the timber. At night we slept in pup tents, and it was pitiful how many men didn't know a thing about camping. At noon rest periods each squad had to cook rations carried in their packs, and a lot of the men didn't even know how to start a fire, let alone *cook* anything. But at that, the Division made it back to camp without any casualties, which was the eighth wonder of the world.

Two months later we got our traveling orders. The division was to jump the Pond to join the fracas in France. Permission was granted for several units to put on a big division show for the town folk, who had already grown rich off the soldiers of the 91st. The cowboys in the outfit gathered every old outlaw horse in the country and put on a rodeo, and the best-drilled infantry company came up with a real snappy Butts Manuel drill team that was something to behold. The engineers built bridges in jig time, the wagon trains and transport outfits wheeled across them just before they were blown to smithereens, and the hospital corpsmen rescued soldiers wounded in the big sham battle and toted them off on stretchers, bleeding profusely (with ketchup). The bronc riders entered the arena on an old stagecoach, dressed in top hats and tails over their boots and spurs. When the stage reached the chutes, out fell the riders, and each climbed on a ready-saddled bronc and turned him out, spurring high and handsome and yelling "Powder River!" This was the war cry that later chilled many a Kraut's blood when we met them on the battlefields of France. It looked like everyone from the whole country had come to watch our going away show, and they gave us a big hand all right.

Packing up a whole division to go overseas was some job, believe me. Every soldier had about as much junk of his own as he had Government Issue. Every outfit had enough mascots to make up an animal show. There were dogs and cats by the hundreds, monkeys, parrots, bears, lion cubs, even snakes. Our troop trains were traveling menageries until we stopped for water at a little Montana town. There the M.P.'s came through the train and threw off all the livestock. I never knew what happened on the trains ahead of or behind us, but I'll bet there was big excitement the next morning in the town our animals were left in.

At every stop, in spite of the M.P.'s, some few soldiers managed to get on the ground long enough to goose all the girls in sight, hop back on the train with a bottle or two, or else throw beer and whiskey to the guys leaning out the windows. Crap games and blackjack in the aisles never stopped day or night and the trainmen had a tough time getting through the cars because of the players. Some fights developed but were soon stopped.

We crossed the Northwest and entered Canada some place, then came back onto U.S. soil, journeying on and on towards the east coast. There, one night, we boarded our transport on our way to the "Big Razzle Dazzle" across the sea.

Forty-five years have not dimmed the memory of my war, nor of its horrors and misery. The period from July 23rd, 1918, when the Ninety-First first set foot on French soil, to November 11th when the guns were finally silenced, was an eternity to me. I could write a whole book on those four months but will give only a few statistics, then go on to more pleasant things. From the Meuse-Argonne, our first battle, to about eight kilometers east of the Scheldt River beyond

Bouche Saint Blaise, our last, the division fought seventeen major battles on six sectors with a loss of 1,454 dead and 4,654 wounded, captured 2,412 prisoners and received 12,530 replacements.

After the Armistice, King Albert, Queen Elizabeth and Prince Leopold of Belgium decorated our pine tree colors with the Legion of Honor at Brussels. Later, along with the Fourth Division (the ivy leaf), we occupied the Moselle and Rhine Valleys. The Fourth stayed on as an Army of Occupation while we of the Ninety-First were sent back to Camp Grant, Illinois, one of the big separation centers for draftees. There, day after day, the boys stood in long lines, inching ahead toward the examining doctors, to be processed out of the army after being punched, probed and tested for war wounds or gassed lungs.

As many of my buddies went on their way, a feeling of lonesomeness came to me, who had never felt lonesome before. I was nervous and irritable, and the burns on my hand, suffered when I had wrested the red hot barrel of a Browning light automatic rifle from the hands of a dead buddy, to mop up a trench of Krauts with, kept bothering me. I avoided the doctors like the plague for fear they would peg me as shell shocked and send me off to the Army Hospital at Ft. Des Moines, Iowa. Time hung heavy on my hands, and when I read a bulletin asking for a few volunteers to transfer to the United States Disciplinary Barracks at Ft. Leavenworth, Kansas, I answered the call.

A year later my service to the colors was up and I took my discharge. The blue skies and shining mountains of the great northwest beckoned and I set out. Montana never looked more beautiful. I was in seventh heaven when I forked my first bronc and went galloping across the sage brush flats once more, smelling the sweet scent of the prairie and looking out towards the snow covered peaks of the great Rocky Mountains in the distance. But still something was lacking and I wasn't satisfied to stay in one place for long. First I quit a good job near Bridger with a mighty fine old cow man who tried hard to talk me into staying with him. Next I took a little branchline train to Cody, Wyoming, where I loafed for a few days until a fellow hired me to trail thirty head of saddle horses inland to a dude ranch he was opening up near Cooke City. I was tempted to stay with him, but all he had for me to do was build some stake and rider fence and I was kind of lonesome to play around with some bronc horses again. So I rode the Cooke City mail stage through Yellowstone Park to Gardiner, Montana, where I caught a train to Whitehall, a little cow town on the Great Northern Railroad. There I made a deal with a rancher to break a few young horses and to take on some others belonging to neighboring ranchers and farmers, using his corrals and pastures while I broke them.

That summer, to teach my string of young horses something about working cattle, I went along on a couple of trail drives across the mountains to the big copper mining town of Butte where we delivered some beef cattle. Later, I delivered the horses back to the ranches and farms that owned them. Tom Jackman, the owner of the ranch at Whitehall where I had been staying, was well pleased with the job I had done on his horses and paid me a bonus of five dollars a head over our agreed price. I felt pretty rich now, having a fairly good stake after collecting the money I had coming all around.

One Saturday I went along with Tom to a little town on the Milwaukee Railroad to help him load some farming machinery at the freight depot onto his wagon. Just as we were about to leave with our load, I spotted the only saloon in town, a typical false front with a high board porch. It looked so inviting that I talked Tom into stopping long enough to partake of a couple of drams of tarantula juice with me before returning to Whitehall.

The bartender was a big beefy dutchman who owned the place, and after our first couple of drinks he set up two more on the house. Those did such a good job of removing the alkali dust from my throat that I declined to leave when Tom was ready to go, so he reluctantly left me and went on home. The array of varicolored bottles on the back bar held a sort of fascination for me as to the probable taste and aroma each might have to offer, so I began to sample them systematically, asking a couple of friendly-acting gents who were setting up a poker table to back up my opinions. As the afternoon progressed I seemed to have met quite a few representatives of the town's male population as they dropped in, and remarked to myself what a fine, friendly place this would be to settle down in.

I guess it was the whistle on a through train that awoke me from my downy couch on the hard board floor on the sidewalk of the now locked and deserted saloon. My mouth tasted like an owl's nest and my head felt as though it had been kicked by a Missouri mule. All the pockets of my levis were hanging outside as though they had just come from a steam laundry. I had been rolled of my money, my pocket knife and even my Bull Durham tobacco.

"Well, cowboy, you shure did cut a rusty caper this time, didn't you?" I remarked to myself. "What in hell you gonna do now?"

While in Butte on a beef drive I had heard that the copper mines were always in need of miners and muckers and that anyone with a strong back and a weak mind could earn four dollars and a half for an eight hour shift. Why not try it a fall? I sure had the right kind of a mind. And there was nothing wrong with my back. So, when a long freight train stopped to take on water at the foot of the divide, I climbed aboard and was on my way.

Butte was booming, with nearly eight thousand miners working the scores of mines on the hill, East Butte and Mederville. Anyone who even looked as though he wanted work could get a stake in Butte. When I explained my financial predicament to the owner of the Walker Bar on East Park Street, he reached in the till and gave me a twenty-dollar bill, told me of a good boarding house and the location of the employment office of the Granite Mountain shaft. By ten o'clock the following morning I was hired as a mucker and told to report on the four o'clock shift at the Speculator shaft. I went to work on the thirty-six hundred level of the deepest mine on the hill.

The old miners I worked with knew that I was a greenhorn at mining and they took good care of me, showing me how to do things the easiest and best way. I was just beginning to think I was a pretty fair miner when a general strike closed almost all the mines in the town, so I moved on to the silver-lead mines in the Coeur d'Alene district of Idaho at Burke. There I worked in the big Hecla Mine until a fellow I roomed with at the Greasy Spoon Boarding House suggested that we move on to Oregon, where his sister lived, before we were entirely snowed in for the winter.

Western Oregon's rainy weather was not to my liking, so I moved on to Southern California and hired out to a man who owned a large hay bailing outfit near Pomona. He had just contracted to bale all the hay on a huge tract of land almost ten thousand acres in area. The work was hard, but I was used to that, and the wages were good. Even with several crews working at one time, there was always more hay ahead of us.

Two Texas boys on the crew who had punched cows in Arizona, were planning to drift back that way before long and asked me to join them. One night in the bunkhouse the three of us got to singing old cowboy range songs like *The Zebra Dun* and *Hell Among the Yearlings,* and that did it. I was ready to go. We drew our wages and moseyed over into Arizona where we hired out to the old Boquillas Land & Cattle Company's Wagon Rod Ranch on the San Pedro River for forty dollars a month and board—equal to a week's work at Pomona.

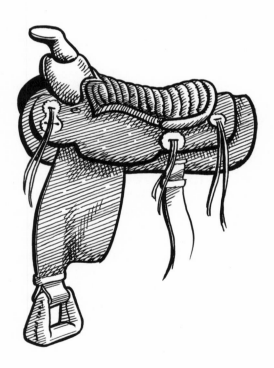

Four   The San Simon Country

Ihad been working a while for the Wagon Rods on the San Pedro
River in southern Arizona. Old Henry Street, the general manager,
was a hard man to work for, but he never bothered me any. But Pink
Murray, his wagon boss, was a big loud-mouthed bastard who riled
me the wrong way every time we got together. I stood about all I
could take of him; and the day he told me to move to the permanent
horse camp in the mountains I sold out to the Boquillas Cattle Company right sudden. I had left a couple of private horses in the pasture
at Fairbanks, so I went down and got them, packed my bed horse,
and rode over the hill to Tombstone. That town was as dead as a
door knob since the silver mines had flooded, so I didn't tarry long
there. I just bogied along, enjoying life without Pink Murray. I had
no particular destination in mind, just looking at the country. Once
across the Sulphur Springs Valley, I rode off up Rucker Canyon in
the Chiricahua Mountains. I spent a night at Charley Rak's ranch,
then took the trail out over the top. I traveled slowly, favoring my
horses, for I didn't know when or where I'd turn them out to pasture
next.

This was in July of 1921, and by the time I topped out on the
ten thousand foot Chiricahua Peak, a thunderstorm was brewing
overhead. Just before it broke loose I got my saddle and bed inside an
old galvanized iron tool shed belonging to the Forest Service and
quickly hobbled my horses up close. I soon discovered that the tool
shed was inhabited by several little spotted skunks. The dirt floor
was full of their holes. The shed also contained about ten cases of
dynamite. Dragging the dynamite boxes together, I rolled my bed out
on top of them for the night. Bolts of lightning continued to strike all
around me, some so close I could feel the earth shake. It would pour
rain for a little while, then the lightning would crash on every side once
more. This kept up until long after midnight, and I sure didn't sleep.
It wasn't pleasant thinking what would happen if the lightning struck
the shed and all that dynamite I was using as a bed.

At long last the lightning stopped, but the rain came down until
almost daylight. I was glad to get my horses and take a forest trail
off the peak as quickly as I could. A bear cub playing with the end of
a pipe at a spring watched me pass. His mother was no doubt close
by. Two-thirds of the way down the switchback trail, it was perfectly
dry. The storm had spent all its fury on top of the mountain. At Rustler
Park I let my horses crop grass for a while, then rode on to the old
mining camp of Paradise. One little store and a few dilapidated old

31

wooden shacks were all that remained of a once thriving camp.

During Tombstone's torrid past, Rustler Park had been a hideout camp for outlaws, and nearby Paradise their source of supplies. The old storekeeper there regaled me with the story of a miner who was sitting on an open keg of single jack heads when a drunken member of Black Jack Ketchum's outlaw gang walked into the store and began cursing everyone in sight. Spotting the miner still sitting on the keg, he staggered over to throw him out of the store. The miner reached down into the keg, came up with a 4 1/2 pound single jack head, and hit the outlaw right between the eyes with it, killing him on the spot. The miners didn't think it fitting to bury an outlaw in a place with such a name as "Paradise" so they loaded his body on a pack mule and dumped him off in Rustler Park after dark. They figured he'd be more at home there.

Around the *esfaldas* of the mountains I rode through White Tail Canyon as far as the Hilltop Asbestos Mine. A little inquiry convinced me there were no sizeable ranches around there, so I started out for the San Simon Valley. A little new cabin perched against a hillside offered a chance to water my horses, so I rode in. I hailed the house but got no answer, although I could hear a man talking. Dismounting, I dropped my reins and followed the sound of the voice to beneath the porch steps. There I found the source; a small crippled-up old prospector, bent over, talking to an old dead shepherd dog. When I had attracted his attention he limped over to me and introduced himself as Jerry O'Sullivan, owner of the property. He explained that his old dog had died the previous night. He told me to help myself to his scanty store of rainwater, which was in a couple of barrels at the corner of the house, and invited me to share a meal with him. Like most men who spend their days in solitude, it was a rare treat for him to have someone to talk to, especially now that his old and faithful companion was dead. I could understand right away that old Irishman's deep love for his dog and what a loss its death was to him.

"Would ye be so kind as to help me bury Neil now?" he asked me after we had eaten. "I named him Neil after the great early Kings of Ireland when he was a wee puppy. And a king of a dog he was. When I talked to him, he understood me, and he wasn't one to argue and harangue, like some people I know. No sir! Never a cross word out of him in all these nine years, and whether I was drunk or sober he never left me alone. I promised him that when he died I would give him a Christian burial, and that I will."

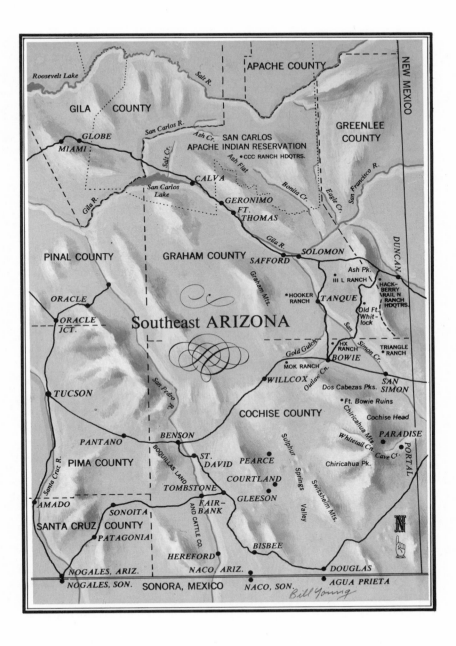

Southeast ARIZONA

APACHE COUNTY

NEW MEXICO

GILA COUNTY

Roosevelt Lake

Salt R.

GLOBE
MIAMI

San Carlos R.

Ash Cr.

SAN CARLOS
APACHE INDIAN RESERVATION

Ash Flat

• CCC RANCH HDQTRS.

GREENLEE
COUNTY

Salt Cr.

CALVA

Bonita Cr.

Eagle Cr.

San Francisco R.

Gila R.

San Carlos
Lake

GERONIMO
FT.
THOMAS

DUNCAN

Gila R.

PINAL COUNTY

GRAHAM COUNTY

SAFFORD

SOLOMON

Graham Mts.

Ash Pk.

III L RANCH

HACK-
BERRY
RANCH
HDQTRS.

ORACLE

• HOOKER
RANCH

TANQUE

Old Ft.
Whit-
lock

ORACLE
JCT.

San

Gold Gulch

HX
RANCH

Simon Cr.

TRIANGLE
• RANCH

San Pedro R.

MOK RANCH

BOWIE

SAN
SIMON

TUCSON

WILLCOX

Outlaw Cn.

Dos Cabezas Pks.

• Ft. Bowie Ruins

Cochise Head

PANTANO

BENSON

COCHISE COUNTY

Chiricahua Mts.

PARADISE

PORTAL

PIMA COUNTY

Santa Cruz R.

BOQUILLAS LAND

ST.
DAVID

PEARCE

Sulphur

Whitetail Cr.

Cave Cr.

AMADO

TOMBSTONE

COURTLAND

Springs

Chiricahua Pk.

SONOITA

FAIR-
BANK

GLEESON

Valley

AND CATTLE CO.

Swisshelm Mts.

SANTA CRUZ COUNTY

PATAGONIA

BISBEE

N

HEREFORD

NOGALES, ARIZ.

NACO, ARIZ.

DOUGLAS

NOGALES, SON.

SONORA, MEXICO

NACO, SON.

AGUA PRIETA

Bill Young

While I was washing up our noon dishes, Old Jerry was seated at the corner of the table laboriously writing a eulogy to Neil, straight from his heart, on an old ruled tablet. Finished, he folded what he had written and carefully tucked it into an empty Prince Albert tobacco can. He rustled up an old piece of blanket and an old oilcloth table cover and went down under the porch. I knew he wanted to be alone so I kept puttering around in the kitchen until he called me. He had wrapped Neil in the blanket and oilcloth and sewed it all up, with the tobacco can inside. I got his wheelbarrow and a shovel from back of the cabin and, with Jerry leading the procession down the hill slowly and painfully, I followed with the deceased in the wheelbarrow hearse. He led the way to Neil's last resting place, an old assessment work prospect shaft. With two ropes we lowered him carefully to the bottom of the shaft, and while Jerry prayed in Gaelic I stood respectfully to one side. When he had scattered his handful of dust over Neil and turned away, I quickly shoveled in enough earth to cover the dog well.

Back at the cabin the old man prevailed upon me to stay the night. He told me he was seventy-five years old. Two of the three copper claims he owned he had sold two years previously. The company that purchased them was to pay off in three equal payments of twenty thousand dollars each over a three year period. The second he had received just a couple of weeks before I arrived on the scene. As near as I could tell by his talk, he had no kin to leave it to. I often wondered what would become of it. He wanted me to stay and help him work his one remaining claim, but I wasn't geared yet to stay in one place very long. There were too many blue mountains and mesas in the distance and I needed to see what was on the other side. When I said goodbye to him he was profuse with his thanks to me for assisting with Neil's funeral. A couple of years later I read in a Globe paper that Jerry had joined his dog. Cochise's Head, (the perfect rock formation of an Apache Indian's face), now watches over them in the White Tail Canyon of the Chiricahua Mountains.

At San Simon, a little cow town out in the middle of the valley of the same name, I bought a few things I needed and rode off north to the old Triangle Ranch. It belonged to old General McKenzie who had come to Southern Arizona as a cavalry officer when the army was trying to round up the fierce Apache raiding parties which were killing and plundering this southeast part of the territory in the 1880's.

After the last of the Apaches had finally been subdued he had returned to stake out this ranch on the San Simon, stocking it with the cattle he and his sons had driven in from Texas. That was the Triangle Ranch. The General and E. Waller and Ed, his two sons, had the reputation of being a real hard-twisted outfit. That first night I spent at their ranch, being new to the country, I hadn't heard anything for or against them as yet. Being in the middle of summer, they needed no extra cowboys beyond their regular help.

Riding north from their ranch a couple of miles, I came to one of their windmills where two fences cornered. While I was opening the gate, I saw the dust of a rider coming fast from the direction of their ranch headquarters. By the time I had remounted Ed Mc-Kenzie rode up, a short 30-30 Winchester in the scabbard beneath his right leg, and a six shooter stuck in the waistband of his Levis, Mormon style. His reins were looped over his crippled left arm.

"Where was you figuring to go, cowboy?" he asked me.

"Hell, I don't know. Just North," I replied.

"Well, go through this other gate," he told me. "The country is all open up that side of the fence."

I told him I was pretty good at finding my way through strange country and as long as I'd started on the side I was, I thought I would just stay with it. Right away he got just as hostile as a disturbed rattlesnake and jerked out his short rifle, cocked it, and pointed it right at my middle jumper button.

"This is Triangle range, and you'll go where I say until you are off it," he said, giving me a real mean look.

"Looks like you're holding all the good cards, so you must be right," I said.

He kept watching me for any sign of a ranny-ka-boo until I had turned back and gone through the other gate. He was still sitting there on his horse watching me as I rode over a little hill and out of his sight, about half a mile beyond the windmill.

I wondered why he was so particular about which side of the fence I was on, so the next high place I found I left my bed horse to graze and climbed up high enough to get a look-see. I spotted his dust cloud away down the country as he headed back toward San Simon on a lope.

I still wasn't too joyful about being told where I couldn't go, so decided to nose around a little and see what was itching him so. Kicking the staples out of a couple of fence posts, I tied the wires down and led my horses across; then fixing the fence again, rode on north up a brushy draw. Well used cattle trails told me there must be a watering hole not too far off. It wasn't long before a noise off to my right attracted my attention and solved the mystery. Two big unbranded calves were tied to small mesquite trees not over a hundred yards apart. A cow, evidently the mother of one, was nervously circling about in the thicket. I got a good look at her brand, and it *wasn't* a Triangle. The soft ground was pretty well plowed up all around with shod horse tracks. I added up two and two and got a dozen.

An hour later the mesquites thinned out as I neared a rocky little range of desert mountains. Heading into a wide pass, I came to an old abandoned adobe house, a tule-grown cienega and some corrals. Here the wagon ruts of an old road lead off North. Following it, about eight miles farther I reached a cow ranch. Two brothers were in camp, and they invited me to alight and spend the night. Their names were Martin. One was the windmill repair man for the ranch; the other was doing the cooking.

Later in the day the cowboys rode in, threw their saddles on the corral fence, and we met and shook hands all around. Ed Gleeson, the ramrod, was the elder son of the owner. Emmett was about seven years younger. Hugh Cavitt was one of the old top hands, and there was a bronco rider named Red Engle. Forest Mulkins, a big chuffy cowboy, wasn't on their payroll but was riding with them for a few days, gathering some of his mother's cattle. Ralph Horn was a fairly new man on the outfit, having come over from the Willcox country just recently from the Monk Ranch for which he had been riding. We squatted around in the corral talking about cattle, the drought and horses, until the cook yelled chuck. After eating, I braced Ed about a job. He asked me if I knew anything about haying, and when I admitted I had done some, he told me they were going down in the valley to cut and put up some wild hay right away, and if I wanted to help, he would hire me.

While we were talking I told him of my run-in with the Triangle man and the tied calves. With a stick I drew a map in the dust of the location.

"Those were Rail N calves as sure as Hell is hot," Ed affirmed. "That Triangle outfit would steal the pennies off a dead man's eyes. I'm going to high-tail down there right pronto, and if I can make it before dark, there might just still be time."

Saddling a couple of fresh horses, he and old Hugh Cavitt took off, leaning over the brow bands. I rolled my bed out on the ground and had been in it an hour or more before they rode in. At breakfast Ed told us that they had found the calves all right and had sleepered both before cutting them loose.

"I'd like to have seen McKenzie's face when he found those cut ropes," he said. "He'll think we may be down there high pointing now, so chances are he will be afraid to make any moves for some time."

That day we got all our camping and haying equipment ready to move down the valley to the old Whitlock Ranch, where we were to stay while putting up hay. That was the abandoned adobe I'd passed on my way to Hackberry, the headquarters ranch. Emmett told me it was so old that no one knew who had built it. There were remains of a second storey over the north end, with port holes all around to shoot from. Every cowboy in the country swore the place was haunted and they had never been able to get anyone to stay in camp there alone for more than a couple of nights. When I asked why, he said they all claimed to hear weird noises at night and he guessed the history of murders and killings at the old place had a lot to do with it. Apaches had taken it once and massacred the people holed up there, losing some of their own warriors in the process. A posse had cornered some outlaws there and killed some of them; and when the Parks family owned the ranch, Jim Parks, the foreman, had had a ruckus with a cowboy working for him and in the gunplay that resulted had killed him there also.

Sounded like an undertaker's paradise. We camped around the other side of the cienega from the house, and the only thing that bothered any of us were some scorpions and centipedes.

For three weeks we cut wild hay on the flats and stacked it, and about a hundred and fifty tons of careless weeds for horse feed. We built fences around the stacks to protect them from the cattle. Before we finished, the boys' father, Old John Gleeson, came up from his home at the town of Gleeson, bringing along three more men to help us.

Along an old sandy road we used, between Whitlock and the haying flats, washes had uncovered some sections of strange clay-like pipes. I had noticed some at different places, so one day I picked up a couple to examine. They were a dingy grey, about a foot long, and appeared to be made of a mixture of caliche and clay. They were very crude and roughly made, all uneven and rough on the outside.

It looked as though they had been formed around a stick of wood, big at one end and small at the other. Then the stick had been pulled out before they were cooked or sun baked. The small end had then been pushed into the larger end on each joint, making a continuous pipeline. There was no doubt that the starting point was the cienega, but we never located the end, although we found some joints seven miles down in the valley.

After we had put up all the hay we could at the Whitlock Ranch, Ed sent the mowers over across the San Simon River to a line camp, (the HX Ranch). John Snow, an old Montana cowboy, lived in that camp. Martin, the windmill man, and I returned to Hackberry to get a chest of tools to take over to the new camp. All the work teams were at the HX and the best animals we could find for the trip were an old locoed saddle horse and a mule left in the pasture. The old horse had never been harnessed before and we had a hell of a tussle with him, but by the time we got beyond the Whitlock place we had him working pretty well. The morning was clear and bright, but clouds began to form, mushrooming fast. By the time we turned west toward the crossing on the bone dry San Simon, lightning was flashing all around us, and in a moment came the deluge. Neither of us even had a jumper along, and in no time we were as wet as drowned rats. Out there on the flats lightning was striking soap weeds and setting them afire. One close miss knocked us both off the seat of the wagon and brought the mule to his knees. Water was running inches deep all over the baked adobe ground. Crossing a shallow dip we got stuck. That old locoed horse refused to pull a pound and the mule couldn't do it all alone. Martin was driving, and after a lot of yelling and cussing and beating on the horse, he finally stopped to figure. We unloaded everything on the wagon, but still that horse wouldn't try. We tried everything we could think of, to no avail. Pretty soon we heard the roar of flood water coming down the San Simon, and now we knew it was no use to go on because we could no longer cross it. We were cold, wet and hungry, and a long way from shelter.

Three beds on the wagon belonged to some of the crew at HX. Leaving the harness and wagon, we put two beds on the horse, one on the mule, and started back afoot leading them. It was just about dark by then and we had about six miles to go to reach the Whitlock ranch, wading water almost shoe-top deep. That was some walk. About half way the clouds broke up and the full moon shone through. A night breeze sprang up and we almost froze. Slogging along through the mud and water, I could think of a lot of places I'd rather have been about then. We staggered into the place, threw the beds on the floor, and put the horse and mule in the corral. Fortunately there was a little dry wood in the house with which we started a fire in the fireplace. Partly dried and warmed, we bedded down.

There wasn't a thing in the place to eat, so around daylight Martin rode the horse bareback on to Hackberry and worked a pasture to get up a horse of his own. He got his saddle there and a pack saddle for the locoed one, packed some grub and returned to me at Whitlock. There we ate hastily, packed two beds on the horse and one on the mule, and again headed for the HX, me riding atop the beds on the horse. Two beds high, I felt like I was nounted on a camel.

This time we took a short cut on a horse trail to the San Simon to cross it. Where the crossing was, horses had worn a deep trail down into the silt banks on either side. Now the river was running bank-full of muddy brown water. Martin, leading the mule, tackled it first, telling me to wait until he saw if he could make it across. Just as soon as they went off the bank, man and mule were swimming, and I could see that the current was stronger than it looked. They had a hard time keeping far enough upstream to hit the trail out on the far side.

Once across, Martin waved me in. That old locoed horse stepped off the bank like a drunk off a roof, and promptly went clear under. When we bobbed up, he rolled over on his side and I fell off. He acted like he had never seen water before, and began trying to climb on top of me as I was swimming ahead of him. Martin rode down the bank and threw his rope to me just before I reached the falls in the river. With a wild grab I caught hold of the rope, but there was no place he could pull me over the bank. Turning his horse back upstream he headed for the trail. I had a death grip on the rope, and going against the current I was spinning like a top under water. Just when I knew I couldn't hold on any longer, he snaked me out on the bank like a mud turtle, and I guess I looked like one. I had swallowed a lot of San Simon mud, and my eyes were plastered shut with it.

That crazy old horse had found some way to scramble out on the bank, but of course it was on the wrong side. Martin cussed and stomped on his hat for five minutes over that. Now he had to swim back across to get old loco and haul him back again. He was really cussing the world by sections by the time he got to that muddy half-drowned old pelican on the opposite shore. This time he didn't bother with the trail either. Dallying old loco up short against his horse's shoulder, he backed off and made a run at the bank above the horse trail. They hit the water in a belly flop that was a dandy, and momentum had them half way across before old loco knew where he was. Even then he tried to roll over, but Martin's horse was stout on a rope and brought him across like "pulling bog." Between there and the HX, if we had met any Digger Indians they would sure have claimed me as a blood brother. Just before dark we delivered the beds. We fed up good, and I rolled in early out in the yard, completely pooped out.

The HX had a small frame one-room house, built on stilts. John Snow had a bunch of chickens, some horses of his own, and an old hound dog in camp. He left the door open to get what breeze there was at night; but to keep the dog out he laid an old chair on its side across the threshhold. Along about one o'clock in the morning his chickens began making a hell of a racket. John jumped out of bed in his drawers, grabbed his shotgun from the antlers on the wall, and ran for the chicken house to kill the skunk. But he forgot about the chair in the door. He turned a coon's ass, head over heels, clear to the ground. Cussing, he got up and ran to the chicken house, threw open the door, and fired away at what he could see of the skunk in the dark. Tally, six hens and one skunk. He was fighting mad by then, but we had a chicken dinner the next day at noon.

After haying, we moved back to the headquarters ranch where I took over the job of freighting for the outfit. All their supplies had to be freighted in from Bowie, a small town on the railroad some twenty miles away. There were about seventeen windmills scattered out over the range, each with a gasoline pump, so I freighted in quite a lot of gasoline to keep the pumps working when the wind was not blowing. For light loads I had a four-horse team and, for heavy ones, a six up. Now freighting is no bed of roses either, and many times I had more trouble than a one-armed man with the dobie itch. The wagon tires were always loose and trying to come off, and it is surprising how many things can go wrong on a twenty-mile trip. So I wasn't unhappy in early September to turn the freighting over to a new man.

The Rail N was about to start its fall works. While we were gathering horses on the range I ran across a fellow riding the high places. He said his name was Bradbury from up in the Clifton country, looking for some mares and colts of his that had strayed. I thought it odd he hadn't come in to the ranch and made himself known first, so I passed the word to Ed Gleeson that evening. He scouted the country next day but saw nothing of the fellow. After we had a remuda together and were shoeing up, Ed went in to Safford to hire a cook for roundup. He was a tinhorn gambler but a good roundup cook all right. All one day he spent scrubbing the chuck box and loading the wagon to have everything in readiness for the first move. He'd bought a new alarm clock in town and he wound it carefully, wrapped it in a bath towel to protect it from the shocks of the wagon bouncing over the rocks. The outfit had hired a half dozen new hands for the works; and quite a few stray men "repping" (representing their ranches) had brought their mounts from the ranches they rode for. There were Monks of Willcox, the Lazy B's (near Steins Pass), the One Hundred and Elevens of Safford and Solomonville, Moore and Moyer of Willcox, the Riggs outfit from Bowie, and some others of the bigger outfits. Even the Triangles had one man with us. Typical of their outfit, he was a tough looking hombre who gave his name as Jones. Then there were a number of small one-man outfits from as far away as Duncan on the New Mexico border that had come to throw in with us while we worked the country nearest their spreads.

By the time we made our first camp at a dry lake east of Whitlock there were probably thirty riders with the wagon. That was on the fifteenth of September. Ed instructed the cook to have breakfast early so they could get off to a good start on the first day's work. That first night there was a lot of conversation around the campfire among men who hadn't seen one another since the previous spring roundup. So it was late before most of them crawled into their soogans to sleep. When the cook got his clock out to set the alarm for about three-thirty so he'd have plenty of time to stir up breakfast for the big crew, he found the clock wouldn't work. Loose threads on the towel had wound themselves solidly around the winding stem until it had wedged. There was no way to fix it in the dark. Figuring he would awaken in time anyhow, the cook went to bed. I heard him rattling the dutch ovens and coffee pots around the breakfast fire early. It wasn't long before most of the men were up and dressed, except for a few old fellows who were still pounding their ear. Breakfast was over pretty soon, and the night hawk and horse wrangler could be heard in the distance bringing the remuda in. Tom Brown, a small rancher from Duncan, and some other fellow were arguing about the morning star, high in the east.

"That's old Jupiter," one said.

"Hell, no," said the other.

It was still too dark to see well enough to rope our horses, so everyone was standing around the fire scanning the eastern horizon for the first glimmer of dawn. Finally one cowboy looked at his pocket watch by the firelight and discovered that it was only twelve forty-five AM. A few went back to bed, but most of the crew sat around the fire and drank coffee until the morning star peeped over the malapai mountains to the east. We sure got an early start that day. With our big remuda of fresh horses and the frosty dawn air, there were a lot of bronc rides as we left camp. Three or four horses were bucking at one time.

As the wagon moved on around the range, rep men would cut their cattle and mounts to return to their outfits, and new ones would join us. One of the new ones was a Mexican cowboy sent by a woman who owned the Prod S outfit near St. Thomas. She had mounted him with a whole string of mares. At the time, we were camped at a line camp of the One Hundred and Eleven Ranch where Thad Adams was living with his new bride. We were working the herd out on the flats when the Mexican arrived. He threw his mares into the remuda grazing north of the place. When the horses began fighting over those mares, the horse wrangler cut them out and boogered them off. At noon when he came in to eat and change horses, the Mexican discovered he was afoot. He overtook his mounts which were headed for home, and brought them back. Ed read him the riot act about those mares and told him to leave them in a side corral after saddling up.

When we went to rope out our afternoon horses from the big round corral, Thad Adams (a riata man) wanted to show off the trick pony he had trained for his bride. Tying the end of his long riata around the pony's neck, he jumped on it bareback without even a bridle, and rode into the milling remuda, to rope his horse. Spotting the one he wanted, he dabbed a loop over its head. That pony whirled to take the jerk on his shoulders. This Mexican was standing in the middle of the corral trying to get a look at the mare he wanted to catch, just as Thad's horse hit the end of the riata. He was standing just right so the riata caught him under the chin and flipped him through the air to land flat on his back. It was a pure accident, but he thought Thad had done it on purpose and he was as mad as a turkey gobbler. He sputtered in Spanish awhile, but was careful not to get too loud, for Thad was a big husky old Mormon boy who would fight a circle saw and give it three revolutions head start. I guess he figured he had come to the wrong place, because he cut his mares and took off for Ft. Thomas pronto. All of us, and the wrangler in particular, were glad to see him leave with those old mares. The short while they had been in the remuda had caused a lot of chewed-up backs from those old horses fighting over them.

The country was pretty open in those days and we worked from the New Mexico border to the Graham Mountains, east and west, and from the Southern Pacific railroad on the south almost to Clifton on the north. It was the fourth of January when we wound up.

That roundup was where I first met Shorty K. Boldin. He was a short, heavy-set cowboy, about forty years old, who had worked all over that part of the country for several years. He was a plumb good cowboy, but he couldn't stay away from booze. He could stand it for just about a month before he had to go on a toot. Every red cent he earned he spent for whisky, or gave away to kids while he was drunk. He sure never spent any on himself. His whole outfit consisted of stuff discarded by other cowboys. He wore an old black hat with no crown and a pair of old boots without heels. He had nailed two big spools on them. He always looked like a scarecrow in some old nester's cornfield.

After we had been on the works for a month, he hit the boss for some money, claiming he had a hell of a toothache and wanted to see a dentist when we got near Safford. Ed gave him twenty dollars just before we moved to Ash Springs. Shorty and I were to go through to help the wrangler move the remuda to the new camp. Everything went fine until we hit the highway between Duncan and Safford. We had to take it for a few miles west before reaching the trail to Ash Spring. Shorty was up in the lead holding the horses back some, while we brought up the rear. We met a pickup truck whose driver stopped to let us by.

"You fellows cowboys?" he asked Shorty.

"Shore are!" Shorty replied.

"Well, I'm a bootlegger," this character announced.

"The Hell you say," says Shorty. "Have you got any samples with you?"

Receiving an affirmative reply, Shorty dismounted, and with his foot on the running board of the truck began negotiations for some firewater. We went on to the new camp. After noon, with the day herd men holding the steer herd on a hill, Ed took the crew and made a small drive into a canyon nearby. We worked the herd within sight of camp. Along about four o'clock, here comes the bootlegger, drunk as a lord, driving his truck over the rocky hillside like he was on level ground, with Shorty passed out in the bed behind. Just before he reached camp, Shorty came to and bailed out over the side, landing in a big prickly pear plant. Wheeling up to camp, the bootlegger announced to the cook:

"I just brought one of your men back!"

Then he looked back to discover he'd lost his passenger.

"Now where do you reckon he fell out?" he asked himself.

Ed sent a couple of the boys to bring Shorty into camp. They removed his shirt and laid him on the redwood box covering the spring and began pulling cactus thorns out of his hide. Shorty lay there awhile, then sat up trying to figure out just where he was. The wrangler had come into camp to cut some wood for the cook, and his horse was standing close by. Shorty got up, staggered around a little, then managed to get up on the wrangler's horse. Weaving in the saddle, here he came; no hat, no shirt, and as tight as a tick. He rode into the middle of the herd, spurring that old horse in the shoulder and yelling,

"Git outta the way! I'm gonna cut out these cattle!"

Ed rode in and led the horse out by the bridle reins.

"You're not going to cut anything, you drunk son-of-a-bitch," Ed told him. "You go back to camp and sleep it off or I'll put a long U across your ass with this rope."

Had it been anyone except the boss, Shorty would have challenged him, but he finally went off to camp.

Riding through some brushy draws a couple of days later, we jumped a bobcat. Some of the boys chased it up a mesquite tree, where it crouched on a limb. Shorty never passed up a dare, so when one of the boys dared him to climb the tree and rope that cat he took the bait. With a cotton tie down rope about three feet long, he went up the tree. Snarling defiance and spitting like water on a hot stovelid, the bobcat kept backing farther out on the limb as Shorty inched closer to him. When they were about as far out as they could get, Shorty built a loop in his piggin string. After a couple of tries, he finally got it over the cat's head and began trying to reel him in. That was a mistake. When that wildcat found he couldn't get loose he jumped right at Shorty's face, biting, and clawing with all four feet. Shorty lost his hold on the limb and the pair of them fell out of the tree in a squalling, fighting heap. That danged cat bit and clawed Shorty everywhere he could reach him, but he couldn't get loose. Getting a strangle hold on his throat, Boldin finally choked him down, then killed him with a rock.

"That kitty cat was sort of fighty, wasn't he, Shorty?" one of the boys said.

"Yeah, but he couldn't whip Shorty K. Boldin, by God," he replied, wiping the blood off of his scratched face.

Every day we were getting many big husky calves to brand, and the flankers were worked to a frazzle trying to keep up with the ropers. There were three, and sometimes four, sets of flankers working on the ground at one time. One day when we had about three hundred big calves to brand, Shorty got paired off with a big, lazy old boy. A couple of good head ropers were bringing those calves out of the herd on a high trot, bucking and bawling at the end of a thirty-foot rope. One flanker would down a calf and hold it by a foreleg, with a knee on its neck, while his partner, one foot braced against the calf's hock, the other leg held stretched out beneath his arm, sat holding the rear end until the branders and markers had done their job on it. The next calf out, they would change over. Now this old lazy boy got tired after a little while of being kicked in the belly and dragged around by those big calves while he tried to get them down. So he began to hang back when the ropers dragged one up past him. Shorty knew the ropers didn't enjoy having to drag a calf up to the fire two or three times before they could get their rope back, so he would step up and flank the calf down. Pretty soon he found he was downing all those husky calves, while his partner was working the easy end. The calves were coming thick and fast and pretty soon Shorty was sweating and blowing. In his addled old rum-dumbed mind he knew he was getting the worst of it. Finished with one big calf, Shorty released it, and his partner just stayed sitting on the ground, waiting for a roper to bring up another for Shorty to flank. Without warning, Boldin dived right on top of that old button and began beating his head with both fists. He really worked him over.

"Now git up, you lazy bastard, and make a hand around here for a change," Shorty told him. And believe me that old boy sure set to work. Shorty had the Indian sign on him.

During the roundup, we picked up over seven hundred big six and seven-year-old Mexican steers of the one thousand head the Rail N had turned loose on the range several years before. We put them in a pasture east of Hackberry. On our last delivery to the railroad shipping pens at Bowie we took them along. We had a stampede just before we reached town, and it was after dark before we got our herd across the tracks near the stockyards. Two other outfits had corralled before us, but they took some of their cattle out to night herd, to make room for us. All of the next day was spent shaping up the cattle for the buyers, and having them inspected. The buyer for the big Mexican steers wouldn't accept delivery on them at Bowie, so after shipping the rest of the cattle, we had to trail drive them clear to Willcox, spending one night on the way at Moore & Moyer's ranch on the west side of the Valley.

We reached Willcox in the rain and spent a wet miserable day there before we were rid of them. On our last night in Willcox, a few of us got drunk, but we didn't leave any of the boys in jail. Paid off, I cut my private horses and left the Rail N, to take on a few horses to break out in the valley. I threw in with an old Dutch nester who had a place south of the San Simon, with some good corrals. Before long I had gotten together quite a few horses to work on.

Things were rocking along pretty well until some of the colts I was breaking began to show signs of going loco. That didn't suit me, so I made a deal with a boy who had a small ranch up in the Dos Cabezas Mountains south of Bowie to move up with him. His father was the foreman on a bridge-building crew for the railroad. He lived in Bowie with his two daughters. One of the girls worked in a little cafe in town, and the younger one was still in school. John, the brother, spent most of his time at the ranch, going in to town often to see them during the times their father was away working on the road.

Riding those colts, it didn't take me long to learn the country up in the Dos Cabezas. Now and then John would get up a beef which we would butcher out. Then he would pack about half of it to town for his dad and the girls, and we would graze on the rest ourselves. Once out of the mountains he usually stayed with them a couple of nights, bringing groceries and grain back on the return trip.

One night while he was away, I awoke to hear riders going by in the creek bed after midnight. Curious as to who would be travelling those dark canyons in the dead of night, I followed the trail they made the next morning. There were both horse and burro tracks leading up a rough canyon about three miles beyond our camp. This canyon branched off into a side canyon among huge granite boulders and thick trees. Hearing movement, I dismounted and scouted on afoot until I came to a bend where, in a little open place, I saw the horses and burros hobbled, grazing. Under a great overhanging bluff, three men were working around a whisky distillery. From behind some brush I watched them for some time, running off a batch of mash. Easing back to my horse I went on. I was no revenue officer, and what they did was no concern of mine. When John returned from town I casually mentioned having heard horses travelling past our camp during the night. For all I knew, he might have had some hand in the deal himself. He told me he knew who they were and that they were moonshining, although he didn't know where or when.

Later on, while we were bringing a few head of cattle off a brushy ridge, we met the moonshiners on a trail. Two were brothers. The other fellow was a short, tough-looking man who was a lot older than the brothers. We passed the time of day and talked awhile before going on.

"Come over to our place and ride the barrel next Sunday," they invited us before we parted.

After they had gone on I asked John what they were talking about.

"They've got a contraption rigged up that bucks worse than a horse. It's a lot of fun to try," John told me. "Maybe we'll go down Sunday and try it a fall or two."

So Sunday he led the way down the canyon a couple of miles, and a little way up a side canyon to where they had a rough board shack on a bench of the creek bank, amid some big oak trees. A long rope, tied in the tops of two big oaks, was strung through holes bored in a large whisky keg. Spliced just ahead and behind the keg were two cotton ropes about four feet long. An old, slick fork Meenie saddle with iron stirrups was cinched on the keg. After we'd shot the breeze for a while we went over to the contraption. Hanging on the off stirrup to counter-balance the saddle, one fellow held on until the other mounted the keg from the left side. Once the victim was in the saddle, the other two took up positions in front and behind, each taking a good hold on the short ropes. When the fellow in the saddle was all set, they began pulling downward on the short ropes, the spring of the tree tops causing the saddled keg to go up and down higher and higher. Then suddenly the man in front would jerk his rope to one side, while the one behind would pull on the opposite side. That damned keg would sun fish worse than any horse could think of. About four or five jumps were the limit any of us could stay on, for that keg was strung on the rope with a hairpin balance, and once that was lost, down came the rider. To keep him from hitting the ground, there was a short rope just ahead of the saddle for the rider to hold onto with one hand. But that didn't keep those old iron stirrups from whacking the rider over the head when he fell off. They had spurred that old keg until its sides were splintered. It was a lot of fun, and we spent the whole afternoon on it.

A month or so later John and I were getting low on chuck, so I took a pack horse and went over the mountain to the mining camp of Dos Cabezas, where I bought a load of chuck. The store had some fancy canned goods that caught my eye so I splurged a little and took several cans each of salmon, shrimp, oysters, crab, and such. A couple of days later John left for town to visit his sisters, expecting to stay for a period of nights. I rode out in the hills on one of my horses and it was dark before I got back. Someone had robbed the camp while I was away. All the canned stuff, sugar, milk, *everything,* had been cleaned out. It was too dark to cut sign for tracks until morning, but the thought struck me that those three moonshiners might be my boys. I was tired, hungry, and hostile, but determined to find out. Catching up a horse in the corral, I saddled and took along a couple of barley sacks just in case. Armed with my old six shooter and some extra cartridges, I jogged down to see the boys. Tying my horse in the canyon, I climbed the bench and thus came up on the back side of their cabin. Light was shining out through the cracks of their house and I could hear them laughing and talking loud inside. Against the house, with my eye to a crack, I took a good look. The men were cooking supper, a glass jug of moonshine on the table. All of the three acted about half drunk. On some shelves and on the table I spotted my canned sea foods and most of the other stuff in plain sight. Easing around to the front door I lifted the latch and stepped in.

Startled at my sudden appearance, their heads swiveled around like hoot owls. "Oh! Come in," the runty one said. "You're just in time. We're cooking supper. There's a drink there on the table. Help yourself."

"No thanks, I won't drink and I won't eat. But I sure as hell came after my chuck," I said, looking him right in the eye. He was silent a moment, and I could see the wheels going around in his head behind those mean little eyes. Whatever he wanted to start, I was cocked and primed to go along with.

"Why, Hell, fellow, we just came by your camp and saw there was no one there, so we figured you and John had gone to town for awhile," he said. "We just brought your stuff over here to keep for you while you were away. There are so many Mexican woodcutters working this side of the mountain from Dos Cabezas we thought they might steal it."

His story was as weak as skimmed Holstein milk and he knew it. Watching him for any sign of war play, I sacked up all I could see of my stuff and eased out. Riding back, I got to thinking what a fool play I had made. Those three were not just run of the mill moonshiners. If they had made a gun play, outnumbered three to one, I might have wound up with some extra buttonholes in my shirt. I had gotten away with it, but my water was bad. Events later proved it.

The Clifton sheriff had been trying to run down a bunch of horse thieves for some time. Horses were being rustled from pastures at night and driven south. The sheriff had traced some of them as far as a canyon just west of Bowie, where another horse had been stolen. The rustlers had a going business which they had been working for a long time. Starting from the Clifton country, they drove by night to one of their hideouts, where they laid up during the daytime. Then they drove across the San Simon Valley to this canyon in the Dos

Cabezas, where again they holed up during the daytime. The next night's drive would take them into Mexico, where they delivered the horses. Now and then, if it came handy, they would add a few along the way from some ranch pasture. The hideout stops were manned by friends of theirs, operating a grapevine to keep the rustlers posted on where the posse was, and any spot to pick up more good horses. The men didn't fool with unbroken or common range horses. They took the best.

This extremely profitable enterprise came to an end, however, when one of their station men sold them out for the reward money and a guarantee of immunity from prosecution. The posse surprised the men in the canyon hideout. In the fight that followed, a young fellow named Miller was killed, also the one from whom I had taken back my chuck. He was operating the station in the canyon for the gang. Only one man got away from the posse, and he didn't have enough head start. He was overtaken by a rifle bullet and killed. That was Bradberry, the man I had talked to at the Rail N. From what I heard later, he was the "king pin" of the gang.

A year later the two brothers sat in at a very high stakes poker game in a back room of the old Palace Bar in Globe. Leaving the game, they went outside, put on different clothes and masks, then came back and held up the game. As they were going out the door with the money a snap shot by one of the gamblers caught the taller blonde one in the back. He lived about four days, handcuffed to a bed in the Globe hospital. His brother went to the Penitentiary at Florence. The newspapers made a big thing of it, as Globe hadn't had so much excitement in a long time. The brothers had done time in New Mexico, and the older one had pulled a seven-year hitch before that in Texas.

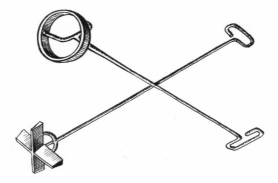

Six   The Gentle Art of Promotion

The Wiley family had a little cow ranch west of John's, and we rode a few days with them while they were gathering. A long canyon on their range had been the site of a gold rush back in the eighties, when pocket gold had been found there. Remains of old miners' camps could be found for miles along both sides of the canyon. In fact its name on the map was Gold Gulch. But after the first flurry, no new strikes in paying quantities had been found.

Crossing the gulch one morning, Westley Wiley (one of the younger boys) saw a piece of float gold in the creek bed. He picked it up and put it in the pocket of his chaps. That night at home he showed the gold to an old man who was working for board for himself and his family by doing chores around the place. A couple of months earlier the family had drifted in to Wiley's ranch in an old burro wagon, broke and hungry. Old man Wiley had felt so sorry for the woman and the three little children that he had let them stay around, even though he didn't really need any help. Well, the old man got the gold fever right away and wanted Westley to show him where he had picked up the piece. Next morning, riding one of his burros, he accompanied Westley, who led him to the spot.

After about a week of scrabbling and panning, the old man traced the vein back up the canyon to a point under a bluff. Stakes and location notices were already posted on the property, naming the owner as a woman living somewhere in California. After some correspondence she agreed to lease him her two claims. Convincing Mr. Wiley that he could pay him back in no time, the old man borrowed a couple of hundred dollars from him and got the lease for two months' time. Right near the surface he struck a small pocket of coarse gold. In Willcox, he hired a couple of Mexicans to do the pick and shovel work, and they began digging. Right away they found a couple of small pockets, one of which was a bonanza. Word of the strike got out, and within days the whole canyon was full of prospectors and camps once more.

The old man took his gold to Douglas each day with a deputy as guard, and left it in a bank. His run of large nuggets was soon over and an occasional small one was all he turned up during the remaining time of his lease. The woman owner of the claims had gotten the news too, so when he called her to renew the lease she wasn't about to. There was some fine gold left but he had no facilities for working it even had he known how, which he didn't. Before his lease was up the gold had petered out, but the old man was mad because the woman had

51

refused him a renewal, so he had the Mexicans blast out the pillars of ground holding up the roof and caved in the whole workings.

Before anyone knew his intentions, he went to Douglas, drew all his gold out of the bank there, and crossed over into Mexico with it. His wife and kids were left stranded at Wiley's, and Old Man Wiley was out the money he had loaned him for the lease. As far as I know he was never heard of again. The prospectors and miners working the canyon weren't even making their beans, and soon they quit and left. Then a new development took place.

Old Bill Bondurant got wind of the strike. He was one of the slickest mining promoters that ever hit the West. After a quick trip out from California to get the lay of the land, he quickly bought up a few leases and patented claims. Hurrying back to California, he formed a company which he named the Gold Belt Mining Company. He gave the papers a glowing account of the recent wonderful gold strike made in the gulch, where nuggets as large as walnuts were scooped up in handfuls, barely beneath the grass roots. His company was going to spend hundreds of thousands of dollars to build a good road into the property, where a huge flotation mill would be erected to recover the millions in fine gold his claims had uncovered. He really painted a flowery picture for the California papers, making sure the eastern papers would get the story also. At Willcox he let it be known that the company wanted to hire at least two hundred workmen right away, plus numerous teams, for the road construction. Soon Gold Gulch was again alive with camps. This time there were road-builders' tents.

While the road work was in progress, Bondurant hired a few miners to start a tunnel in the face of a hill. After it had been drifted in about thirty feet and all nicely timbered and shored up, he brought in some mine rails and an ore car. The track laid and the car in place, he was about ready to set the stage for his play. Filling the ore car full of rocks, he had it placed just ahead of the adit, or portal, of the tunnel. Grouping his miners around the car, together with Tomlins (his superintendent) and a couple of fellows in choke bore britches and miners' hats, he had them pose with wide grins and beaming countenances. All held sample picks and wore high laced boots. He himself stood in the foreground holding up a large rock, supposedly pure gold. His photographer snapped picture after picture of this ecstatic group, from all angles.

The few miners were then paid off and sent on their way, and Bondurant left on the next train out of Willcox. Tomlins, the time keeper, and the road workers remained on the job.

Bill Bondurant had some of the prettiest and most artistic engraving jobs one would ever see made up on his stock certificates. On beautiful bonded paper, spread across the top like a rainbow, was a wide belt with ornate buckle, all of pure gold. Beneath, in fancy lettering, were the words: "The Gold Belt Mining Company, of Gold Gulch, Arizona." A sharp clear picture showed the ore car and the jubilant men around it. Only now, the actual glitter of gold shone from the rocks piled high on the car. In Bill's hand were a glowing account of the assay per ton, a fine report by a mining engineer, and a wonderfully-worded description of the work the company had done and expected to do in the near future, along with an architect's picture of how the property would look upon completion of the mill. I would almost have bought stock in the company myself after reading the certificate. There was a lot more, proclaiming that only a very limited amount of this gilt-edged Gold Belt stock was being reluctantly released for purchase to a *very select* group of people fortunate enough to get in on the ground floor of such a once-in-a-lifetime opportunity.

Armed with a suitcase full of these masterpieces of art and doubletalk, some fake assay reports, and some *real* high grade gold ore samples, Bill went East to clean up. He wasn't only slick; he was slippery. I had left that part of the country long before the completion of the story, but I ran across some fellows from Willcox who filled me in. I also read an account in the papers of the demise of the Gold Belt Mining Company, and the indictment by a California Grand Jury of Tomlins and some others I did not know for operation of a fraudulent mining scheme and for selling fraudulent stock. Bill Bondurant slipped between the fingers of the law and got away with most of the proceeds. I heard that the mill they finally built was only a little one horse affair, and never even went into operation.

Years later, I ran across Bill Bondurant again, still up to his old tricks and going strong. His last venture that I recall was his attempt to promote the sale of stock in the "Mine with the Iron Door," a legendary Spanish lost mine in the Catalina Mountains near Tucson. Harold Bell Wright had written a book with that title while he was living near Tucson years before. Purely fiction, like all stories of lost mines and buried treasure, it stirred the imagination and interest of the readers until many people got to believing it was a true story and there actually was such a mine. Old Bill Bondurant knew human nature, and such a story was just made to his specifications for another crack at the pocketbook of a gullible public. The trouble was that by the time he had gotten around to promoting it, new "blue sky" laws had been enacted to protect the public against just such a fleecing as he had planned. These were laws with sharp teeth, that even he couldn't escape. His whole sand castle came tumbling down around his ears after he had spent a lot of money baiting the trap.

In his heyday Bill was a flashy dresser and a high liver, spending money like water and traveling in the best of style. He was one of the old school of western mine promoters who bled the eastern seaboard of millions of dollars and gave the western mining business a shady reputation which it took a long, long time to overcome. The last time I saw him was at a little shipping corral on the Black Canyon Road north of Phoenix. He was trying to pawn his gold nugget watch chain to a cattle buyer for a few dollars to eat on. So passed into limbo Bill Bondurant; old and shabby and broke. But, thinking back on it, that cattle buyer *might* have been smarter to have had that watch chain assayed first. Who knows?

Early in the Fall of 1922, I was riding up Bonita Creek. I had passed several ancient cliff dwellings, perched like swallows' nests in the canyon walls, before I came to a ranch house tucked away around a bend. I stopped to ask about the trail on ahead, and the lady who answered my hail invited me to rest a while and drink some coffee. After we had talked about cattle prices, the weather, and the usual subjects ranch people discuss, I asked if she had heard of the gun fight between the Clifton posse and the gang of horse thieves down in the Dos Cabezas.

"Yes," she said quietly. "Jonny Miller was my son."

I didn't quite know what to say. I had said too much already. Thinking about it as I rode along up the canyon, I wondered if this hadn't been the other hideout station the gang had used on their route to Mexico. This wild isolated canyon would have been ideal for the purpose.

Missing the trail at one point, I found myself boxed in a dead end, with barely room between the towering walls to turn my horses around in order to back track out of there. Just before dusk I climbed the steep zig zag trail at the head of the canyon, to find myself atop a high malapai mesa. There were no signs of habitation, so I camped where I was for the night.

The next afternoon I came to the Ash Flat headquarters ranch of the Chiricahua Cattle Company on the Apache Indian reservation. The men were shoeing up to begin their fall roundup and still needed a few more cowboys. When John Osborne, the foreman, returned from the bull pasture he hired me. Every cowboy in Arizona had heard of the "Cherrys" (as the ranch was dubbed), and how mean their horses were, so I didn't know whether or not I could make a hand with that outfit; but I was willing to try. Tom Ranier was their straw boss, and he cut me a reasonably gentle string of horses to work on.

The country being too rough for a wagon, the Cherrys used a string of pack mules for the cook outfit, and every man had an extra horse on which to pack his bed. Those first few days of shoeing were real exciting, but hard on cowboys and old clothes. About nine out of ten of those big old Cherry horses had to be tied down to shoe, and they sure weren't docile about that. There were a lot of skinned up men and horses both, before we were finished.

Bill Sparks was the cook for the outfit, and two Apache Indian boys wrangled the horses. Our first camp was made at some big corrals out on Ash Flat, a few miles from headquarters. Andy Green, Charley

Engle and Cotton Evans were the three rough string men; but from what I'd seen of the horses the outfit needed several more. That first afternoon they spent letting the hammer down on their mounts. One would call out the name of a horse, and a mounted cowboy would rope and drag it out of the remuda. Once the horse was saddled, the rough string man would mount, and the show was on. After his horse had bucked itself out, he would pull off the saddle and retire to the fence to rest while the next man was drawing his horse.

Some of those old owl-headed horses sure took their tails in their teeth and turned handsprings in that big square corral. Andy Green rode one big grullo named "The Bull Pup" which bucked so hard with him he had to lie down a long time after he had dismounted. Charley Engle drew a black horse from his string that was real waspy to saddle. Before he could reach the cinch the black would throw a fit and loosen it. After several attempts, Charley got hot under the collar and fought that crazy horse around until it got alongside a big boulder sticking up through the ground. Jumping from the boulder, he landed astraddle of his horse bareback and, with a handful of mane, he fit his spurs to both shoulders. Every time that black hit the ground he bawled and grunted like a wild boar. He was really leaping for the moon, Charley digging him in both shoulders on every jump, until they reached the far fence. Too late, the horse tried to turn, and they hit the fence broadside with a jar. A sharp snag caught Charley under the rib and jerked him off, to fall in the corner. He was hurt and couldn't get up. Tom Rainier and a couple of the boys ran over to him, and I saw Tom look down, then turn away acting sick. The other two boys had pulled open his shirt where a lot of blood was coming out of the hole in his side. One jumped on a horse and headed for the camp in the draw to get some bandages. Tom Ranier was still leaning on the fence with his head on his arms trying to keep from being sick. That was the first time I realized he was one of those few people who couldn't stand the sight of human blood. The boys quickly patched Charley up and helped him back to camp, while Cotton Evans and Andy Green went ahead and topped out the rest of his horses along with their own. They were a rough and ready crew, those Cherry cowboys.

That evening in camp, Bill Sparks, the cook, began horsing around with some of the cowboys, all in fun. He sneaked up behind Fats

Chapman who was sitting on the ground, jumped astraddle of his back and wrapped his arms around Fats' neck in a strangle hold. It looked as though he had him completely fouled. But Fats was a strong husky old boy. Struggling around, he finally got on his knees and from there to his feet. With one arm loose, he reached back and got a hold on the cook, pulled him loose and flanked him like a big calf, throwing him to the ground with a thud. Sparks couldn't get up. He was hurt bad, in the back. Fats felt pretty badly about it because he hadn't intended to hurt him. It was all done in fun; but that lick removed Bill Sparks from the roundup, and the outfit had to hire another cook, Dixie Taylor, to finish out the job.

Riding for the "Cherrys", a cowboy needed a lantern more often than a bed. The days were long and hard, and two hours of night herd on cattle, plus two more on horse guard with the remuda regularly every night, rain or whatever, sure didn't leave much time for sleep. In fact, it got plumb monotonous. Beef and beans, biscuits and coffee every day grew old too, pretty fast. Every time the company truck came out from Globe it brought a load of cowboys and took a load back.

For two days we trailed a big bunch of cattle, divided into three herds, to the shipping pens at Calva on the railroad. The lead herd was all big steers, three years old and up. The second consisted of about five hundred head of yearlings. And the third was a mixed one of old bulls, cows, and calves. The first night out, the big steers stampeded early, and the yearling herd made a run off the bed ground at about eleven o'clock. No one got more than a couple of winks that night. At Calva, many of the big steers got bogged in the quicksand crossing the Gila River, and we were a long time getting them snaked out on to solid ground. Our cattle cars wouldn't arrive until the next day. The dust was so thick around the cattle pens that it was hard to breathe, but close to the pens was the only place flat enough for us to roll our beds out on when night came. Fats Chapman and Concho Bill Wheeler talked to the station agent who told them no trains were due before morning over the line. So, to get out of the dust, they carried their beds up the track a ways and bedded down right between the rails. Along about midnight an extra freight train coming from Globe rounded the curve through a cut, rolling along slowly. The engineer saw the beds on the track, pulled the whistle cord, and set the brakes. Fats and Bill sat up and saw that big headlight looking them in the face, and I guess they thought hell was a-poppin'. Running like they were chased by a mad bull, they took off barefoot down the track, clad only in their drawers. The brakeman came up ahead of the engine and threw their beds off the track, and the train went on. By then they were awake enough to hobble back over the cinders to their soogans, but they didn't try sleeping on the tracks any more. Tom Ranier went off to some Indian's wickiup along the river with one of the Apache boys and came back as drunk as a boiled owl late in the night. They had been drinking "tulapi," a mash beer made by the Apaches. He was so sick the next day he couldn't help us load the cattle. We all ate enough dirt around those dusty corrals to plant a potato patch in. I was mighty glad to see the last of the cattle enter the cars that day.

The upper outfit working on the Blue River finished up first and came down to throw their gathering of wild steers in with ours. A week later we made another trail drive to Calva. That wound up the little ball of yarn for all of us except the steady men, who were going to stay on the ranch through the winter. The morning I got my two private horses from the pasture, the rest and good grass had them slick and shining. My saddle horse was feeling so frisky that he took me for a bronc ride before I was able to ride him out of the corral.

My first night away from the "Cherrys" was spent in the tules along the river bank at old Fort San Carlos. A week later I was riding through the Tonto Basin country north of Roosevelt Dam. Stopping one afternoon to water my horses at a ranch, I talked with the owner, Harry Howell, for a while. I told him I was looking for a job riding, but he knew of none. A couple of days later near Pine a fellow stopped me and said he had had a phone call from a Lower Tonto rancher instructing me to come back to ride some colts. That was how I became acquainted with George Felton and the Cross Seven Ranch.

Felton's range lay on the east side of the Tonto River, extending several miles up and down it from his big adobe house. Eastward, it went to the high rimrocks of the rugged Sierra Ancha Mountains. Along the river the flats produced good "filaree" or Alfilaria, and the foothills and lower ridges of the mountains were well covered with rooted grass. Higher, the country was rough and brushy with manzanita thickets, and shin oak taller than a horseback rider's head.

George Felton was a huge man. He stood about six feet four and was heavy. His wrists were as big around as my legs, and his hands looked like hams. His wife, a pleasant Swedish woman years younger than he, was rather short. Her mother lived with them, and they had one son, Louis, a big hulk of a boy at nineteen, but a little touched in the head, somehow. I soon found out that Lou was a bone of contention between his mother and Old George since he was an only child and not bright. She was the protective hen with a lone chick, while George saw him only as a big, strong, disappointing lout who couldn't remember anything he was told to do for more than five minutes at a time.

George was a lover of good horses and he owned nothing but good ones. The eight colts he wanted me to ride were a fine looking group. None were raw broncs. They had all been ridden and were gentle, though none were bridle-wise yet. George watched me handle and ride Shiner, a tall sleek black and the one he thought most likely to act up. He seemed satisfied with my performance, so we got off to a good start together. Whenever I had any spare time I chopped up a lot of wood and kept the box in the kitchen piled high, thereby keeping my rating high with the women folk also. Lou liked everyone, unless crossed, so he was no problem to me. I spent almost two years with the Cross Seven, and I learned a lot from Old George during that time.

Here in the mountain country, cattle were worked California style, as opposed to the more open country where they were worked the Texas way. For those who do not know, I shall try to explain the difference. On the flat lands, at the start of a drive, the crew loped for miles across the country, all of the men starting out together. The boss would begin by dropping off a man here, then another a mile or so farther on, gradually creating a great semi-circle of cowboys until the last man had been dropped out. Then these men would begin moving in toward a distant prearranged spot where the roundup was to be held, driving everything ahead of them. If one man was having too much trouble, another would lope over to help him a little, then go back to his own place in the drive. By the time they all had reached the roundup point, there would be the cattle, like fish in a huge net. Now, about two or three men on the best cutting horses would ride into the herd and begin cutting out the steers to be sold. As these were dodged out, they were driven several hundred yards away from the main herd, where they were held up by a couple of riders.

On the flat lands, it is a cardinal sin to allow a horse to turn his head away from the animal being cut out until it is well on its way to the cut herd. After all the steers are cut out, a branding fire is built on the opposite side of the main herd, some distance away, and the irons put in to heat. That gives the herd time to settle down, and the calves the chance to find their mothers. When the irons are hot, one or two good ropers ride into the herd with rope in hand, a loop hanging down alongside of their horses. They never swing the loop around their heads, but cast it in an overhand throw that fits the loop right around the calf's head. The second the rope touched the calf's neck, the horse whirls and heads for the fire at a trot, with the calf bucking and bawling at the end of a thirty foot rope. The flankers on the ground quickly throw and hold it, pulling the loop from its neck so the roper can ride back into the herd, coiling his rope for the next loop on the way. One man branding and one marking with a sharp knife can be finished with a calf before it knows what happened to it. When the last calf has been caught and branded, the irons are removed from the fire and, leaving the main herd where it is, the crew drives the steer herd away to pasture or turns the steers in with the day herd when there is no pasture available. With plenty of horses, when work is heavy a cowboy may change horses three or four times a day. Every man has a job to do, and on a well-run outfit everything goes along as smooth and fast as a circus sets up its tents.

That is the Texas style of working cattle. In the mountains the work is done differently. Here each man has only three or four horses, and chances are the one he leaves camp on in the morning is the one he rides all day. Each man feeds his horse a *good* feed of rolled barley, or oats, the first thing in the morning. If he is a good cowboy, he takes care of his horse's back, seeing that his saddle blankets are clean and that there are enough of them to cushion the saddle properly. I have worked for outfits where the horses' backs were washed with warm water and soap before saddling every morning and again at night after coming in to camp. And it pays off well, too.

Most mountain cowboys carry from two to three tie-down ropes on their saddles, plus a longer rope (usually tied behind the cantle) with which to neck some old outlaw steer or bull to a tree. Here the horses travel at a walk, for the country is all up or down, and steep. Steel horseshoes are used instead of the softer iron shoes of the open country because here, where a horse is traveling on rocks all day, iron shoes would wear out inside of a week or two. From past experience a mountain rancher knows the best way to work his particular country and lays out his drives accordingly. He also knows where his wildest cattle run, and where almost all of their get-away trails are. Since most of the ranch houses are down in the canyons, along the creeks and rivers, the horses have to start climbing soon after leaving camp. The men travel single file, with the boss usually leading the way. Frequent stops are made to let the horses catch their breath and rest on the steep climbs. Most mountain men use breast collars on their horses to keep saddles from slipping back on uphill climbs, and to help their horses pull when leading wild cattle. Having reached the country to be worked that day, the boss tells each man where to go and where they are expected to get together for the first drive. From then on each man is pretty much on his own. He watches every thicket for any movement of the brush that might indicate cattle hidden in it. Within a short while the country appears empty of men or cattle. Then a cowboy is seen high on a brushy mountainside working his way around it, across side canyons, up and down until the brush begins popping, and briefly red flashes of color show where cattle are running ahead of him. He follows their trail like a blood hound, working above and below to turn them in the direction he wants them to go. On another ridge, perhaps a half mile away, another rider may show up. On each high point he will stop to look over the country. If he spots hidden cattle the other man can't see, he usually waves his hat up or down to indicate to him where they are, and waits to see if he gets them before moving on. As long as the cattle are on the move in the right direction the drive goes along steadily. But when some wild cattle try to turn back to make a get-away, the drive stops until a cowboy either gets them turned in the right direction or ropes them and ties them to a tree. All the men try to work through a piece of country together as much as possible.

Often the drive is held up for a half an hour or more while some old brush hand tries to out-maneuver a wild steer or bull that has turned back too far to bring in to the drive. It's hard and dangerous work to catch and tie such a critter in the mountains alone. Men have been killed doing it, and horses have been gored so badly they never recovered. It sure is no job for amateurs. Most mountain hands carry a short de-horning saw along with which to tip the horns of such cattle. About a couple of inches off the tip of the horns does the job pretty well.

There are tricks to all trades, and tying a big bull or a steer to a tree calls for a lot of know-how plus some luck too. Even a small tree like a cedar as big around as a man's arm will hold the largest animal if tied right. To do the job properly, just the right distance from the tree is required. If tied too close and the steer falls down, he may die because his head is held so high. Too long, he may get tangled in the rope with a forefoot, or break loose. Every knot must be tied so it can be untied again when someone returns to lead him to a corral or pasture. As I say, it takes a lot of know-how.

When the men get together with the morning's drive, the cattle are allowed to rest awhile as the men unsaddle, shake the sticks and leaves from the saddle blankets, and allow their horses' backs to dry off a bit. Saddled and ready to move the herd, one cowboy rides ahead to hold the leaders back and to show the way. The rest, ropes ready, on all sides, move the cattle to follow the lead man. They watch every move the cattle make and can practically read the mind of any animal before he breaks for the brush in an attempt to get away. Sometimes it takes a mile or more of close herding before wild cattle settle down to traveling instead of trying to escape. Now, a couple of men wing out from the herd to brush out the country on either side. They give the herd time to get ahead some, then work the side hills and canyons, throwing the cattle they find into the herd as it travels along.

When the drive reaches a corral, first the calves and orejanas (long ears) are branded. Usually two men rope together, one catching the head, the other both hind feet. Except for the very small calves there is no flanking done. Then they part out the steers. Lined up abreast across the center of the corral, the cowboys form a division fence of horses. Mountain horses aren't usually much shakes as cutting horses, and sometimes a rider drives four or five head together along the fence. The line of cowboys tries to let through the ones that are wanted, yet turn the others back into the bunch. Once the steers are cut out, the riders surround them and drive them to the home pasture.

Gathering wild cattle is hard, exciting, and dangerous work, and any man who can out run and outsmart those kind of cattle in a rough mountain country can well deserve the title "top hand."

Eight or nine men are an average for a mountain roundup. Cattle that had to be roped and tied to trees are led in either the first or the second day after they have been tied. By then they have wearied of fighting the tree and their heads are sore from the tie rope. Afoot, the cowboy lays the loop of his rope over their horns, upside down so it will not loosen. Cinching his saddle good and tight he rides his horse close against the animal, takes a couple of dallies on the horn with his rope, then, leaning over the animal, unties the head rope. Once loose from the tree, for a while it is nip and tuck as the steer tries to hook the horse and rider and get away from them at the same time. However, a good cowboy will have him leading within a mile. He never jerks too much on the sore head, only dallying when the steer is pulling away. Most of the time he just goes along holding the rope in one hand. After a while the steer is leading along on a slack rope against the horse's shoulder. All this sounds easy, but it's harder than it looks to be.

At the Cross Seven my hardest job at first was to get along with the ranch dogs. George Felton had used cow dogs to work his cattle with for years, and he still had about ten of them when I came there. His best one, a big black, was named "Nig". He was getting old and had a bad forefoot which made him lame if he worked too hard. He was a catch dog. Kaiser was a small Australian shepherd, a good heeler. The rest were mostly young dogs and pups. The ranch house yard was fenced with a high woven wire fence where the dogs were kept when not out working. The whole pack was vicious toward strangers, and no one dared enter the yard until some member of the family came to the gate to escort them in. But they were worth their weight in gold working the cattle. Old George always carried a long bull whip on his saddle and many a time I have seen him drive thirty to fifty head of cattle for miles with only the help of his dogs. He would crack that blacksnake a couple of times and the cattle would string out on a rocky trail while George followed up in the rear. If some cattle got too far off the trail, George would motion to one of his dogs and he would go up alongside and put the cattle back in line again. Kaiser, the heeler, came along behind George and when calves would slow down too much he would nip their heels and put them up in the bunch fast. Working the high country, the dogs would climb places a horse could hardly stand on and bring wild cattle out of the brush as well as a half dozen cowboys could.

George's wife was a pretty good hand herself, and rode all the time with us. I got along fine with the colts, and they were doing right well on their second roundup. Soon I knew most of the people in the basin and surrounding country pretty well. There were the Chilsons who owned the Bar T Bar, the HI and the H Bar ranches; the Griffins of the Seventy-six Quarter Circle on Rye Creek; Walt and Polly Brown, the J Slash X Ranch on the Sierra Anchas, and many other outfits. And I met and worked with a number of their cowboys.

Each Spring and Fall after roundup we made a trail drive to Phoenix in the Salt River Valley. We usually started from Tonto with only our own cattle, but at intervals along the trail we ran across other outfits and all traveled together. If the weather held good it was bad enough; when it stormed it was hell.

The first day's drive down the river wasn't bad, though the mesquite thickets were hard to get through. There were a couple of corrals and a small wire trap at Old Fort Reno, our camping place for the first night. The second day was a nightmare, for just as soon as we turned the cattle out of the gate we were faced with a maze of huge granite rocks, many as large as houses, and thick brush on a steep climb up the side of Mount Reno (of the Mazatzal Range) to the pass. It was a fight all the way to force about three hundred head of cattle up that steep mountain. Men and horses would be exhausted and skinned up breaking their way through the stiff, sharp brush to the top. Just before reaching the pass, we came to the remains of the old military road which had been built by the army between Fort McDowell on the Verde River and Fort Reno, the outpost on the Tonto, when the troops were fighting the Apaches in the late 1800's. Beyond the pass, it was only a few miles to some corrals on Sycamore Creek, belonging to the Colcord Ranch, where we corralled for the night.

The next day's drive was comparatively easy, as the cattle were tired and hungry from the ordeal of crossing the Reno Pass and were glad to browse on the low shin oak brush and what grass there was along the trail. By now quite a few were sore-footed, and this day's slow travel helped them a bit.

Just before sundown we reached the Dos S Ranch, owned by Bernard Hughes, where there were several large, strong brush corrals. Although they were the strongest along the entire trail, we often had a stampede there, and once lost several head, killed in the pile up, before the stout fences fell from the weight of cattle against it. Bernard was a work-brittle oldtimer, and we would hear his crew coming in to the ranch with the day's gather hours after dark. Then the men would be up and away before daylight the next morning.

We encountered the most difficult section of the entire trail the forenoon of the day we left the Dos S Ranch. The cattle, already sore-footed from Reno Mountain, quickly had their hoofs worn down to the quick by the sharp granite rocks on "Screw Tail Hill." The cattle had to traverse a long rocky series of switch-back road, all down hill, before we reached our noon camp. In our chap pockets all of us carried pieces of old horse shoes which we had cut in two before leaving the ranch, and a couple of the men had a shoeing hammer and some small horseshoe nails along. When an animal grew too sore-footed we shod him along the way. On some drives we had as many as fifty head shod by the time we reached the Salt River Valley.

Nooning at the foot of "Screw Tail Hill," we were over the worst of the rocks. It was an easy drive from there to the ranger station, our next night camp. This was an old abandoned place with a couple of wire corrals. Quite often here we would meet with Jeff Adams' herd, also on its way to Phoenix.

Old Jeff was an early day Sheriff of Maricopa County. With his son George and his daughter-in-law Maggie, he operated a small ranch on the western slope of the Four Peaks, (the southern end of the Mazatzal Range). From this camp we all traveled together. Six or seven miles down a wide sand wash leading to the Verde River we

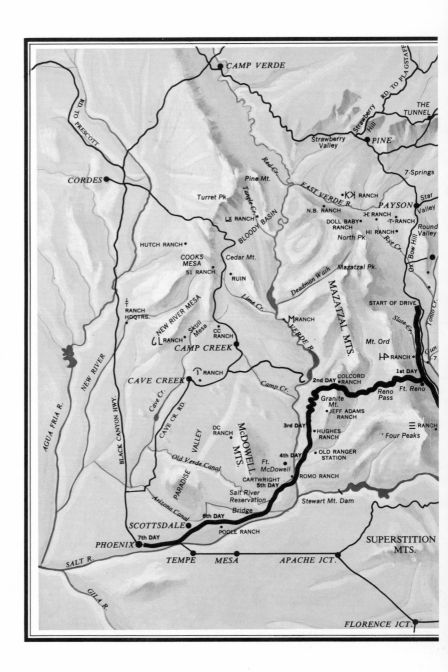

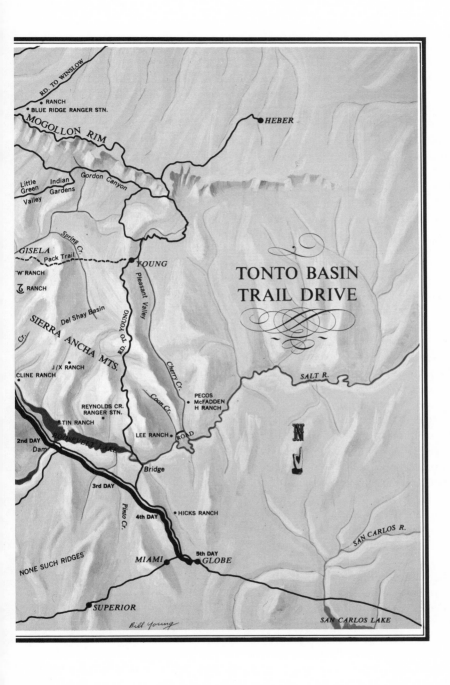

RD. TO WINSLOW

• RANCH
• BLUE RIDGE RANGER STN.

• HEBER

MOGOLLON RIM

Little
Green
Valley

Indian
Gardens

Gordon Canyon

GISELA

Spring Cr.

Pack Trail

• YOUNG

"W" RANCH

RANCH

Del Shay Basin

Pleasant Valley

SIERRA ANCHA MTS.

Cr.

RD. TO YOUNG

J/X RANCH

CLINE RANCH

Cherry Cr.

Coon Cr.

SALT R.

PECOS
• McFADDEN
H RANCH

REYNOLDS CR.
RANGER STN.

TIN RANCH

LEE RANCH

ROAD

TONTO BASIN
TRAIL DRIVE

N

2nd DAY
Dam

Bridge

3rd DAY

Pinto Cr.

4th DAY

• HICKS RANCH

SAN CARLOS R.

NONE SUCH RIDGES

MIAMI

5th DAY
• GLOBE

• SUPERIOR

SAN CARLOS LAKE

Bill Young

trailed to the "Old Romo Ranch." Here we usually nooned for this day, reaching the crossing on the Verde River just below Old Fort McDowell in late afternoon.

The river crossing there was tricky, as beds of quicksand often shifted from place to place, and where we crossed last year might *now* be impassable. Sometimes the river would be high too, and we had to swim the herd across, a risky job at best. By the time we got the cattle and pack mules across, it would be almost dark.

About half a mile west of the crossing was an old round stake corral at the foot of a malapai mesa. All the trail drives had used it for years, and it had been torn down so many times by stampedes that it was a wreck. Every outfit spending the night there went around propping up the fence; then, after corralling the cattle, left a couple of men to ride around the outside and sing to them on two hour shifts all through the night. This kept the cattle from becoming too spooky.

The following day's drive was across the Fort McDowell Apache Indian Reservation, and to a wooden bridge across the Arizona Canal. By this time we were getting too close to civilization to suit these mountain cattle. Every tail boss dreaded this bridge, for if he hadn't had a run *before* he reached it, it was a cinch bet he would have one here. On a drive I helped make one spring, the Cline outfit from Lower Tonto was stuck here for three days trying to get across the bridge. Their cattle were wilder than most, and the first rattle the floor planking made when the leaders stepped on it brought them back in a wild run, time after time. They finally had to swim the cattle across the canal above the bridge, and we saw where their animals had torn down the banks on both sides for half a mile. The Salt River Water Users Association made the ranch pay for the costly repair work that had to be made on the canal.

When we came within sight of the bridge, George would have the lead cattle held up. Then just before the drags and sore-footed ones caught up, he had them worked off around the flank until they were in the lead. Easing them up to the bridge, he had us hold the sides close and keep quiet. Pretty soon some old gentle, or sore-footed animal would venture onto the bridge. Once the leader had started across, we kept easing others on behind him. After we had a little bunch on the bridge, George would signal the boys to bring up the rest, and they would follow the leaders. As the boards rattled and bounced they would jump and try to run ahead. But the slower cattle in front kept them slowed a bit until all the drags were across. Even then we always had a stampede, but it was on the other side of the canal, in open country. Usually, inside of a couple of miles we had the cattle together once more.

Soon after crossing the bridge, we turned west in the desert for another five miles, to reach the Poole Ranch. The ranch consisted of a couple of big alfalfa fields belonging to the widow of Dan Poole, who was one of Quantrell's Raiders in the Civil War. She lived in Scottsdale but kept a man at her place to irrigate and look after the property. Here we always let the cattle rest up a couple of days before going on to the stockyards at Phoenix, to ship.

The last day's drive to town was the most edgy of all. The cattle had never seen cars or many people afoot, and were already tired and nervous from the long seven-day trip from their mountain home. The least thing could tap them off, and very often did. Skirting the little town of Scottsdale on the south, we cut across Papago Park east of Phoenix and came out on Van Buren Street, then unpaved. We drove along a canal bank between the Tovrea Packing Company plant and Pueblo Grande, (pre-Columbian Indian ruins), to come out on Henshaw Road, another unpaved street running east and west. Henshaw led us across the south side of Phoenix to Seventh Avenue. There, turning north a few blocks we came to the railroad shipping pens. After working the cattle into carload lots, we rode north to Madison Street where we stabled our horses at the Star Livery Stables; or sometimes to Jefferson Street where we put up at the big yard of Billy Van Doren. Leaving our beds at the livery stable, we would head for the center of town to sample some of the fruits of civilization.

The boss never paid us off until the cattle were shipped, knowing cowboy failings. Once rid of the cattle, however, we had three or four days to spend our money and head back for Tonto. By pushing the pack mules along, we would make the Dos S Ranch the first night, and Tonto the second. Once, stopping at the Verde River crossing to lunch on canned sardines and crackers, I got a leaky can and a case of ptomaine poisoning. The river stood on end, and the big cottonwood trees began to spin around and around. The remainder of the trail home was no fun. But cowboys are tough, and I survived.

Franz Cooper owned the H FOUR Ranch across the Tonto River from the Cross Seven. He had a lot of old wild steers that ran on Mount Ord, and the Forest Service had been trying for a long time to make a count on his cattle. His range was so brushy and the cattle so wild the count was well-nigh impossible. But after we had delivered the Cross Seven Fall shipment to Phoenix, George loaned me to Franz to help him gather out some of those old moss-horned steers from the mountains. Franz's wife Ella was a plumb salty cowboy herself, having been raised on her father's ranch in the Tonto Rim country. So she and Franz, his brother Chester and myself, plus a couple of good cow dogs, spent several months catching and leading in big steers. One day we'd catch and tie, and the next lead off the mountain to a pasture along the river. That was a rough two months. Those old steers had bruised our shins with their horns so badly that every time we rode through some stiff brush we couldn't help hollering, it hurt so. By February, we had about a hundred and fifty head of those big old rough steers in the river pasture. Some were still hobbled, and others had their heads tied to a front foot, to keep them from jumping out.

Cattle buyers were as scarce as hens teeth right then, but Franz did get one out of Globe to come and look at his steers. We rounded up the pasture so that he could look at the cattle, and he began cutting out the ones he didn't want. I guess he figured he had Franz over a barrel, and sure enough those old steers were no prize beauties. Many of them were lame and skinned up plenty from their trip in from the mountains. This buyer kept whacking deeper and deeper, until he had cut more than half of the herd back as rejects.

Franz was getting madder on every cut. Finally he rode into the herd and had a pow-wow with this fellow. However the buyer reasoned that Franz couldn't afford to argue much on the way he cut the cattle as he knew that the Forest Service was threatening to file a trespass fine on Franz, and even cut his forest permit number by at least half. But he didn't take into account the fact that Franz was about half Indian and had a very unruly temper at times. Sitting on their horses out in the middle of the herd, the two men jawed a while, and I heard Franz tell the buyer to get out of the cattle and stay out. The buyer had begun to back track a little by then, but he was wasting his breath because Franz called over to us to catch the ones that were tied and cut their ropes off.

"We'll turn the whole damned bunch out!" he shouted. And that is just what we did.

The district Forest Ranger about had a stroke when he got the news. Free once more on the mountain, most of those old steers never were gathered again. Franz sold the outfit rather than concede an inch to the Forest Service or to any chinchy cattle buyers.

Times were getting rough on ranchers along the Tonto. By spring many outfits were desperate, so when a man named Howell came into the country offering to contract a lot of their cattle at a fairly good price, many ranchers jumped at the chance. Howell looked like Santa Claus to them.

In those days there weren't many preliminaries to a cattle deal. Once an agreement was reached between buyer and seller on price, kind and number of head, and when and where the cattle were to be delivered, a handshake clinched the deal. I've often seen two men, squatted down on their boot heels, close a deal involving thirty thousand dollars worth of cattle without a scrap of paper involved. No forfeit money was put up, no contract signed. The word of two honest men was enough. Things are a lot different now.

By the first of June of that year, all the cattle Howell had bought took the trail for Winslow. The Bar T Bar, the Booths of Gisela, the Seventy-six Quarter Circle, Frank Holder of Payson, and numerous other ranches had cattle in that drive. I had hired out to Dick Taylor on the East Fork of the Verde River to go through the herd belonging to him and Doll Baby Smith. We were all to get together just north of Payson as one big trail herd. By the time we reached the Tunnel Road where we climbed out on top of the Mogollon Rim, there must have been close to three thousand head of steers in the drive.

Once on top of the Rim, the thickets of jack pine were hard to get through without losing any of our steers. Poison weeds caused us to have to leave three or four along the way to our first night's stop. During the second day on the trail the cattle were badly in need of water and we figured on watering them at Hart Tank that night. When we reached the tank it was dry, and after a couple of hours of trying to hold those thirsty steers on night herd, the trail boss decided that we would have to let them walk.

Trailing about three thousand head of cattle through a heavy pine forest in the night was like playing blind man's bluff. Except for the faint light of stars peeping through the tall pines now and then, it was as black as the inside of a well. How we kept from losing a lot of steers I'll never know. By the crack of dawn we were skirting Jack's Canyon where the timber was thinning out into open country. Once we were out of the timber, the boss sent a man on ahead to scout out a place to water the herd. We laned the steers and made a count, finding that we had lost about twenty head. Several men turned back to see if they could find them while the rest of us went on.

By now the cattle were traveling fast, gaunt for lack of water. The scout came back and led the way to a lake near the Winslow water works. Once the steers caught the scent of water, there was no holding them back. The last mile was a regular stampede, and the cowboys were hard put to keep the animals from piling up on top of one another in the lake and drowning. It took hours before they were all watered out and on dry land once more. In the meantime the boys who had gone back found most of the little bunch we had lost in the dark and had brought them up to the herd.

From here it was only a short drive to the old Hash Knife Ranch where Howell was to receive the herd. He had sent a little one-team wagon and about twenty-five head of Navajo Indian ponies, wrangled by a Navajo boy, along with his foreman (an old Texan) to meet us there. After about thirty straight hours in the saddle, we were glad to see the last steer go through the gate into the huge Hash Knife corrals.

After feeding our horses and ourselves, the job of tallying out the cattle began. Each animal had to be put through the chute, branded with a tally bar as his age and owner were entered into a book. That turned out to be a three-day job. Out here on the flats it was hot, and we scattered a lot of sweat branding out those steers.

Howell had a lot of desert country leased between Holbrook and Navajo Springs, his headquarters, and he intended to scatter this herd all along between those two places. He offered us pretty good wages to go on through with him clear to Navajo Springs, and several of us hired out to him. If I had known what was ahead of us I would have turned back right there with the boys who returned to Tonto. But ignorance is bliss, I guess.

During the heat of the day all we could do was let the cattle lie in what little shade they could find under the fantastic formations of sandstone rocks that dotted the country. In the evening we would string them out and drive by starlight, stopping from time to time to let them rest a little.

The thirty-three miles to Holbrook took us two days. Here we had to cross the Little Colorado River, a thin trickle of water at this time of year, right in the middle of a wide expanse of quicksand that would bog a saddle blanket.

By watching some old desert cows come in to water we found the most solid crossing, but even then we had several head bog down before we got across. Those old desert cows would feel their way step by step towards the water. When they began to sink in the quick-sand they would ease back slowly, then begin again in a new spot. Once they had found a place firm enough to get to water on, they would travel single file until all were where they could drink. Coming back, they would again take the same trail single file. They sure knew how to get through by being slow and careful.

The days were too hot to sleep and we drove most of the nights, so we were all cranky and tired as we made our way along the sandy Puerco River, where the winds blew cutting sand and silt into our eyes and noses. Two or three fights developed in camp over trivial arguments just because of edgy nerves and lack of sleep and rest. This was a god-forsaken-looking country, compared to ours on the Tonto, and we were sure glad when we had covered the fifty-odd miles between Holbrook and Navajo Springs. Drawing our pay, we wasted no time hitting the back track. At Holbrook we left a couple of the boys who had tied on a big jag to come on when they sobered up enough. At Winslow I bought a new rope at a mercantile company store, after a night on the town. Driving our pack horses ahead of us, we hit the road for Payson.

Along Jack Creek another old boy and I found a cow trail off the bluffs where we could get down into the canyon to water. The other boys stayed on the road with the pack horses. After drinking through our handkerchiefs at a slimy green hole of water, I threw my new rope in to soak it up a little. We had spotted some big steers on the opposite side, grazing on a malapai mesa, and figured to stretch our ropes a little. Out on the mesa a little way I billed to a big black long-horned steer and hung my twine over his horns. When he hit the end of the rope my partner heeled him and jerked him down. About that time we looked up to see an old touring car heading our way coming from the east. As quickly as I could I jumped off my horse, ran down to the big steer, and pulled my rope off his head. The two men in the car were coming on as fast as they could over the rocky mesa, bent on seeing who we were. By then they were getting too close for comfort, and to discourage them a little I pulled my short 30-30 rifle from the saddle scabbard, lay down on my belly behind a malapai rock, and began laying down a few bullets just a bit in front of their car. After they saw the dust fly out of a couple of rocks in front of them, they took the hint and veered off, making a big circle away off to one side. I mounted up, and we made deep tracks on into the timber south of us.

Neither of us knew the country on this side of the canyon and we got thoroughly lost in the tall pines that night before reaching the Blue Ridge Ranger Station where we had planned to spend the night with Elmer Piper. He was an old cowboy camped there to look after some Chilson steers on their summer range. It was about midnight when we rode into Blue Ridge and bedded down.

The next morning Elmer Piper told us that the telephone line had been buzzing with rangers trying to head off a couple of fellows who had been seen attempting to butcher a beef belonging to the Heart Cattle Company near Chevalon Butte. The men had shot at some Heart men and escaped into the timber, but rangers were guarding the roads at the Brown Ranger Station behind us and expected to capture them at any time. We didn't let on that we knew anything about the deal, and as soon as breakfast was over we hightailed through the timber and rode off the Rim as soon as we could.

At Payson we met up with a couple of brothers who had made the trip with us as far as the Hash Knife, and I threw in with them and rode along to their little ranch at Round Valley, a few miles south of town. They were a pair of wild old boys who would do just about anything that struck their fancy. An older brother, with the real first name of Jesse James, lived in Pleasant Valley on top of the Sierra Ancha Mountains. An older sister was married to a carpenter and lived in the smelter town of Cottonwood, near Jerome. One young sister, Mary, lived at home with their parents.

Those three boys were pegged as renegades, in a country full of renegades. They were not outlaws but they came near being just that at times. Like the time one morning when the three of us rode into Payson, tied our horses in an alley behind Boardman's store, and walked down the street to A. J. Franklin's Pool Hall. A couple of Deputy Sheriffs were in town from the county seat at Globe. They were having breakfast at a boarding house and, having finished, came down the steps just after we had passed by. A minute after we walked into A. J.'s they came in behind us. I had sat down at a poker table, brother Fred was at the bar talking to A. J., and brother Dallas was shooting a few practice shots on the pool table. One Deputy stepped onto a side porch, the other started around the end of the pool table near Dallas. As quick as a rattlesnake could strike, Dallas swapped ends with that pool cue and rapped the Deputy right between the horns with the heavy end, laying him out cold on the floor. It all happened so quick that Dallas was out the side door and gone before any of us got our mouths closed. The other Deputy and A. J. worked over their fallen companion for quite a spell before he came to enough to sit up. Fred and I had a hard time convincing that big Deputy that we had no idea of why Dallas had swung on his partner. He took our names and addresses and went looking for Dallas all over town. But Dallas had gotten his horse and was long gone to the tall uncut. The Deputies came out to the ranch at Round Valley and quizzed his folks, but he hadn't been there. Three months later he came riding in to Round Valley in the middle of the night, slept three or four hours, got some clothes and left again before daylight. He still wouldn't say why he hit that Deputy, but I always thought he believed the law was after him that morning in Payson. Actually they had never *heard* of him until then. During that time he hid out in Pleasant Valley with his brother, Jesse James.

Fred and I were sleeping in a side room one night when we awoke to hear horses coming, about four o'clock in the morning. We pulled on our levis and boots and went out to see who was riding in at that time of night. It was the older brother, Jesse James, his wife Ella, their young baby, and Dallas. They had three pack animals loaded to the hilt with the damnedest collection I ever saw. The animals carried five gallon cans of honey, new overalls, horse hobbles, cow bells, bridles, spurs, dutch ovens, razors, canned foods, sacks of barley, breast collars, three rifles, two extra six shooters, cartridges, a telescope, and heaven knows what else. Jesse's mother and his wife got busy cooking breakfast for the tribe, while Dallas and Jesse began hiding all that stuff they had stolen. A lot of it they put in a hole under the heating stove in the living room. The barley went to the barn, and some of the rest of the loot they hid out in the rocks and brush surrounding the place. Old Jack, the father of the boys, was off working on Doc Risser's ranch at the time.

The baby wasn't more than a couple of months old, and on that trip they had carried it horseback for more than fifty miles, over some of the roughest country in Arizona. Ella didn't look as though she was more than seventeen years old to me. She wanted to wash up some clothes for the baby and herself right after breakfast. Along about ten o'clock she was working at the tub just outside the back door while Jesse was cleaning an old cedar-handled six shooter on a bed by the window. On the wall hung an old fashioned crayon

portrait of Jesse, in an oval frame. After cleaning his Colt and reloading it, Jesse looked up at his picture and said:

"By God, Jesse, I'll just shoot your eye out!"

With that, he snapped a shot that broke the glass and picture
all to hell and gone. His mother, who was washing up dishes in the
kitchen, ran in, and Ella put her head in the back door to tell him
he should be ashamed to do such a thing in his mother's house.

"I just feel like shooting this morning, so get to dancing before
I shoot your boot heels off," he told Ella.

She paid no attention and sure enough he began shooting around
her feet so close that the gravel stung her ankles. When he had fired
his last shot, she dashed inside, grabbed up Fred's rifle standing in
a corner, levered a shell into the chamber and aimed it right at his
belly.

"Jesse, you son of a bitch, I've took all I'm ever going to from
you, and if you ain't out of sight in about two minutes I'm a-going
to kill you!" she said. She was mad enough to do it too. Jesse dived
out the door and around the house like a scared wolf, with his mother
and Mary screaming at Ella not to shoot. Dallas was laughing so
hard at the sight of Jesse in full flight he couldn't catch his breath.
All the shooting had set the baby to crying, and altogether it made
quite an uproar. The old lady finally got Ella calmed down some,
but she wouldn't give up the rifle, setting it against the house where
she was washing, just in case. Jesse stayed out in the brush all day,
and only came in just before supper after Fred had gone to tell him
that Ella had promised not to shoot him if he behaved.

Jesse set himself up as a pretty tough hombre, but actually he
didn't have the guts of a winter snow bird. Dallas was the only one
of the younger generation of that tribe with sand in his craw. I guess
he was the only one who had the nerve of his father and uncles.
Old Jack had been a United States Marshall in Oklahoma Territory
in its outlaw days. He was honest and had tried to raise his family
so, but now old and sickly, he had lost the upper hand. Disgusted,
he stayed away from home as much as he could.

Poor old Jack had a lot to live down on account of his family.
Its early history in Tonto Basin wasn't savory. From old timers this
is the way I heard it. First to come to the Tonto was Andy. Down
in the Sulphur Springs Valley he went by the name of Carrel. He
carried too long a loop in his rope to suit the ranchers down there,
and they finally invited him either to migrate or decorate a tree. On

the Tonto he bought a little remnant (sixty head) of an old mountain ranch and settled down there to increase his herd. To assist him in that endeavor, he sent for another brother, Bill, who was living in Oklahoma. Someone had shot an eye out of Bill back there, but it sure didn't prevent him from seeing any neighbors' calves that had escaped the branding iron. The brothers' first year's calf crop was about four hundred per cent, after which the neighbors to the south built eight miles of fence between the two ranches as a protection against losing any more calves.

Andy took a trip to Phoenix to establish an alibi, and while he was gone the wires were mysteriously cut between every post along the whole eight miles of fence. He was arrested and tried in court for that, but his alibi paid off and he was freed. The owners of the fence never rebuilt it. I guess they knew it would be cut again if they did.

Bill's kids were too small, but Andy used his own two boys and Jack's three, plus a few long loop cowboys, to work for him, and he had a system hard to beat. He had little brush and pole pens hidden away in almost inaccessible places on his range. There he kept big calves penned until they quit bawling for their mothers and their brands peeled. Ranchers from a long way off kept finding dead cows on their country which had been suckling big calves, and the calves were always missing. There were no signs of what had killed the cows. They had not been shot, their throats had not been cut, nor were there visible signs of why they had just lain down and died. But dead they were, and their calves were gone.

It was a situation too serious to ignore, and the ranchers got together to have a pow-wow about what to do. Finally they formed a pool and hired a couple of range detectives. These men high pointed the country early and late, but could never catch Andy or any of his men. Two strange men in the country stuck out like a billboard on a highway and Andy's outfit laid low for a while. However, the presence of these two hombres stopped the cows from dying, while they were around. Quite a spell after they had left the Tonto, cows began dying again.

Early one morning, a rancher found one that had just lain down and wasn't quite dead yet. Examining her closely he saw that she had been bleeding internally. After putting her out of her misery with his six shooter, he operated on her to see what had caused the bleeding. He discovered that her womb had been torn from the inside with an instrument such as a three-or-four-pronged hook of some kind. A cow thus torn might live for several days before dying of internal bleeding, but she could not travel far. Andy well knew that, even if anyone should stumble onto one of his hideout pens full of calves, no one could prove ownership of the calves, with their mothers dead. In cow country the only absolute proof that a certain calf belongs to a certain cow is to *see* the calf suck its mother cow.

The rancher spread the word of his find to the other cowmen, and the Tonto country was soon buzzing with talk of taking the law into its own hands. Even though they hadn't been able to catch any of Andy's outfit red handed, the ranchers knew he was guilty, and they didn't aim to let a court of law release him a second time just for lack of an eye witness.

Andy's own brother Bill saved him from the wrath of the Tonto ranchers. Old one-eyed Bill killed him. Working the hideout pens one day, Bill found a calf he recognized as one of his own, freshly branded in Andy's brand. Right away he hunted Andy up and, warning him that if he (Andy) enjoyed life and expected to reach old age, he had better never try to steal another calf from him. Andy pretended it was all a mistake, but Bill knew better.

This happened in early spring, just a couple of days before Andy was to throw a thousand steers on the trail to Flagstaff. Bill was to go along on the drive. The morning of the drive, just a few miles north of the Gisela ranch, Bill rode over from his little ranch to throw in with the herd, already on its way. On his way over he looked in at another hideout pen and found a second calf of his carrying Andy's brand. That cooked Andy's goose with Bill. When Bill rode over the last brushy hillside where he came in sight of the trail herd, Andy was out in front of the steers, leading the way, mounted on an old white horse he liked to ride on trail drives.

Bill rode to within about fifty feet of Andy before he pulled his short-barrelled 30-30 rifle from its scabbard under his right leg and shot him once from the hip in a sudden, snap shot. Andy started to fall from his horse, but saved himself by holding the saddle horn. He was hanging on one side as his old horse began turning around slowly on one tight rein. Bill watched a minute, then rode closer and shot him again.

"Fall off, you son-of-a-bitch!" were his parting words as he reined his horse around and rode back over the hill.

Andy's oldest boy was the first to reach him, down on his knees in the dust, opening his shirt to see where he was shot. No one made any attempt to follow Bill. That second shot had ended Andy's rustling days for good. Andy was wearing an almost new pair of boots, and two of Jack's boys almost had a fight over who was going to get them even before his body had been tied over his saddle to take back to the Gisela ranch.

At Globe the Sheriff of Gila County was notified and came out to bring Bill in. When he found him, Bill was at home drinking coffee, as unconcerned as a successful duck hunter. He went along to the county jail at Globe for his preliminary hearing, made his plea of not guilty, posted bond, and was soon home again to await his trial.

Although Bill had worked for Andy, the ranchers all felt that he had done a good piece of work for them that spring morning. Many of them secretly put up money to hire a good defense lawyer for his forthcoming trial. Andy had been such a downright *mean* man, even to his own family, that public sentiment in the Tonto country wasn't very strong on seeing Bill swing for his demise.

It was a long time before the case came up on the court docket, but when it did the court room was jam packed with both witnesses and spectators every day of the trial. The prosecuting attorney contended that this was a case of willful murder of an unarmed man, a loving husband, and a wonderful father. The defense shot that picture as full of holes as a flour sifter. Witness after witness described how they had seen Andy kick his boys (eleven and fourteen) out of bed at three o'clock in the morning, day after day, to do a man's work, until long after dark. They told how he had whipped his sons with the blacksnake whip he always carried, for the least mistake, until they were a mass of welts all over.

Objections flew thick and fast as the lawyers wrangled and jockeyed for position, day after day. The only eyewitnesses, of course, were the men on the drive; and one by one they told about as many different stories of the shooting as there were witnesses. The judge helped the proceedings once or twice by stating his opinion that the north end of Gila County must have been peopled by direct descendants of Baron Munchhausen. With the exception of Andy's two boys, every witness called swore he had *never* seen Andy without the German Luger pistol he always carried in his right-hand chap pocket, with a handkerchief wrapped around it to keep out the dust. Yet apparently when he was laid across his saddle after the shooting, the pocket was empty. Since Carrel, his oldest boy, was the first to reach him, it was believed by most that he slipped it into his own shirt before the rest rode up. This was never proved, one way or the other.

The prosecuting attorney, a pompous individual, insisted that Bill re-enact the shooting in the court room for the benefit of the jury, and for his *own* aggrandizement. Bill's own saddle, and his rifle in its scabbard, were brought into the court room and strapped to the rail in front of the judge's desk, to represent the horse. Bill was told to mount his saddle, while the prosecutor was to represent Andy.

"Now, where was Andy in relation to your position there?" asked the prosecutor. Bill told him where to stand.

"Now sir, will you demonstrate *just how* you managed to pull your rifle out from under your right leg, cock it, and shoot your brother from the hip, all in one motion, using *only* your right hand? Remember now, you have sworn under oath that you were using your *left* hand to hold your bridle reins. *I* contend it is an impossible feat, and I defy you to demonstrate to the court, and the jury, how you performed this legerdemain."

Enthralled by his own histrionic abilities, the prosecutor was unprepared for the suddenness of Bill's reaction. In one smooth motion, like the strike of a rattlesnake, the rifle was in Bill's hand and the hammer had fallen on the firing pin with a loud snap heard throughout the silent court room. That prosecutor jumped at least six inches off the floor. The whole court room went wild. Such a surge of belly laughter arose that the bailiff's call for silence couldn't be heard for minutes. Even the judge was snorting into his handkerchief, trying to get his face straight and to maintain the dignity of the court. The members of the jury were practically falling out of their seats.

That one maneuver did more to acquit Bill than all the testimony heard. When the case finally wound up days later the jury wasn't out long enough to butter a turnip before returning a verdict of not guilty.

Andy's widow had prevailed on her sons to work for a conviction no matter what they had to swear to, and the word had gotten back to Bill during the trial. So he had done a little message-sending of his own as to how Tonto Basin was liable to be too small to hold all of them if the jury did see things his way.

Andy's widow saw the handwriting on the wall as to what the outcome of the trial would be. She gathered her boys and sacked out of Globe before the verdict was in. She sold the Gisela Ranch to the Hazelton family practically "jaw bone," and went to California to live. Bill came back to Payson, sold his little bunch of cattle in the House brand and went to work for the county highway department.

Old Jack's boys were such a renegade lot that every time they rode by people would begin to wonder where they were headed and what deviltry they were up to. Dallas borrowed my old grey pack horse to carry his bed to the Pitchfork Ranch on top of the Rim when he went to ride roundup for the outfit.

The Sheriff's office at Flagstaff phoned to Jim Cline (the deputy at Payson) that a bootlegger with a pack horse load of whisky was seen headed for Payson from the west. Jimmy put his horse in a trailer and drove to the bridge on the East Fork of the Verde River, where he unloaded him and rode on toward Pine, figuring to meet Mr. Bootlegger along the way. At the same time, Dallas was on his way home, having just come off the Rim on Strawberry Hill Road. About a half a mile apart they sighted one another. Right away Dallas quit the road and hit the pine timber. Jimmy, convinced that Dallas was his man, took after him. When Dallas saw that his pursuer was gaining, he turned my pack horse loose with his bed still on it, and put on the speed. Now Jimmy was raised in the country and was a real brush popper himself, but Dallas showed him a clean set of heels in that race. Jim came back and got the horse and bed, recognized the horse as mine and left it at the Baloosa place at the Verde Bridge. The bed he took to Payson where someone identified it as being Dallas's. He took it to Round Valley, but Dallas didn't come home for almost a month after that scare. He was sure one of the wild bunch.

In August, when Payson put on its annual Rodeo, Dallas met a chippy whom Old Majorie Stoderman had imported from Globe to wait table at her hotel. The two got drunk together and thought it would be a hell of a caper to get married, so they took the mail stage to Globe and did just that. Dallas brought her home to Round Valley, and it wasn't long before the local boys had trails beat out of the brush leading into the Valley when Dallas was away. Right from the start, the newlyweds fought like cats, and it was a toss-up which one stayed drunkest longest.

One night Dallas borrowed a suit of clothes from me to take her to a dance in town. They drove in in his dad's wagon with a team of mules. About two o'clock in the morning I heard the wagon come into the yard and heard her yelling for me. I got up and went out to see what was the trouble. She had driven home with Dallas passed out cold in the wagon bed. I unhitched the team and pulled the harness off while she tried to arouse him. He must have been drinking mash out of a fruit jar from the looks of the wagon bed and my suit of clothes. He sure had been sick. His wife finally got him boosted high enough to drape over the side of the wagon, whence I put him over my shoulder. I carried him to the house while she opened doors.

"Don't put that drunk bastard on *my* bed. Dump him on the floor of the porch," she ordered. That's where he slept the rest of the night.

It wasn't long until she left him and went home to Globe. He followed, they had another fight and he beat her up. She had him arrested, and he paid a twenty dollar fine. About an hour later he showed up in City Court with another twenty which he offered to the court in advance. He said he intended to work her over again.

"The course of true love," as the saying goes.

The Seventy-Six Ranch on Rye Creek was about to go on roundup and Alec Cox, the foreman, hired me as a member of the crew. Cliff and Laura Griffin, the owners, were a fine couple of old timers and grand people to work for. Cliff was as deaf as a door post, and his deafness was a big handicap when working that rough brushy country of his. So most of the time he left the cattle work to us and spent most of his time working in his garden. Laura, his wife, had been raised in the Pleasant Valley country, and was a real ranch woman. She kept a little old .41 caliber derringer on the mantle over the fireplace, and she could shoot at close range with it as well as anyone.

One afternoon she was sitting on the front porch shelling peas from Cliff's garden, when she heard a noise and looked up to see quite a sight. It was old "Quien Sabe" the Apache. He made the rounds up and down the Tonto country pretty regularly and I thought everyone knew him, but I guess Laura had never had the pleasure before. He was one of the old long-haired Apaches who thought civilized clothes were for the birds. His entire wardrobe consisted of an old union suit that he wore in winter and carried rolled up under his arm in summer. So when Laura looked up she was some little surprised to see an old grey-haired Apache standing on her porch naked as a jay bird, with his union suit rolled up under his arm.

"Me Quien Sabe, want sugar," he grunted.

Laura jumped from her rocker so quickly she scattered peas all over the porch, as she made a grab for the broom leaning against the wall. Quick to sense danger, old "Quien Sabe" jumped off the porch just as Laura took a whack at him with the broom. There was a living ocotillo fence about four feet high across the front of the yard and that old buck cleared it like a fox-hunting horse without looking back. Laura ran into the house to get her derringer but "Quien Sabe" was long out of shooting range by then. That old Apache was about eighty years old, but he was a wiry and tough as a mule. All the cowboys kidded her about him for weeks.

Cliff sold his steers to a Globe man that year and we were to deliver them to the shipping pens at Radium. It was a five-day drive from Rye Creek. When we reached Lower Tonto the Cline boys threw their herd in with ours and we all drove together from there on.

The third night we night-guarded the cattle on a point of land that ran out into Roosevelt Lake above the Dam. The road went across the top of the Dam and we wanted to get across it early with these wild mountain cattle before too much daytime activity began. Workmen had been doing some cement work and had left a big pile of gravel against the inner bannister of the dam. We were lucky and were able to get our steers started across before any cars came along. Those wary old big steers in the lead took plenty of time crossing the dam, sniffing the air and looking at everything with a suspicious eye. One walked up atop the gravel pile and was gazing eastward across the lake when another old long-horned steer came up behind him and hooked him in the rear. He jumped, and fell about fifty feet into the lake, came up swimming, and headed toward a spit of land across the lake almost half a mile away. We kept watching him until he waded out almost to dry land, then danged if he didn't change his mind and start swimming back.

About then we hubbed some trouble just after we had crossed the Dam and were working the herd in small bunches on a narrow road past the houses of Roosevelt. Some Indians afoot climbed a bank to let us by. After two or three little bunches of cattle had passed, the Indians thought that was all, so jumped back into the road right in front of still another bunch. The whole rear end of the herd stampeded back, but took the Salt River fork of the road instead of re-crossing the dam. I was between two bunches when the run began, and I knew it was going to be a horse race to overtake and pass the leaders down that narrow winding road with bluffs on one side and the canyon on the other, with no wide place within miles. And it *was,* believe me! It was four miles or more before I got them stopped and some of the other boys were able to get through to me to help drive them back.

That run cost us a half a day's work. By the time we had passed through the town of Roosevelt again that old swimming steer had re-crossed the lake and wound up in the cement lined intake ditch that skirted the lake on the south shore. The ditch ran all the way to the bridge on the Pleasant Valley Road. One man had to follow that steer the entire distance before he could get him out.

That night we camped by the roadside on Pinto Creek. The next day's drive was all up-grade and slow. We made Mark Hicks' ranch at Wheatfield by late afternoon, and by noon the following day were at Radium. It had been a hard trip.

Actually, Cline's herd was made up of cattle belonging to several people. Some were George's, some Oscar's, some Leck's, and some belonged to the Flower Pot Ranch, owned by Mrs. Lann. Her son Burrel was along on the drive. She came near losing him while we were loading the cars at Radium. He got drunk and crawled under the cattle cars in the shade to sleep it off. A brakeman, walking up alongside, spotted him and dragged him off the track just before the switch engine coupled on to move the cars.

George Cline's eye was bothering him pretty badly. Heading and old wild steer out of a mesquite thicket on our way down Lower Tonto, he had scratched the eyeball on a mesquite thorn, and now it was giving him trouble. In Globe he saw a doctor who wasn't able to help him much. After we shipped, George went on to Phoenix to an eye specialist. He did the best he could, but George lost the sight in that eye. He was a real top brush popper and roper. Even after losing the eye, he followed the rodeos all over the country, winning most of the calf roping money wherever he competed. All the Clines were top cowboys.

Returning from Globe, I drove the pack mules, staying one night at Roosevelt. On Lower Tonto next day, a character who called himself Scissor Bill the Outlaw hailed me and I stopped to talk with him. He was supposed to be a harmless old coot, somewhat locoed. Every now and then he would show up at some isolated ranch or farm and scare hell out of the women folk. The law would pick him up and send him back to the State Hospital at Phoenix for a while. There he more or less had the run of the grounds, and when he got tired of it he'd just take off afoot for his old stamping ground on the Tonto. He wore an old wide brim hat with the front of the brim pinned up and "Scissor Bill the Outlaw" written across it. He always carried two six shooters and an old long-barrelled rifle, and he was a rough-looking old boy for certain. While he and I were passing the time of day on the road, John Corn, driving a county road grader, approached us. As he got close, Scissor Bill stepped out and held his hand up in the stop position.

"Just hold up there a bit fellow, I'm visiting with my friend here," he ordered John. With that, he pulled one of his six shooters and twirled it around on his trigger finger for a few revolutions. John didn't know him from Adam's off ox, but that performance was convincing enough to cause him to set the brake on his grader. Scissor Bill resumed his conversation with me, standing by my horse with one hand on my knee. After awhile, with the words, "Well I'll see you, old Partner," he waved John to come on and stepped into the brush by the side of the road. John came on up to me and stopped again.

"Who in hell was that?" he asked me.

"Scissor Bill the Outlaw," I told him.

"By God, I thought them kind went out with the Pleasant Valley war. Is he a sure enough outlaw?"

"That's what *he* says, and I'm not going to argue the point as long as he carries all that hardware," I told John. I left him scratching his head.

The next I heard of Scissor Bill was from Charley Cole, a local bronc stomper. He and Shorty Pratt had taken on a bunch of horses to break for some ranches along the Tonto and were camped at an old cabin and corrals up in the Sierra Ancha Mountains. Shorty had gone to town for a couple of days, leaving Charley alone in camp. That night Charley was sitting by the fire reading an old wild west magazine he had found in the cabin. He heard the door hinges creak behind him and looked around to see a rifle barrel aimed at his head as the door opened wider and Bill stepped inside.

"Sh-----, I'm Scissor Bill the Outlaw," this apparition told him. "You jest sit still and do as I say and I won't kill ye. I'm on the dodge and I need food. You fix me up some chuck and don't reach fer no guns, or I'll blow ye to Kingdom Come.''

Charley said he was danged near petrified, and he sure wasn't intending to argue the point. He set out the bean pot and made some coffee, and Scissor Bill ate a bait that would founder a wolf. Charley gave him a sack of cold biscuits and the rest of the beans in an old empty fruit jar, and Scissor Bill backed out the door, still keeping the drop on Charley with his old long tom rifle. Charley was so nervous he couldn't sleep that night, and it wasn't until Shorty Pratt returned that he learned who his night visitor was. During the next trail drive to Phoenix we passed in front of the State Hospital on East Van Buren Road, and there was Scissor Bill sitting on top of the brick gate post.

"Good looking bunch of cattle you got there cowboys," he greeted us. "Want me to auction 'em off fer ye?"

Then spotting me, he said, "Why hello thar neighbor! How's things on the Tonto? I'll be back up to see you when the weather gits better.''

And sure enough he was. He claimed he had walked the whole way barefooted. And maybe he had. He was tough enough.

The Hazeltons, who had bought Andy's outfit from his widow during Bill's trial, had let the ranch go to pot so badly they were about to go broke. Andy's oldest boy, who was now working in Nevada, convinced his mother back in California that their only chance of holding on was for them to return to Gisela and take the ranch back themselves. It must have been a hard decision for her to make, as scared as they all were of Bill. Carrel gave up his Nevada job and all three moved back to the Gisela Ranch, having their furniture shipped from California.

I was in Payson the day they hit town to stock up on supplies for the ranch. The two boys came in to A. J. Franklin's Pool Hall (and bootleg joint) late in the afternoon to wait for their mother who was doing some last minute shopping. They were sitting at a poker table talking when the county road truck drove up. Old Bill, with a double jack sledge hammer over his shoulder, walked in the door and set it on the floor before approaching the bar to talk to A. J. His one eye caught those boys at the table and he stopped like a cutting horse, dead still, not saying a word, just looking at them.

The brothers went out that side door real quick, hunted up their ma, and left town in a hurry. Bill was no longer on the war path, but they didn't know it.

After the Hazeltons turned the ranch back to them, they figured on having an early roundup to see how many cattle were left, so they sent word they would need a few cowboys in about a week. I rode down to Gisela and was hired. First there was a lot of packing to do to stock up their Soldier Camp place on the mountain, and the horses to shoe up. When we finally got going on roundup, George Hazelton rode with us the first day. He had evidently never expected the boys to come back to the Tonto, and had started feathering his own nest by branding every calf he could find into his own brand, regardless of what was on the cows. Carrel made him vent so many brands that first day that he sacked out for Phoenix that night and didn't come back. That didn't hurt my feelings a bit, as he and I had had a little set-to at the Seventy Six Quarter Circle ranch on Rye Creek the year before. He had jumped on me in the corral to give me a licking. Only he didn't, because I had pulled my Bowie knife out of my boot top and tickled his short ribs with it a little. He had climbed the fence, mounted his horse, and crossed the river to the house while we were finishing the branding. By the time we reached the house he had left, telling Laura Griffin that he wouldn't work on an outfit where the cowboys carried Bowie knives. He was a big, mean, overbearing yahoo, and no one liked him much.

Sheep Basin Mountain was a big brushy U-shaped mountain on the boys' range. The day we worked it, Carrel sent me with Alec Cox and his nephew Leland Larson to climb to the top from the north side and work down the main canyon. About halfway down the canyon was a spring in a tangle of grapevines, sycamore trees and brush. The rest of the crew had skirted the mountain and spread out at the mouth of our canyon to hold up the cattle we drove out ahead of us. At the spring we found quite a bunch of cattle, some wild ones among them. As we were boosting them on down the canyon, one big wild steer hit a side trail out on top of the west ridge. Leland, who was a big old wild kid of seventeen, followed that steer, hoping to get a chance to rope him on top to show us what a salty hand he was. The rest of us had our hands full working our cattle down the canyon. Lower, where the canyon widened, Alec got out on the side hill where he could see his nephew still after that big steer. The top of the ridge was covered with high stiff oak brush, and

Leland was chousing that steer trying to get a throw at him. Just as he was about to throw, his horse fell down. Alec watched and saw the horse get up and go on without Leland. There was no place where he could break a way to the top anywhere along the canyon. He figured that Leland might be badly hurt and wanted to get to him. He kept riding around the ridge trying every once in a while to get out on top, but the brush was so thick he had to back out every time. We moved our herd out on some open ridges where we could see Alec still trying to reach Leland. Finally he did, to find that old kid standing on his head in an oak brush so heavy Alec had to saw a bunch of limbs off with his dehorning saw to get him loose. Leland was skinned some but not hurt. Alec caught the boy's horses, and it took them a long time to get off that ridge.

We were four or five miles away by this time and, looking back, we saw little puffs of white smoke begin to spring up along the base of the ridge in three or four places. The brush was dry, and before we lost sight of the ridge as we crossed over a hill the whole lower slope of Sheep Basin Mountain was burning uphill. We all knew they had set it afire. This whole country was on the Tonto National Forest and the rangers would get as excited at a puff of smoke in the brush as a bunch of hens with a hawk in the chicken house.

The fire lookout on top of Diamond Point, east of Payson, spotted the fire and phoned the approximate location in to the Payson Ranger Station. The Payson ranger had gone to Flagstaff to attend a meeting and had left another man in his place. He rounded up a crew of fire fighters in town and they headed for the fire. Only they couldn't locate it. They rimmed around in the canyons and rocks most of two days trying to find a way to get to the smoke, and by the time they did get through to it the fire had burned off the whole west side clear to the top, where it had burned itself out. When the regular ranger returned from Flagstaff, he came to the ranch trying to find out who had set the fire, but he got no information that would do him any good from us. Yes, we'd seen the smoke. Must have been dry lightning, or the sun shining through an empty whisky bottle, or something. No sir! None of us would think of setting any fires on the national forest. The ranger knew when he was licked and went back to Payson, talking to himself. It would take a forest of pulp wood to manufacture all the paper wasted in correspondence between him and the regional office in Albuquerque, New Mexico, and Washington, D. C. over that one little brush fire.

Five miles east of Payson was a small valley in the pines called Star Valley. A. J. Franklin's old home place was there, and it was said to have been an outlaw hideout shortly after the Civil War days. Frank and Jesse James' names were carved pretty high up on an old aspen tree not far from the ruins of an old cabin. Maybe someone else had carved them there, but it had been done long ago, because they were pretty faint by now.

From Star Valley eastward to Green Valley and Gordon Canyon, along the head waters of Tonto Creek, the whole country was settled by a big family named Haught. They and their relatives by marriage numbered in the hundreds. Just about any cabin one came to, back in that heavy pine-timbered country under the Tonto Rim, was lived in by Haughts. Old Sam (Pappy), Babe who was Zane Grey's hunting guide, Jim Sam, Henry and Zeke were some of the older members bearing the name. Whole generations of that family had been raised back there in the vines, and most had never been farther away than Payson or Pleasant Valley in a lifetime. Like most mountaineers they were clannish. Old Babe, however, seemed to be the only one of the clan who never mingled with the rest.

There was a story making the rounds in Payson about a fellow on his way from Globe to Flagstaff riding a bicycle. At Payson he got off on a wrong trail and wound up out in Haught country. He spent each night with a different family of Haughts. Each morning they would put him on some dim trail, supposedly leading to the road to Flagstaff. Once again he would get lost and wander around afoot pushing his bicycle all day, then wind up spending yet another night out in the woods with yet another Haught family.

After about three days of this he finally got on the road back to Payson. At Star Valley he met the Forest Ranger from Payson and stopped him to ask if he was on the right road to town.

"Mr. Haught," he said, "how far am I from Payson?"

"About five miles," the Ranger told him. "But my name is Little, not Haught."

"By God! Shake hands, Mr. Little. You're the first man I've met in three days that wasn't named Haught," the wanderer exclaimed. He was back in civilization.

Once a year, in July, the Haughts had a family reunion at Green Valley. All day long they would come in out of the vines by wagon, horseback, afoot, or riding old mules. The whole valley would be full of them by night. They built a rough plank platform on which to dance and they had kegs of moonshine whisky stuck behind every bush to liven up the proceedings. That first night they would fiddle and dance and have a high old time. The next morning was devoted to foot races, wrestling matches, and a number of stunts they had thought up to entertain themselves. At noon they had a big picnic and barbecue, and afterwards a calf-roping and bull-riding contest on the flat east of the big spring. In 1924, Frank Pyle and I rode the twenty miles from Payson and stayed three days for the whole show. I saw old Babe ride by, but he never stopped. I guess he was the only Haught missing. One of the younger boys was *actually* named Cowboy Haught. I had worked some with him and he was a good one. When he got after wild cattle in the timber he broke limbs from the trees as big as my wrist with his shoulders.

Typhoid fever hit their part of the country soon after the reunion and thinned out the tribe pretty badly before it was checked. About the same time it struck the little Mormon settlement of Pine, west of Payson. It took a number of residents there before it was traced to the community ditch water used by the whole town. Then, to cap the climax, smallpox broke out in a little bunch of Tonto Apache Indians camped on a hill at the west edge of Payson. Following their age-old custom, those pox-ridden Indians took sweatbaths, then a quick jump into cold water. This remedy for illness of any kind quickly killed practically every one of the smallpox victims.

Every morning about sunrise, the eerie death chants of the squaws could be heard coming from the brush wickiups atop the hill. By the time the county health officers came up from Globe, the living had disposed of their dead and no amount of persuasion could make them reveal where they had put them. Vaccinations were carried on, both in the Indian camp and in Payson for some time.

Later that year the town was buzzing with excitement. News came that a moving picture company was coming in from California to film Zane Grey's story of the Pleasant Valley War between the sheep ranchers and the cattlemen. Nothing like this had ever happened to Payson before. The two little stores began laying in supplies of things they hoped to sell, and Marjorie Stoderman started fixing up her hotel to take care of the influx of actors. Even A. J. Franklin took to bottling up a big stockpile of Hilligass' famous moonshine whisky in brown beer bottles to tide him over in case of a rush. A new boarding house opened in town. Payson was really perking up from the sleepy little cow town it had always been. Soon elements of Lasky's Famous Players began arriving. There were advance men, trucks of equipment, costume people and hair dressers, stunt men, and some horses. The actors were the last to arrive, just before the actual filming was to begin. Every cowboy or rancher in the country who owned any sort of horse or mule brought his animals into town to rent out to the movie company. About a quarter of the residents of the country were soon on the payroll, at wages they'd never dreamed of before. Every normal activity was suspended in favor of the making of that picture called "To the Last Man."

Right away two blonde sister actresses got themselves lost in the timber about a mile out of town. They told a harrowing story of being treed by a bear all night before they were rescued. They posed for pictures all over the place, and the reporters wrote up a big yarn about their ordeal. This made all the local papers, the nearest of which was published at Globe sixty-five miles away. Payson had made the headlines and was real happy. Dances were held almost every night in the school house to afford the movie people a bit of entertainment, and A. J. Franklin's old warped pool tables were in constant use at night until quite late.

Constance Bennett's colored maid came into Boardman's store one morning while I was buying some horseshoes, and asked to see some gloves. Bill Boardman waited on her as she examined and tried on about every pair of lady's gloves he had in the store. Deciding on a pair, the maid told Bill to wrap it up and charge it to "Miz. Bennett." Now Bill didn't know the maid, nor had he ever heard of "Miss Bennett" so he dubiously asked the colored maid if she was *sure* Miss Bennett could pay for the gloves.

"Can she pay for them? Miz. Bennett? Well I *hope* she can. She only *makes* ten thousand dollars a week!" replied the maid disdainfully as she strode out of the store muttering something about hick storekeepers and how glad she was going to be to get back to Hollywood again.

For part of the picture, a whole false front town was built at the foot of Ox Bow Hill on the old H Bar Ranch. During the filming of a wild shooting episode, the whole town was burned down, with bodies and ketchup gore all over the place. It made a real impressive picture, I guess.

Only a small portion of the movie was actually shot in Pleasant Valley for there were still old-timers living there who had lived through the real thing and they weren't keen on having any re-enactment of it, even if it *was* only make-believe. Zane Grey had found these old-timers an almost impossible nut to crack when he was doing research work before writing his book. He did the best he could, but most of his information came from hearsay sources, not from the actual survivors of the war. Old wounds are a long time healing.

By the time the picture was finished, the honeymoon was over between the Lasky Famous Players and the natives. The picture people claimed they had been robbed blind by the natives and the natives accused the Hollywood group of shamelessly corrupting the morals of their daughters and wives. Me, I wouldn't offer any opinions. I guess it was sort of a Mexican standoff. The movie people left a lot of fresh money in the town, and several of the local girls ran away to Hollywood. Bill Boardman's good looking blonde wife skipped town about that time, too. However, most people claimed she ran off with a handsome cowboy who followed the players to California. I dunno.

Life soon settled down to about what it had been prior to the invasion. A hair-pulling fight between old Doc Risser's wife and old lady Pyle on Main Street, an occasional run-away team, and Marjorie Stoderman on one of her fighting drunk sprees were all the town had left to gossip about.

I sold my horses and saddle and went to the little copper mining town of Miami for a change of atmosphere. I had done some mining during the course of my checkered career, so I went to work for the Miami mine for a couple of months. Shift work never had pleased me too much, and when a little widow woman got to playing up to me too strong, aiming on a steady meal ticket, I figured it was time to move on. I turned in my brass check at the company office, drew my wages, paid my board bill, and caught the stage for Phoenix.

Nine　　　　The Three-V Cattle Company

In 1926, the Three V Cattle Company was just about the biggest cow outfit left in Arizona. Owned by the Pacific Loan Company of California, it was made up of fifteen or twenty ranches which had been gobbled up over a period of years through purchases or foreclosures on loans. It also had a land lease on practically the entire Hualapai Indian Reservation. The outfit owned an estimated twenty-five thousand head of cattle, enclosed by enough fence to surround several eastern states.

The rub was that the land was short on water. It was located on the high plateaus of Northern Arizona which, geologists explain, were formed from cinder beds of extinct volcanos, pushed up eons ago to their seven thousand feet above sea level. The surface soil of volcanic ash and decomposed malapai rock was rich, and it was a natural for the waving black gramma grass that covered the country. Earthen dams built across draws caught water from summer rains and from melted winter snows. But wells were as scarce as hens' teeth. There were only three on the whole outfit, and two of those were side by side at the old Rose Wells Ranch about forty-five miles north of the little town of Seligman. The remaining one was Frazier Well, at the head of Aubrey Valley on the Hualapai Indian Reservation. The Company had paid out almost a million dollars to drilling companies, punching down holes at different locations around the ranch without success. It seems that wherever they did tap underground water, the water sank downward because of the porous nature of the cinder beds. So the ranch had to depend on the surface tanks. Those had been neglected so long that many had filled up with silt. Flash floods in summer had broken the dams on others, because the spillways weren't deep enough to carry off the surplus water before the dams gave way.

Winter snows had been light, and summer brought only a few scattered showers, spotted far apart, that first year I worked for the Vs. A few big dams on the east side of the range held the bulk of the remaining water, so the roundup crew kept pushing more and more cattle over onto that part of the ranch as they worked the country. Charley Hiler, the wagon boss, scratched his head, with a long face, as he watched little promising thunderheads form day after day way off across the Cataract Plains, only to dissipate into a few scattered showers in the July afternoons. Tom Cavness, the general manager, drove out from his headquarters in Seligman almost daily to watch those same disappointing clouds build up, then break apart into showers

GRAND CANYON
OF THE COLORADO

GRAND CANYON OF THE COLORADO

Havasupai Indian Res.

HILLTOP

GRAND CANYON PARK

AUBREY CLIFFS

CATARACT PLAINS

CABIN

To Cn.

D.C. RANCH

CO RANCH

Pine Springs   CABIN

SHILOH   REDLANDS

ANITA

Natural Bridge

FRAZIER WELL   Thornton Tank

Bridge Canyon Damsite

Diamond Cn.

CABIN

PIPELINE

ROSE WELLS

SANDY CORRAL

WILLAHA

Sullivan Pasture

Long Point Dam

More Tank

VALLE

Red Lake   MESA   PASTURE
4½ TOWNSHIPS

Blacktanks

HUALAPAI INDIAN RESERVATION

AUBREY CLIFFS

PEACH
SPRINGS   PASTURE

KESAHA
RANCH

SHEEP
RANCH

Bishops Lake

QUIVERO

PASTURE
¼ TOWNSHIP

MARTIN DAM
PASTURE
1 TOWNSHIP

PRIMITIVE ROAD

AUBREY VALLEY   137 MILES

PICA
STOCKYARDS

Trinity Pk.

BURRO
TANKS
PASTURE
4 TOWNSHIPS

Mt. Floyd

RED LAKE

OLD KY
RANCH

VALENTINE

TO KINGMAN

N

A-A
RANCH

AA PASTURE
7 TOWNSHIPS

WILLIAMS

SELIGMAN
STOCK PENS

24 MILES

NORTH TRACK   SANTA FE

SOUTH TRACK

ASH FORK   20 MILES

Bill Young

that barely settled the dust where they fell. This was normally the rainy season for the country. If it didn't rain during July, no more moisture could be expected until September. It was a *serious* time for the Vs.

I had been working with the wagon since early May, and as yet we hadn't touched the part of the ranch which lay east of Ash Fork. Most of that was taken up in two big pastures: the Double A, with seven townships under page wire fence, and Martin Dam Pasture to the north, with one township fenced the same way. Since cattle can exist for quite a while on scanty feed, the situation was grave only because of lack of water for them.

Orders came through from headquarters for the roundup crew to start gathering for a drive to the railroad shipping point. Within four days our thirty-man crew had a couple of thousand head of cows and calves together and on the trail to Pica, a siding with shipping pens on the Santa Fe Railroad west of Seligman.

When we reached Pica, the buyers from California were already there. We worked practically all of one night, fighting the bawling cows and their calves into long strings of cattle cars. Just before sunup we ate our breakfast in a pall of dust stirred up by the cattle. That dust would continue to hang over the area for a day or two after we had quit working there. The wrangler came in with the remuda, and we roped out our mounts to saddle for the return trip and a new gathering.

We were working the hardest hit west side of the range first, and made a bee line for Pine Springs on the Reservation. Here there was a big concentration of cattle hanging close to the only two watering places, the Park and Pine Springs. This was timbered country, oak thickets and yellow pine, and the cattle running in there were pretty snakey. We hadn't time to gather them too close, and many calves were dogied because we were too rushed to mother them up properly.

Once we had skimmed off a few shipments from that part of the range, we began on the middle. We delivered and loaded one drive of one thousand yearling heifers at Seligman. After we had shut the car door on the last of them the Superintendent blew us all to a meal at the railroad Harvey House. While we ate, he told me that he wanted me to move over to the Double A Ranch northeast of Ash Fork and help the steady man there look after eight hundred head of big steers in the seven township pasture until the crew could get around to shipping them out in late October. So I threw my gear on the truck, loading supplies at Pitt's Mercantile Store in Seligman, and by late afternoon had my first look at the Double A and Demus Yoder.

My first impression of Demus was favorable. His hand clasp was sincere and the quick flash of his smile — what I could see of it through his red whiskers — was friendly. He was slender (almost skinny), about 5 feet 10, with sandy hair and bushy eyebrows over bright clear eyes. Being fair complected, his face was wind-and-sun reddened, and the backs of his hands freckled.

This was our first meeting, although we had been in the same outfit at Triers, Germany, in the Army of Occupation, after the Armistice of World War One. He had been with Headquarters Company, and I in Company E. His father and two brothers had had a small cow ranch northeast of Williams before the war. Demus was the only one of the Yoder boys to be drafted, the other two having gone into railroading on the Santa Fe. His dad had held onto their little ranch until Demus could return and give him a hand with it.

The war affected different men in different ways. In Demus' case it sure wasn't for the better. He lost his own personal war, to booze. Once he was out of the army and home again, it didn't take his dad long to see that it was a lost cause to depend on Demus. So when he'd had a fair offer for his ranch from a big company he went out of the cattle business. After the proceeds of the sale were divided the old man used his part to buy a combination meat market and store in Ash Fork, a cowtown and railroad division point about thirty miles west of Williams.

Demus went on about a six-month bender, trying to drink it up faster than the distilleries could make it. Many of his old cowboy friends gave him help along that line. When he finally sobered up, he had not only spent his part of the ranch money but also owed about five-hundred dollars which he had borrowed during his spree. The clothes he had on, his bed, and an old worn-out saddle were all he had left. All he know how to do was punch cows, so he hired out to the Three V Cattle Company as a cowboy. The Double A was his permanent camp when I arrived there.

The ranch had a big old yellow frame house, some sheds and corrals, and a sandstone dam in a draw just north of the house. Demus loved animals of any sort. He had a string of old horses (eleven I think) in the trap, and a few extras which he never rode, also some chickens and a couple of cats. One of the roosters had been hurt somehow and was crippled in one leg. Demus had named it "Tom Cavness" after the General Superintendent who had a permanent limp, the result of a horse falling with him years before. He staked me to a mount of horses; some of his own, and some of the extras.

For a couple of days we stayed pretty close to camp shoeing up some of the barefoot horses before we began riding the pasture. Demus and I soon became good friends. I believe the biggest hit I made with him right off was in keeping a clean camp. I had lived with old boys whose camps looked like boars' nests but I had never enjoyed them and had always tried to keep mine fairly clean and as neat as I could when I found the time. I also carried water from the dam and washed up a sackfull of the dirty clothes I had brought with me. Demus seemed to see that as a favorable omen.

The steers were doing all right, so our chief concern was in keeping the fences up so none of them would leak out before shipping time rolled around. East of our pasture there were a lot of sheep belonging to the Grand Canyon Sheep Company. This was a subsidiary of the Pacific Loan, so the sheep really were a part of the V outfit. They weren't supposed to graze any farther west than our fence, but sheepherders the world over love to steal feed and those Basques weren't any exception to the rule. Every now and then we would find sections of our fence tied up high enough to let bands of sheep under them. Only once did we catch a band inside, and Demus threw a good scare into their offending herder. We searched until we found his camp, took his 30-30 rifle and ejected all the cartridges from it, and threw it up into a sotol plant. The Basque herder was hidden in some rocks on a bluff watching us. We scouted around and located him. When he knew he was discovered he stood up with one hand behind him, holding a rock. Demus cussed him in English awhile, and then Spanish, and though he pretended not to understand, he did. When Demus told him to round up his band and put them back under the fence, he gave us a big argument and acted as though he wanted to bean old Demus with that malapai rock. He simmered down quickly enough when he saw the cedar handle of my old Betsy peeping out from under my jumper, and sent his dogs out to bunch the band. After we were rid of the sheep we made him come back, unhobble his burros, strike camp and move it outside also. He was a real mad Basque.

One day we got word that the Super had set up the date for delivery of our steers. He wanted us to come over to Seligman about the middle of September to help out with the loading of a big delivery of cattle. Then he would send a crew over to the AA to help round up our pasture, and we would ship our big steers from Ash Fork. So, early in the morning of the 16th of September, we headed for Seligman in Demus' T-model Ford. It was an old relic, rusty from sitting out in the winter snows and summer rains. The top was gone and three of the four fenders were loose and flapping. Just before we left camp, Demus went out to the wood pile and got the axe.

"May as well make her a muley," he stated. So he chopped off all the fenders and threw them into the junk pile.

When we reached Williams, about 18 miles from camp, where our road joined the paved road to Seligman, we found a celebration in progress. This was Mexican Independence Day, and the big Mexican population of the town was putting on a rodeo and many other events. The rodeo field was right alongside the road as we entered the outskirts of town. Activities were to start at 12:30 but already the cattle and broncs were in the corrals, and goats for the goat roping were being unloaded. We stopped and talked with several of Demus' friends before going on into town.

Knowing his own failings well, Demus gave me almost all of his money to keep for him, with instructions not to let him have it if he got drunk. While I was in a store buying a pair of gloves, he cut out with some of his friends. About an hour later he showed up, already oiled to the gills. He insisted we stay for the rodeo before going on to Seligman, which was O.K. by me.

Out at the field, Demus wanted to enter the jackpot calf roping. I argued that he couldn't possibly catch a calf in the shape he was in, but he begged so hard for the entrance fee that I went over and entered him. He had borrowed a good roping horse from Walt Brown earlier in the day.

The saddle bronc event came off first, and then some goat roping. Those goats had been roped before and they were plenty smart on dodging and out-figuring the ropers. Joe Evans ran one black goat way down the field, and just as he was about to get a good throw, the goat saw a crack in the door of the women's "Chick Sales" and ducked inside. Joe, about half drunk, bailed off his horse and jerked the door open to get the goat out. A Mexican girl inside screamed bloody murder and the crowd roared.

Came the calf roping, and Demus' turn. He threw a big old blocker loop in the general direction of his calf, and promptly fell off his horse like a big tumble bug. He also skinned his knuckles up in the fall.

Late in the evening he finally got around to going on to Seligman and we pointed the old Ford in that direction. Just a little way out of town at the top of the Williams Hill he ran off the road and butted heads with a pine tree. We weren't making much speed, so a broken headlight and a dented radiator were the only casualties. I wanted to drive, but Demus claimed nobody in the world knew that Ford's tricks but him, and pretty soon I found out he was right.

Once on the long down grade of the Williams Hill, we chugged along hugging the mountain side of the road until we were about four miles from the bottom. Every once in a while Demus would take a swig from his bottle, then hand it to me. I guess the road got to dodging a bit, for all of a sudden he steered completely off it and away we went, careening down an open hillside at a steep angle. Demus fell out over the door on his side. I jerked the emergency brake but there was no brake, and the Ford picked up still more momentum. Twisting the wheel wildly, I ran the car into a hole on the mountain side and we stopped with a jar. Demus came hobbling down through the rocks to congratulate me on making a good stop.

It was just about dark by now and we climbed back up onto the road, hoping we could flag down a car going our way and get a ride in to Ash Fork. After a while four big highway trucks came grinding up the hill on their way back to Williams. The drivers looked over our predicament, got a number of long chains out of their trucks, and about an hour later they had our vehicle back on the road. It was somewhat the worse for wear, but still able to navigate.

Demus seemed to feel that after such a near disaster his nerves needed fortifying, so on the way into Ash Fork he lowered the Plimsoll line on the whisky bottle once more.

Out on the western edge of town, the highway made a sharp jog to the left for a couple of blocks before resuming its direction towards Seligman. With only one headlight giving off about as much glow as a burning corn cob, Demus missed the turn and ran off into some high rocks behind the Harvey House. There we highcentered on a big boulder. By now Demus was so drunk that he didn't realize what had stalled us, and I sure wasn't going to enlighten him. I figured that the remaining thirty miles to Seligman might be just a shade risky, with him at the wheel in the shape he was in. I knew that his dad lived in town somewhere so I took off afoot to hunt him up. After nosing around awhile I located him at the lunch counter of the Harvey House.

Demus' drinking bouts were an old story to his dad, and he took my description of our hair raising trip from the Double A as calmly as a summer boarder eating his hash. We found Demus passed out on the seat of the car, but he had removed the switch key and lost it. We searched his pockets, the floor boards and everywhere we could think of, but found no key. Some fellow came out of a highway shop building to see what we were doing there. He went back and got a fingernail file which worked as well as the key.

After we had pried the car off the rock Mr. Yoder drove up the hill to his house. We pulled off Demus' boots and put him on the bed. I talked with his dad for a while and then bedded down to sleep beside Demus.

About daylight I awoke to hear Mr. Yoder starting a fire in the kitchen stove. A dent in the pillow was all that remained of Demus. Looking out the window I saw his Ford still sitting in front of the house where we had left it.

I helped Mr. Yoder cook breakfast and while we were drinking our coffee Demus came in. He was raring to get started for Seligman right away. I noticed a suspicious bulge under his shirt but said nothing in front of his dad. Demus wouldn't eat, but he did siphon a cup of hot black coffee before we left the table. He sure was a high powered scrounger to have rustled up a new bottle of whisky before daylight in a little town like Ash Fork. Once out of town he produced a vinegar bottle, already lowered somewhat, and I took a mild nip. He seemed to have a towering thirst, and kept wetting the neck of the bottle all the way.

In sight of the stockyards where we saw the dust of the loading crew, we branched off on a dirt road leading to the shipping pens. Just as we crossed the spur track Demus turned the car over. Some of the boys were watching our approach and rode over to where the Ford was lying on its ribs, tied on to it with their ropes and pulled it back up on its wheels. With their help I deposited Demus alongside the stockyard fence and left him to his dreams.

I helped load cattle the rest of the afternoon. Along about four-thirty we had wound up the little ball of yarn on that herd. Most of the boys went in to town to dampen down the dust they'd swallowed, so we took Demus along and bedded him down in a box stall at the Company's yard.

The following morning, he still wasn't feeling like running any foot race. He bogied off and came back after a while with a bottle of some sort of crack skull wine. We bought supplies at Pitt's Commercial Company store, loaded up the old Ford and headed back for the Double A.

At Ash Fork Demus bought two new tires for the car, and we went on to Williams without mishap. Before we got out of town he had to get one more quart of firewater to see us over the rough places between there and our camp.

At a farm a couple of miles north we bought a case of eggs. We put them in the back on top of the load and as we came to the cattle guard in the fence, Demus misjudged a little and ran into one of the side posts, scrambling about half the eggs. That upset him so much he had to have a couple more snorts out of the bottle. We rattled along over the weed-grown malapai flats, and just as I began to have hopes of being at the ranch within the hour, he cut across a turn in the road and blew out two tires at one lick. While he lay draped over the steering wheel trying to remember where he was, I put on the two new tires, and it wasn't easy, believe me. The lugs on those old tire rims were rusted on, and hell to get off.

Before I was finished Demus came to, bleary-eyed but determined to make the final sprint to the ranch. Crossing the last open flat before we came into the cedar breaks, with only one skinny little cedar tree way off to one side, he pointed Old Reliable straight toward it and stepped on the gas.

"By God, Demus, you're going to hit that tree in a minute," I said.

"Hell no, we won't come close," he replied, just as we *did*. The impact threw us both out. That tree may have been little but it was tough. While it was only skinned up a little, the Ford had a broken wishbone and a dished left front wheel. It had climbed the tree as far as it could and was sitting there at about a forty degree angle, the front end up in the top of the tree.

"Guess we'll have to pull up a fence post, pry the car off that tree and fix it," Demus said.

"Looks to me like you've already fixed it for keeps," I replied.

Old man Robinson had a little cow ranch just north of where we were, and I knew that he was shoeing up his horses for the works that were about to start. I suggested to Demus that we hoof it over to his cabin and spend the night. But Demus had a one-track idea about getting the car out of the tree and fixing it. I left him tinkering around and cut through the timber, reaching Robinson's just before dark, where I stayed the night.

After sunup the next morning I hiked back to see how Demus was making out. He was humped up over a little grass fire, out of whisky and out of sorts. There were little black spots all around the flat where he'd had little fires during the night. About half a dozen empty green chili cans were lying around, plus some egg shells. By now he realized that we couldn't do anything about the Ford alone. He figured that the crew coming over to work our pasture would have reached the Double A by way of Martin Dam from the north. So he set out afoot to hike the last ten miles in to camp. His boots wore a few blisters on his heels, but he made it. The boys were there, and they said that he was so dry he just waded out into the tank and sat down, letting that muddy water run into his mouth.

The boys brought Demus back to the car and, after a useless attempt at towing it, jacked up the front end and chained it to the truck bed, then towed it as far as the old KY Ranch. No one lived there and the place was overgrown with high weeds. Demus removed the battery and the two good tires from the Ford and we left her sitting there, a gallant monument to a great car builder — Henry Ford.

Lord rest her rusty old soul.

We had some exciting days gathering out our big steers. Joe Evans, riding Blue Ribbon, a rough string horse, didn't come in off a drive through some thick cedar country, so we went looking for him. Pretty soon we cut his sign and trailed him up. The tracks showed that he had jumped a big buck deer and had evidently tried to rope it from his horse's back. Every little way we found the ground plowed up. Evidently Ribbon had fallen to staves and thrown a bucking fit. There were deep tracks, far apart, showing where Joe had coaxed his horse into a run once more, trying to gain lost ground on the buck. Then we found more signs that the horse had bucked again. We found Joe at the holdup ground when we got back, still riding Old Ribbon.

"I could have roped that deer if this damned jug head hadn't broken gait so often," Joe swore.

Bill Chestnut, an old Verde Valley cowboy, roped a big, snuffy, brindle, five-year-old stag trying to make his getaway in the timber. Bill's horse forked a tree going full tilt. Bill was thrown and stag and horse piled up at each end of the rope. Bill wasn't hurt, just skinned up a little, but his temper was riled.

Back on their feet, the horse and stag were having a real set-to. Some cowboy had once tipped the stag's horns, but he sure gouged that old pony every time he got within reach. When he did, the horse hit the end of the rope hard and jerked the stag down. Just as soon as he'd get a little slack, the stag would jump up and go to his end of the rope and jerk the horse down. Bill sat on the ground off to one side and rolled a cigarette, just watching the performance.

"That horse will learn to keep his head to that stag pretty soon." Bill predicted. Two cigarettes later, both animals were standing head down and panting, facing one another, each willing to give up the fight. They were wet with sweat and had a lot of rope burns, but they had sure learned they couldn't get away from that rope.

"That's the best education this old pelican's had since he was broke," Bill declared.

Once we had our steer herd together near the corner of the pasture nearest Ash Fork, we had to take down a section of the fence to get out, as there was no gate within miles. Then we worked the drive down off the sandstone benches to a big weed-grown flat where the shipping pens were. Just as the men on point had the leaders eased up close to the wing jutting out from the stock gate, the steers stirred up a bunch of hogs sleeping in the weeds. These went woofing off in every direction, and we had a stampede on our hands. Luckily we had a big flat on which to turn the steers. Whipping over and under we finally got them into a mill, but it took us until after sundown to get the herd inside the wing fence and into the stock pens. We had come very close to losing the works. We shut the gates and tied them fast with ropes for the night, for the cattle cars would not arrive until the next day.

Once the steers were shipped, we were no longer needed at the Double A, so the super sent us to work with the roundup wagon. That Summer and Fall the Vs shipped out about twelve thousand head, thus relieving the pressure of the critical water shortage. In early November I quit and returned to my old winter stomping grounds around Cave Creek and Bloody Basin north of Phoenix where the winters weren't so severe. Demus stayed on at the Rose Wells camp.

The following spring I returned to work with the V wagon once again. It was a month or more before we got around to Rose Wells, to work that part of the range. Demus was still camped there. There was a big old ranch house at that camp and numerous corrals. We always camped the roundup wagon just outside of a fence north of the house. Demus came down to our camp that first evening and he and I swapped yarns around the camp fire until late in the night.

Rose Wells was situated on the western edge of the Cataract Plains, a great open expanse of country without trees farther than the eye could see. Near the big barn was an "outhouse" which had been built before Abe Caufman, the former owner of Rose Wells had had a bathroom installed in the big house. One afternoon when we had finished the branding early, Tom Vest, an old Texas cowpuncher, made a visit to the outhouse and dropped his cigarette as he left. someone noticed the smoke pretty soon, but by then it was too late and up went the structure in flames.

The wagon seldom camped in one place more than two or three days, so we moved on soon after that episode. It was about another month before we made it around to Rose Wells again. In the meantime Demus had exercised his skill as a carpenter and built a new outhouse which was wonderful to behold. It was somewhat larger than the previous one, with the seat part about six feet wide. Demus had sawed out the oval holes with a keyhole saw, exactly in the center. Anyone using it was forced to sit with his feet straight out before him. The super came out in his car one day and looked in the door at Demus' masterpiece.

"What in hell did you build that holer like that for?" he asked Demus.

"So old Tom Vest could sleep and smoke at the same time," Demus replied dryly.

Our roundup cook Ed Byers was a slightly greasy individual who talked incessantly, sucking on his old hod of a pipe. He had cooked for the outfit for several years. Because he talked so much Demus, who had a name for everybody, called him "Old Victrola." There was no love lost between the two. Any chance he had to job old Ed was a red letter day for Demus.

While we were at Rose Wells, Ed took the opportunity of going up to the big house to use the bathroom facilities there rather than use Demus' outhouse. Once in the house, he would talk Demus' ear off for an hour or so. One morning after the crew was out of camp on circle drive, Ed waltzed over to the big house bent on using the bathroom, only to find the toilet seat wired shut hard and fast with about ten strands of barbed wire criss-crossed over and around it, and twisted so it couldn't be untied. There was a big printed "Out of Order" sign on the door. Demus had ridden off to one of the pastures to look up some bulls he had been feeding, so old Ed got a pair of wire cutters and cut the toilet open again. When Demus returned he was as mad as a wet hen. He knew where the water pipe line coming from the wells was buried, so he went down into the corrals, dug up the valve box about four feet underground, shut off the valve and sawed the stem off even with the pipe. Then he reburied the box and took great pains to sprinkle dust over the freshly turned earth to disguise the spot. On Ed's next trip he found no water. For the next three days Ed spent all of his spare time digging in the corrals searching for the valve box which he was sure was there somewhere. On the last day we camped there Ed finally located the box, only to discover the valve cut off slick and clean, even with the pipe so it couldn't be turned on. He was cussing whoever the dirty so and so was who had cut the valve off when Demus came riding inside the corral to water his horse. Demus sat there on his horse listening to old Ed sputter and cuss. Then, smiling under his red whiskers, he said,

"Well Ed, every son-of-a-bitch has his troubles," and rode off, happy again.

That summer and fall I again rode with the roundup wagon, and Demus stayed at Rose Wells. By the time I left the outfit for a warmer winter climate, the Vs had shipped out several thousand more head of cattle, once again because of lack of water.

The company owned another big ranch south of Seligman called "The Grant," because it had been part of an old Spanish Land Grant when the flag of Spain flew over the Southwest. That same summer, (my second with the Vs), a manager was needed at the Grant, so the Company sent Charley Hiler and put Demus in his place as Wagon Boss.

About this time, because buyers and feeders put a penalty on horned cattle, the company decided to de-horn all the calves as they were branded. We took out the little wagon with a skeleton crew, just to brand and de-horn calves. Our wagon crew consisted of Demus, Miller (a New Mexico waddie on the dodge), Owen Susonatomie (a Hualapai Indian) and myself. Old Ed, the roundup cook, had been left at Frazier Well on the reservation to pump water and take care of the ten miles of gravity-flow pipe line carrying water down to the Pipe Line Pasture in Aubrey Valley.

We took along a small remuda of about forty horses, with one team on the wagon. When we moved, one man would drive the wagon, make camp and do the cooking. The rest would drive the remuda through, then gather what cows and calves we could, brand and de-horn. We took turns on the wagon and doing the cooking. Whenever Owen's turn came to move camp he would drive way off the roads to keep from meeting any Indians, as he felt that it would hurt his prestige to be seen driving a wagon. Up in the timber country where the wagon couldn't get around, we would carry about a dozen horn-searing irons on our horses, loose herd little bunches of cattle till we had roped and tied down the calves, then build a fire for our irons, brand and de-horn, then turn the cattle loose again.

At one time we camped down in the bottom of Prospect Valley, a wild isolated canyon, the northern end of which jumped off into the Grand Canyon. There were always many wild cattle in there, and we figured on catching some mavericks. We had run out of meat, so Demus rode away from camp to see if he could find anything fat enough to butcher for beef. He didn't, but on the way back he shot an antelope not far from camp. We gathered up a couple of pans, the meat saw, and some knives, and walked back with him to butcher out the ante-lope. He had killed it at the foot of a pine tree, a little way out on a flat. Each of us grabbed a leg and began skinning it out. Working with our heads down, we didn't notice when Demus dropped the leg he was working on and slipped away. He circled and came up behind us, and spoke in a gruff, deep voice: "Hello! What are you fellows doing?"

We were all startled, but Miller, the man on the dodge, was plain unvarnished scared. He tried to run but his feet slipped on the pine needles and he fell down. I guess his first thought was the same as ours, that the Indian Police had caught us. Demus enjoyed his laugh on us for a week. At that time there was a fine of one thousand dol-lars for killing antelope on the Reservation. I know, because that was the fine the Cole Campbell Sheep Company had had to pay when Leland Larson, one of the company employees, had been caught with one on his truck not long before.

One morning as we rode out from camp we came across the biggest steer tracks I had ever seen. It looked as though someone had set down a series of dutch oven lids in the dirt. That old ox had sneaked right out past our camp during the night, We followed his trail out of the valley, up on top of the divide, right to the park water lot where he had gone for salt. The park was a deep open draw be-tween two timbered hillsides. A big pine log dam on the north end formed a tank. The whole area was fenced with ten strands of barbed wire, and several heavy oak stays between posts. A dividing fence across the center made it into two big lots. Pine pole corrals at the south end made it a good place to work cattle. The gates on either side of the lot were always left open except when we were trapping cattle there or when the Hualapai Indians were using it to work wild horses.

As we eased down the trail we saw that big old moss horn licking salt with other cattle in the lot. He took a long, hard look at us as we appeared, then headed for the opposite gate. We charged off that hill-side like the Light Brigade, rocks flying, in an attempt to head him off. Owen beat him to the gate and I ran my horse through it to the outside, in case he jumped over or tore the fence down. He turned toward the other half of the water lot, then ran into the fence just as Demus roped his horns and Miller got his line on one hind foot. That steer plowed right on through the fence, bringing both of the horses right along with him, pulled by the ropes tied to the saddle horns. By then I had caught up with him on the outside of the fence, and I made a lucky throw and caught both front feet. With three ropes on him, we had a tussle even then to down him. Owen dismounted and tied him hard and fast. He looked like an elephant lying on his side. He had a big DS brand on his hip, and one horn was only a four-inch stub where it had been broken off years before. The DS was an old abandoned ranch in Prospect and the brand hadn't been used since the owners had sold out sixteen years before. So we knew that steer had to be sixteen or seventeen years old. We hobbled and side lined him and left him in the pine pole corral overnight.

Next morning we came back and led him to Pine Springs where we rested him for a while, then took him on with some more cattle to the Pipe Line Pasture. We had about fifty head of big steers there, and he loomed up a foot or more over the largest among them. We thought he might die, because sometimes old wild steers like him grieve themselves to death in captivity, but he didn't. In the fall we shipped him to Phoenix.

On our rounds we reached the nine section Trinity Pasture, near Seligman. Demus had worked hard and had stayed out on the range much longer than usual without going on a bender. But I know he was thinking of us as well as himself when he suggested that we rest our mounts for a few days and go to town. At Seligman we drew our pay and got on a local train, and we had to give Demus a little boost to get him aboard since he had acquired a little "Old Tanglefoot" prior to the train's arrival. The chair car had very few passengers aside from us, fortunately. Pretty soon Demus went to the men's room at the end of the car. Someone before him had left the wooden seat hooked up, and Demus, too drunk to notice, sat down on the bare bowl and promptly fell asleep. Not long before we were to get off at Williams, the brakeman came through and found him, still asleep. The train, going around the curves of Bill Williams Mountain, had jiggled him deeper down and he wasn't able to get out alone. The brakeman called Miller over to help, and holding the door open with one foot they each got an arm and heaved. Demus came out easier than they had thought, catapulting clear into the car aisle, his pants down around his ankles, bleary eyed but triumphant. The brakeman hastily shoved him back inside.

We were a wild-whiskery crew when we reached Williams. At the first clothing store we saw we purchased some clean clothes, then headed for the San Tan Barber Shop to get "gussied" up. While the rest of us were being roached and shaved, Demus entered the bath in the rear. After a good hot bath, out he staggered clad in the pristine glory of a new union suit. Somehow he had gotten it on *upside down*. His legs were in the arms, and arms in the legs, with the seat making a lovely hood to frame his bushy red beard. He realized that something was wrong, as he asked the barbers:

"What in hell's the matter with this union suit? Just don't seem to fit no place!"

They really got a laugh out of that.

Williams wasn't much of a town in those days, and its entertainment facilities were too meager for his taste, so along in the evening Demus suggested that we all migrate to Prescott. Williams suited us fine, so we declined the invitation. He was to meet us back in Seligman on the tenth, but he didn't say of what year. When he didn't show up by the morning of the eleventh, we picked up Foster Marshall, a Supai Indian cowboy, to fill in and returned to Trinity Pasture to resume the work. Ten days later the CO Bar truck on its way to that ranch's Redlands camp, dumped Demus at Rose Wells, broke, sick, and sorry. That's where we found him. And was he a mess. We remained in camp two days longer than we'd intended to, pouring canned milk and strong black coffee into him, wondering whether he'd live or die. He pulled through, but barely. The Super never found out that we had covered for him.

At Pine Springs we threw up a small wall tent to sleep in, out of the rain. Owen was the only one of us who never took shelter, no matter what the weather.

About two miles west of camp, at the head of Pocomatay Canyon, "Doctor Tommy", an old Hualapai medicine man and a sub chief, lived with his little group of Indians. Owen rode over there after supper one evening. When he returned he told us that the Hualapais were going to have a sing two days later for all the "Squidgidees" (ghosts) of those who had died earlier in the year, and that we could come. Miller didn't want any part of it, so we left him in camp while the rest of us rode over to the site of the sing, after dark.

There must have been more than a hundred Indians in attendance. We tied our horses in the trees and sat on the wagon not too close, so that we remained in the background. Owen, being a Chief himself, was to take part. Three fires burned in the glade and the sing was already in progress. It had started at sundown and was to continue until sunrise. Naked except for breechclouts, the dancers and singers were to all intent the wild men of the forest of centuries ago. The eerie wails and chants for the spirits of the departed, the firelight reflected on the background of dark pine trees in this gloomy isolated glade, and

the boom of the dance drums transported the scene backward in time until we could scarcely recognize these people as those we knew and worked with in the present day.

About midnight, there were signs that many of the Indians were getting drunk, so Demus and I eased back into the trees, got our horses and rode back to camp. Owen rode in just in time to change horses and start out on the day's work with us. To look at him, one would never have guessed that he had danced and sung all night. We knew that after we had left, the choice belongings of the dead had been heaped on the fire and burned; saddles, blankets, spurs, bridles, cradle-boards, household goods, everything. Then the ashes had been taken by certain designated "keepers of the dead" into Diamond Creek Canyon. There in a burial cave known only to the Indians, the ashes had been deposited with their owners, before sunrise. We knew that only through Owen's standing in the tribe were we white men tolerated at the sing. Not even the Agent of the Reservation knew when or where a sing was planned, let alone being given a chance to view it. Owen himself died the following year of tuberculosis and I often thought of *his* sing when I chanced to look off of the rimrock into the impenetrable depths of unexplored Diamond Creek Canyon. He was a good friend and a good cowboy. The following year a young brother Claude wrangled horses for the Vs roundup.

From Pine Springs we moved to Frazier Well where Ed Byers, "Old Victrola", was looking after the pipeline and pumping water for stock. With far-sighted deviousness, Demus had long before approached the Superintendent about borrowing Ed, if he was needed, to help out with the stock. Although he could ride a gentle horse, old Ed was a total loss working cattle, as Demus well knew. So when he asked Ed to ride out with us one morning Ed brought up every excuse he could think of to keep from going. Demus insisted he just *had* to have him that day, so reluctantly Ed agreed.

Demus staked him to a big raw-boned horse with a churn-dasher gait, named "Old Drum" Everyone mounted, Demus led the way at a fast trot uphill and down, through the heaviest thickets of jack pine and scrub oak he could find. Without chaps, Ed's knees and shins took a beating in the brush and timber, the legs of his bib overalls crawling up as he stood up in the stirrups to absorb the jar of Old Drum's rough trotting gait. Unused to riding, I'm sure Ed's side was aching before we'd gone a mile. Demus just pretended that he thought

Ed was enjoying the ride, and he almost trotted us *all* down before he circled back toward camp.

We finally found four old bulls which Demus insisted should be driven back to camp. They wouldn't be hurried, and it took most of the afternoon to get them back to Frazier Well. Old Ed practically fell off his horse, he was so weary. The inner sides of his legs were galled.

"Now tomorrow we ought to work that Dutch Bell Tank country," Demus began.

"Hell, Demus," sputtered Ed, "I *can't* go with you tomorrow. My pipeline's busted about six miles south, and the tank in the Pipe Line pasture is about empty, and I've got to pump this well," and he rattled off a dozen more things he just *had* to do. I noticed the tell-tale quirk of Demus' smile beneath his red whiskers and knew this was another of his red letter days. Any time he could score on Ed his day was made enjoyable.

Taking no chances, Ed was out of the gate and chugging down the pipeline in his old Ford pickup next morning, before we even had our horses caught. And he didn't return until dusk that evening.

Frazier Well was about four hundred feet deep with a huge old Fairbanks Morse gas engine on the pump. This was enclosed in a pump house of galvanized sheet iron. The starter crank to rotate the big fly wheels took both hands and a lot of energy to operate. I didn't have to *see* him do it to know from what followed that Demus had slipped down to the well at night, removed the spark plugs, poured gasoline into them, then replaced them. When Ed went down before breakfast to start the pump, the engine backfired at about the second turn of the fly wheel. It threw Ed, crank and all, through the roof. We heard the commotion and went down to see what had happened. Ed slid down off the low roof, white and shaken, and just a little skinned up.

"Jesus Christ, I could have been killed!" he stuttered. "That damned old engine backfired and threw me clean out through the roof. Just look at that hole I made," he pointed.

Demus was so sympathetic and over-solicitious over Ed's accident that it was a pure give-away he'd had a hand in it. Days later I'd catch him smiling off toward the distance.

I stayed on until snow forced us to store the little wagon at Kesaha until next spring, and the rest of the boys went into winter camps. Then I went south with the birds once more.

Eleven   Horses and Men of the V's

In early March, I had a telegram from the Superintendent asking me to come up by the fifteenth to ride some colts. I knew it would be bitter cold up there at that time of year, so I stayed on where I was until the first of April. As it was, there was still quite a lot of snow on the ground when I dumped my saddle and bed off at National Tank. There Demus and a short crew were making ready to gather a remuda of horses out of Prospect Valley as soon as they could get in.

Expecting me in the middle of March, Demus had been grain-feeding the colts I was to ride ever since the first, and they were hard and in good shape; *too* good. Only two were colts: a four-year-old roan and a five-year-old sabino. The other, a wild-eyed sorrel named "Tomatoes" was nine if he was a day. I'd seen Charley Cole, one of two bronc stompers working for the outfit, ride him at Kesaha a couple of years before, and he wasn't having any easy time of it. I also knew that Tomatoes hadn't been ridden since. I was due for some rough days ahead.

National Tank was situated just on the north slope of a divide, where the drainage ran into the Grand Canyon of the Colorado River. Two big water lots, a squat log house, some corrals, and a section (640 acres) horse pasture about made up the place. Malapai hills, pine covered, surrounded it on three sides. There was open country to the south. Four miles to the north National Canyon joined the Grand Canyon in a spectacular dive of a mile in space, almost too frightening to look upon.

Demus had already hired a cook for the summer works, a little old Irishman who looked as though he had escaped from the chimpanzee cage of a circus. He wouldn't weigh more than a hundred and five pounds soaking wet, but he was a pugnacious old cuss. I had run onto him before, as he had cooked for the 51 Ranch in Yavapai County during roundup one year. His nickname was Dad, and his rear handle was McCaughey. Demus had brought the specially made roundup stove on its trailer cart up from the sheep ranch for Dad to cook on. He had also brought up the Pine Springs wagon, a big double-tired rock wagon with a big, high chuck box.

Some of the men were sleeping in the log house and some in the wall tent outside. I chose the tent because of the spotted skunks who lived in the old log cabin. It snowed most of my first night there, and Demus and I had to get out and scrape the tent off twice to keep the ridgepole from breaking down.

Next morning while the wrangler was working the horse pasture,

I went out to feed my colts in a side corral. After breakfast I decided to let the hammer down on the roan and the sabino and save Tomatoes until later in the day when it had warmed up a bit. I spent about an hour on each of the horses in a good, tight, round corral, then took them out to the big water lots to gallop around awhile. Fresh, they wanted to buck and cut up, but they weren't too hard to handle and out-maneuver.

Tomatoes, however, was another story. He was a spoiled, dirty, conniving, wise old pelican who had shucked off so many cowboys he considered that to be his life's work. He was hard to mount in the first place. He would kick you if you stood a bit too far back, and paw if you were too far in front. On a tight rein he'd fall backwards, and on a loose rein he'd rear and jump forward, to hit the ground buck-ing. Any way you tried to mount him was wrong. Whenever a rider let him get his head he buried it between his front feet and all hell couldn't drag it up again.

I had an old leather blind in my war sack, so I got it out and used it on him. That fooled him for a while. Once I was in the saddle he couldn't buck me off. He could fall, however, or scrape me off against a tree or fence. So I got in my licks first, while he was fresh. I had tied my rope on the corral gate in a slip knot, laying the loose end on a corral pole. After he had bucked out, I rode him within reach, pulled the slip knot loose and the gate swung open. Once in the big water lot, I really took to him. One of the boys opened the outside gate and I rode out into the big open country. Fourteen miles south was a little red lake. Tomatoes was going strong when we topped the hill where we could see down to the water. Some antelope and a few head of cattle watering there scattered at sight of us. From the lake I turned back and loped him all the way to the water lot gate again. It had been a twenty-eight mile jaunt.

When I slipped off to open the gate, Tomatoes tried to jerk loose and kick me, but I was expecting it and he didn't get the job done. Then he stood on his hind legs and leaped as high as he could when I remounted. As usual, he hit the ground bucking as hard as he could, but I still wasn't napping and didn't land in the back seat as he had expected me to. Every time he hit the ground I spurred him in both shoulders as hard as I could stab him. After about ten jumps like that he wanted to get away from those punishing spurs, so he broke into a run. He was wringing wet with sweat when I pulled my rig off him, but just as ornery as ever.

Demus and the crew left early next morning for Prospect to get the remuda. He figured they'd be back in three or four days. I had National all to myself now. The following morning broke cold and clear, so right off I made Tomatoes my project for the day. As I started to mount him he leaped in the air and came down broadside on his ribs twice. I was on him as he got up from the last fall. That made him *very* unhappy, so he bucked and bawled all over the lot trying to slip the pack. Now that I was alone, I *had* to ride him. This time I pointed him toward Lagoon Tank eight miles west of National, and poured on the coal. I avoided the ridge trail through the thick timber, riding in the canyon instead, where I had a better break with him. At Lagoon I dismounted and tied him to a solid post while I built a fire to warm my hands and feet a little. There were three adjoining corrals so I picked the back one to mount him in. When I hit the saddle he was turning handsprings toward the next corral. As he went through the gate between them, he whacked my left hip-bone a hell of a lick on the big juniper gate post. It hurt like the devil all the way back, but I knew I could never get back on him if I quit then, so I toughed it out. That night and the next day I laid around camp, too sore to do more than cook and feed my horses. However, I knew that rest was pure poison to a horse like him, and that I *had* to ride him to keep him in my pile while I had him going.

This was one of the toughest days of my life. With every quick move I made, that cracked hip-bone gave me fits, and Tomatoes seemed to turn on stronger than ever that day. I sure didn't show him any sympathy either, but beat and spurred him until by nightfall he looked as though he had been in a fight with a den of bob cats. When the crew returned with the remuda, Demus was undecided which one of us needed the liniment in the wagon worse, me or Tomatoes. After that he let Owen ride with me whenever I took Tomatoes out. The other colts I needed no help with.

The company truck came out from town with a load of cowboys and their outfits, and for the next three days everyone shod up their mounts. One big old chuffy boy who'd hired out as a rough string rider didn't even know how to shoe. I watched him bend and throw away about a half a box of nails while trying to shoe one horse. The day we pulled out for Lagoon to begin the Spring roundup, this old boy was riding Chili Bean, a big rough string bay horse. Except for two men who had gone with the wagon to guide the way and to make camp for the cook, the rest of us helped the horse wrangler get the remuda on its way. The road crossed over a dam about a mile from National. Chili Bean was slinging his head and trying to get up among the remuda horses, getting madder by the minute at being held back. When they came to the dam Chili Bean exploded. On about the third jump he threw that old kid off, and down the riprapped side of the dam the boy slid on his belly. The rocks really knocked the bark off him. Demus had to stop the wagon and let the fellow ride to Lagoon on it, then he told me to cut through and see if I could find something fat enough for beef.

It was cold and windy and spitting snow before I reached Lagoon. I had picked up a fairly good heifer on the way, and at the edge of Dad's camp I roped and tied her to a tree. Old Dad had his camp set up fine in a little open place in some pinon trees. Inside the cook tent, his stove going good, a big roast was in the oven and coffee was boiling on the top. Everything looked hunky dory to me. But not to Dad. He'd already taken down with the gripes.

"By God," he exploded, "just look at the sand blowing up under the tent, and that snow and wind outside. If this ain't a hell of a country. Here we are, living just like barbarians did ten thousand years ago. If I ever get out of this damn wilderness I'm shore going to *stay* out!"

I tried to josh him out of his mood, but he was constipated and refused to be convinced there was any worse place on earth. The Super came by on our last day there, and Dad tried to quit. But Tom soothed his ruffled feathers by telling him that he would take him to see a doctor in town when we reached Frazier Well. The next move was to Frazier, and Tom took Dad to town from there.

The only doctor in Seligman was an ex-veterinarian now working for the Santa Fe Railroad and selling Chevrolet cars on the side. He gave Dad about five pounds of salts, with instructions to take one heaping tablespoonful each day. The salts worked, all too well. In about a week old Dad weighed several pounds less and was weak as a cat. Demus and I both told him to quit taking the stuff, but he was hard-headed and said he was going to take the whole five pounds if it killed him. It danged near did.

Dad always slept under the wagon, and at Kesaha where we had five hundred big steers to move to Trinity, Demus asked him to get an early breakfast, about four a.m. Dad set his alarm clock for three-thirty and went to bed. That old clock would raise the dead, and when it jangled right alongside his ear next morning Dad sat up so quickly he bumped his head on the bottom of the wagon. That set him off on a cussing spree. Next, fumbling around in the dark trying to get his clothes on, he got both skinny old legs in just one leg of his baggy britches. When he stood up to pull them on he fell down again. That really got his Irish up. Demus and I just had to laugh at his choice of cuss words, and that did it.

"All right! Laugh you hyenas. Go ahead and laugh yore fool heads off! And cook yore breakfast while you're laffin'—cause I quit!"

And this time he sure enough had. Demus and I wrangled up breakfast for the crew that morning. On our way to Trinity with the steers, we met the Super in his Buick. To his query of how things were, Demus had to tell him we no longer had a cook. Tom thought that perhaps once more he could talk Dad out of his peevish spell, but he guessed wrong.

For the next two days we all pitched in to wrangle the pots until the Company truck deposited a new cook in our midst. He was a big old yarn socker, bib overalls and all, who claimed to be an ex-policeman from Elko, Nevada. He may have been a policeman, but he had never been a cook. He actually couldn't boil water without burning it, and he was filthy, which was *the* cardinal sin with Demus. He had the damnedest bed I ever saw in a cow camp. It was a big old lumpy double bed mattress, with a mess of old soogans sort of wadded together in a ragged old tarp. When the boys were loading the bedrolls to move camp, it took about three of them to wallow it up onto the wagon. And it was always coming untied.

From the start Demus wasn't a bit happy, with either the cook *or* his cooking. We stood him for about a week until one morning when we were moving over into the Cataract Plains, near Shiloh Camp. Just after the cook had got on the wagon and picked up the lines, the boys holding the four-horse team stepped back to let them make their runaway start. Before they had gotten a hundred yards out of the camp ground, part of the cook's bed fell off. Hollering "whoa" at the teams, and setting the brake on the wagon, Old Nasty shouted at Demus.

"Have somebody put my bed back on the wagon."

Demus rode over real polite-like.

"Why sure, fellow," he said. "But first I think that since we have no pitchfork on the wagon, you better go back and shock it up again."

The cook climbed down and began re-rolling his bed, and Demus told Jim Fancher to take the wagon on to Shiloh. By the time our cook realized what was happening we were rolling on. Fancher threw the rest of the cook's bed off, and the last we saw of him he was sitting on it, out on the lone prairie. A couple of well drillers who were on their way to Seligman for a broken part on their rig picked him up and delivered him in town.

Our third cook of the summer was a Jim Dandy. He was about thirty years old, from California. The Super had to pretty near shanghai him, because he definitely wasn't looking for a cooking job. He had been breaking horses in Nevada, and only agreed to cook until the Super could get another one. We all hoped that he would stay all summer, for he was a bang-up good cook, – and clean. He did stay almost two months, until we made a delivery of a thousand yearling steers at Seligman. Then he was on his way.

Demus got drunk in town, and came up missing when we were due to go back to gather the next shipment. I pinch-hit in his place as wagon boss for the next week. The Super came out once during that time and asked where he was.

"He just went over to scout out the feed situation in the Sullivan pasture," I lied, knowing that Tom couldn't get in there with his Buick.

The next day an old cowpuncher came driving into camp with Demus draped over the back seat of his battered-up car. He said that the wiring had caught fire back a ways and he had had to throw sand on it to keep the whole car from burning up. Demus, still drunk, had tried to help and had burned his hands pretty badly. He laid around camp that day, then rode out with us next morning. Cutting calves and branding, he must have got dirt in his burns, because they soon became badly infected. A fellow named Tyree came along from Martin Pasture, in his Chevy pickup, and we convinced Demus to go to town with him. The Super sent him on to the Veterans Hospital at Prescott immediately. Doctors kept him there for almost a month. They cured his hands, but not his thirst, and he was nursing a sizable hangover when he returned to us.

Soon after Demus' return we started another drive to the railroad. We were within fifteen miles of it when the buyers headed us off. Their pasture deal had fallen through in California and they needed a few days to arrange for another pasture before receiving the ship-ment. Trinity had plenty of feed and water to hold the cattle that long, so we put the drive in there. We hadn't time to go back and gather again, so we had a few days at loose ends. The Grand Canyon Sheep Company had been crying for burros for a long time, so we decided to kill time by looking for a few. Each of us saddled the best mount we had, and early one morning made a circle drive in the big four town-ship "Burro Tank" pasture. The pasture was full of wild burros, and when we reached the holdup ground next to Trinity fence we must have had four hundred wild jackasses together on top of a little hill. We all stopped some distance from them to blow our horses and cinch up. Three old boys eased around to open a gate into Trinity and make a wing out from it. Then we began trying to ease those nervous asses off the hill, down to that gate. We all knew our chances for success were mighty slim.

About half way to the gate the burros began to boil over. In about a minute they were going in every direction, "hell-to-toot." We man-aged to get about thirty through the gate of one bunch. There were cowboys after burros all over those malapai hills. Some roped only one, and several caught two apiece. A few caught and tied as many as three each. We had only one casualty, Henry Romo. He was a Mexi-can from the Verde River country, near old Fort McDowell. His horse stepped in a dog hole while running full tilt, and Henry's head made a duck's nest in the ground where he hit. Dang near broke his neck.

We led the tied burros into Trinity and returned to camp for the day. Next morning we made another drive, and had about eighty to-gether this time. Most of them got away, but we did save enough to keep those sheep herders busy for many a day, breaking them to pack. Henry rode the wagon to town when we delivered the yearlings out of Trinity and went back to the Verde country where there weren't any prairie dog holes.

The afternoon we loaded the last of our cattle, the Seven Drag outfit came in with a drive of chow horses. The horses, corralled in the stockyards, were a sorry sight to behold. There were many old cow horses too old to work hard any more, and fifty or more range mares and colts, wild and unbroken. To keep them from outrunning the riders and getting away, the boys had caught the mares and colts and sewed their nostrils shut with baling wire. Thus, when they tried to run, they couldn't breathe enough air and would choke down.

Demus and I were uptown at a thirst parlour that evening when the boss man of the Seven Drag came in and made a long distance phone call to Rockford, Illinois, to get a price quote on his horses. Then he put in another call to some chicken feed plant in Los Angeles. We couldn't hear the other end of the conversation, but we could hear his. He was dickering for a higher price and we heard him say he would phone again next day.

There was no water in the stock pens, and those old horses and mares and colts were gaunt for lack of water. They had probably been hazed for a day or two before being caught and it was a cinch they hadn't had water in a long time. Demus and I got our heads together and discovered we were both thinking of the same thing at the same time. We knew the stockyard gates were kept locked at night. After dark we just happened to locate a pinch bar, and just happened to find ourselves at the stockyards. Somehow, the gate came open and every critter in there took off for the tall uncut. Early next morning, Seligman's Livestock Inspector, Bob Jones, was as busy as a bird dog trying to find out who had released all the Seven Drag horses. He even questioned us, but we were plumb innocent. The Seven Drag boss sent his waddies out to try to get as many back as they could find, but they only got a few.

Demus and I were surrounding some ham and eggs in the Chinaman's cafe while the Drag boss was coffeeing up and telling his tale of woe to anyone who would listen. Demus pushed his plate aside, wiped the coffee from his mustache, and surmised as how every son-of-a-bitch has his troubles, as we strode outside into fresher air. That mystery must have given the townfolk something to cogitate about for a long time.

Just before the Fourth of July some of the boys allowed as how they wanted to go to Prescott for the annual Rodeo. Demus passed the word to the Super, who was agreeable. So on the morning of the third a whole truckload of us took off for Prescott. Yaqui Ordunus was going to enter the saddle bronc riding; Jim and Johnny Fancher, the team roping; and Bob Adams the bulldogging event.

Once in Prescott the crew scattered like blackbirds. The town was swarming with cow hands and bronc riders, many of whom we knew. This was in the days before professionals made a business of rodeo competition, doing nothing else. These old boys were real working cowboys who competed at rodeos more for the fun and hell of it than for the money. And many of them were plenty good too. Yaqui took second money in the bronc riding, and the Fancher boys also won some money. The rest of us had variously a good time or a good drunk. Demus had the latter. Yaqui Ordunus felt nigger rich after his winnings, and bought a second-hand car. He'd never driven a car, so he got Demus to drive him back to Seligman, which was a mistake. Between Ash Fork and Seligman Demus wrapped it around a telephone pole. Neither man was hurt, but the car was, to the tune of a seven hundred dollar repair bill. Yaqui sold it as was to a gambler.

By the last of September Tomatoes and I parted company until the following Spring. He hadn't been able to throw me away—yet, but I knew he had plans for next year.

In November I had a telegram from the Super to bring Gus Tipton, an old cowboy I had worked with in the Basin country, and come up to help deliver a big shipment of steers. From Seligman the truck took us to the wagon camped at Long Point Dam.

The S.P. Pasture we were to gather was twelve miles across from east to west, and fourteen from north to south. It took us four days to work it out. Each day's gather was put in a small pasture atop a long cedar ridge nearby. The weather was cold and clear. Each morning as we loped out across the rolling hills of the pasture, the frost sparkled like millions of diamonds on the dry grass. At times we would see as many as two hundred antelope in a band, running ahead of the drive. The evening of the last day, we worked the smaller pasture and eased everything into the big fenced water lot at Long Point. We had two thousand one hundred head of steers in it that night. They walked the fence all night, and several times bunches of them spooked and hit the fence. All of us slept with our clothes on, expecting a real stampede before day. But the fence held, and by good daylight we turned the cattle out of the gate toward Black Tanks.

For the first four or five miles the herd walked along at a good pace. Then some of the steers began to graze. As I looked back from my position on the right point, the drive was strung out for three miles or more, a sight I was never to see again. The days of the big trail herds was almost over.

At Black Tank we spent the night. The next day's drive was through thick cedars in Malapai country and was much slower. Just before sundown we reached an open flat where we held the herd to cut out the big steers. There were over four hundred of them. Once the steers were separated, the main herd went on to Trinity about six miles farther on. At the same time some of the boys took the big steer herd west to the Sheep Ranch Pasture.

It was eleven o'clock at night when we finally reached Trinity. Many of the steers were sore-footed from that day's drive through the rocks. Daylight found us working Trinity and making the last day's drive to the railroad. Once rid of that shipment, we returned to the Sheep Ranch to bring in the big steers. They were to go to Phoenix. Gus Tipton and I were to ride the train with them.

It was night before our train left Ash Fork, and somewhere around Skull Valley we had a small wreck. We felt the jar back in the caboose and walked up towards the engine in the dark. Our cattle cars were at the head of the train, directly behind the engine. The fireman started back, carrying an open torch for light. The conductor was just in front of Gus and me. At about the center of the train a tank car had jumped the track and fallen on its side, tearing a hole in one end from which gasoline was leaking. We could smell the fumes before we reached the toppled car. The conductor shouted at the fireman to douse his open torch before he blew up the train. After a pow-wow, the train crew cut the cars ahead of the wreck and pulled on into Prescott with our part of the train.

We had a long wait there until a wrecker went back, removed the tank car and brought up the rest of the train. So it was night-time once more before we reached Phoenix, our destination. Those old big steers were tired and cross, and we had billy hell unloading them in the dark. One of them kicked Gus on the leg so hard it popped like a firecracker. I thought sure that kick had broken his leg.

Early the following morning Ed Cavness, the buyer, was at the yards with some horses. Gus and I and Ed's men took the steers out of the yards and drove them to Ed's feed pens, a few miles west. Then we went into town. Gus swore he'd never get caught in another deal like that. I think it took him a week to get warm again.

It was the following May when I rejoined the V wagon, near Bishop's Lake. The boys were shoeing up, and right off I had my eight head to plate. There were a couple of new cowboys, one a fellow about fifty-five years old. In the afternoon he got ready to shoe another of the horses they'd cut to him. Many of those old

V horses had to be tied down to be shod and this was one of them. The old cowboy and one of the younger ones were bedding that old fighting pelican down, and having a hard time of it. They finally got him down, and this old boy was trying to get the front and hind legs crossed and tied. The horse fought and struggled the entire time to keep him from doing just that.

The old cowboy was hot and mad by then, so he just sort of *half* tied him. After a lot of puffing and cussing, he got one shoe on, but he had pretty well given out by then. I had finished the horse I was working on, so went over to give him a hand. While he held the pole raising the horse's crossed legs, I leveled and shod one hind foot. Bent over clinching the nails, I was in an awkward position when the horse threw another of his fighting fits. The tie-rope came loose and he kicked me in the mouth with the edge of a shoe, breaking my upper front teeth off even with the gums. It all happened so quickly I was spitting out blood and broken teeth before I realized what had taken place.

The nearest dentist was at Williams, sixty miles from Seligman. Getting into Seligman, waiting for the train, and the trip to Williams burned up a lot of daylight, so it was dark by the time I reached Williams. At the dentist's office I was faced with a note on his door announcing that he had gone fishing and would return in ten days.

Since he was the only dentist at Williams, I again had to wait for a train, backtrack to Ash Fork, wait for another train there, and finally reach Prescott, still in search of a dentist. There I spent the small hours of the morning suffering from the fierce ache of those broken teeth, until the dentist came down to open his office a little after eight o'clock. He got right to work, extracted all the roots, and snipped some broken bones off level. That night I was back at the camp, ready to go on with the works.

Tomatoes was as salty as ever, but by now my disposition matched his, and I combed his old sorrel hide every time he even humped up. At Rose Wells one morning I mounted him in a corral, on the fly as usual. While he was bucking and bawling, I got a quick short wrap around both hands with the split bridle reins, then sat back as hard as I could to pull his head out from between his forelegs. I succeeded, too darn well. The top of his old hard head smacked me right in the face, breaking my nose once more. I wasn't going to let him think he'd won anything, so I rode him out on the drive. Later in the morning while in the lead of a little herd going up a draw, he took another bucking spell, scattering the cattle in all directions. I spurred him to a standstill and that simmered him down until we reached camp. The blood from my broken nose had run down and clotted in my whiskers, and at camp I had to soak my face in a pan of warm water quite a while to loosen it up. I whittled out a smooth cedar stick and wore it stuck up one side of my nose for a few days, except when riding Tomatoes.

Bud Pendergast, a Salt River Valley boy I had once worked with, came to the wagon to work for a while. He claimed to be a pretty good bronc man, so with Demus' O.K. I staked him to Tomatoes as one of his mounts. Bud had a new saddle, and he got away from camp the first time without trouble. About a mile down the fence line was a gate. Just as we reached it, Tomatoes threw one of his bucking fits. Bud was digging him with his spurs at every jump, until suddenly Tomatoes sort of sucked back beneath him. Bud, saddle, blankets, bridle and all, skinned off over his head right into a growth of wild roses. Someone roped Tomatoes, going down the fence, and led him back. Bud re-saddled him and came on with us to where Demus scattered the circle. Demus had watched the performance at the gate, so he told Bud to stay with me the rest of the morning.

Tomatoes felt pretty cocky, and every little way he'd grab his tail tight and act like he was going to buck again. I think that dive into the briars kind of chilled Bud's nerve, because he was awfully careful not to let his spurs touch Tomatoes when he acted up.

"Next time he does that, comb his hair good and take it out of him," I warned Bud. "If you don't, he'll think he's got you bluffed." But Bud wouldn't try him out, and old Tomatoes kept acting up more and more often all morning. By the time we got back to camp Bud was plumb scared to death of him. I traded him another horse for Tomatoes, and *he* bucked through an old dead fallen tree with Bud right away. That did it. We lost another cowboy. Bud rolled his bed and went back to the Valley to stay. He spread the word down there that the Vs had the meanest horses in Arizona, and he was about half right.

We always had a few head that were in no regular string. Whenever a horse-fighter with the reputation of abusing his horses hit the outfit, Demus would slip one of those to the man, and it wouldn't be long before he quit. They were too rough to ride for any fifty dollars a month, in anybody's country. Doney, Black Lightning, Scorpion, Skunk Tail, Brown Hog, Black Jack, Pero, Sailor, and Trigger were all more or less outlaws, just to name a few. Yes, the Vs had some rough horses.

Old Doney was a real "wart hog." During his life at the Vs he had shelled off more cowboys than an ear of corn has kernels. He wasn't a fancy, showy bucker, but his results were good—for him. At least his bucking talents got him out of a lot of hard work. Chuck line riders and cowboys had talked about him around many a camp fire. Even cowhands who had never seen him had heard of him. Even when he was fat, which he seldom was, being a hard keeper, he wasn't much to look at. A big-headed bay, cat-hammed, and ill-built, he sure didn't *look* like he could buck off a wet saddle blanket. His looks were right deceiving.

Charley Cole, a Tonto Basin bronc stomper, took a job with the outfit one summer to snap out a string of horses. For a partner he had Yaqui Ordunus. They set up their first camp at Kesaha, where they rode out their first string. Then they moved over to Rose Wells for their next bunch. By late summer they had knocked the rough edges off quite a few horses. Yaqui had met his match a couple of times so far; once with a blue roan, and once with a palomino. But Charley was going strong, and thinking the outfit didn't have any horses *he* couldn't ride.

We were eating our noon meal one day when Charley rode in to our camp. After he'd scraped his plate and tossed it in the roundup tub under the chuck box, he squatted down by Demus to pick his teeth and palaver a bit. He'd heard of Doney and had some idea that he would like to try him a fall. Demus sent one of the boys to the horse trap and in a little while Doney was in the corral, with a sort of dejected look like an old Iowa plow horse. Charley walked all around him, sizing him up, and I don't think he was impressed. Bill Chestnut and Joe Evans, both of whom had lost "coup" to Doney at one time, began telling Charley how hard he was to ride. I could see with half an eye that Charley had them pegged as a couple of amateurs, which they very much weren't.

Anxious to show his prowess on one of the Vs' most famous horses, Charley carried his saddle into the corral and asked one of the boys to catch Doney for him. Now Old Doney never wasted his powder on fighting a man or a saddle on the ground. He allowed Charley to saddle and mount and get his feet in the stirrups without untracking. Then Charley hit him between the ears with his hat and jabbed both spurs in this shoulders. That was insulting, so Doney responded. Doney was barefooted and his feet were worn down almost to the quick from running in the sandstone pasture. The little corral was real rocky too, and Doney didn't buck very hard because his feet hurt. After a few jumps he slacked off to run around the corral and stop. "He can't buck," Charley grinned. "I've got a half dozen raw broncs in camp right now that can lay him in the shade."

"We were just going out into the pasture to drive in a few heifers," Demus replied. "Why don't you come along and help us?"

"Fine," says Charley and came.

Doney trotted along like any old horse until we got out onto nice soft ground. At one place where our horses had to step off a little cutbank about a foot down Doney suddenly pulled the pin on his grenade and exploded. Charley was sitting deep and straight from the first jump. On about the third, Doney had him loosened, and on the fourth he stacked him neatly on his head, as limber as a dish rag. When Charley got up and brushed himself off old Doney was cropping grass as unconcerned as though nothing had happened.

"By God, he sure caught me napping," Charley allowed. "But he won't the next time."

So he piled back on Doney mad as all get out, and fit the spurs to him, right off. Old Doney responded right pert. This time he threw Charley up astraddle of his neck while both feet were still in the stirrups. Then he pulled his head out, leaving Charley hanging upside down in front of him. Determined to lose his rider entirely, Doney was spinning and jumping at the same time. It all happened so fast it was hard to follow the action, but one front hoof must have stepped on the side of Charley's head, because by the time we had got Doney by the ears and had cut a stirrup leather to get him loose, Charley was almost missing one ear, and all the meat was off that side of his head. He was really bunged up. I'll give him credit though, for hurt as badly as he was, he got up without help. A couple of boys helped him up behind Demus and took him back to camp, where they bandaged his head as well as they could. Doney had scored again.

Charley spent a month in the Prescott Veterans Hospital. The doctors saved his ear, and the hide grew back on his head, but a lot of scars stayed with him to remind him of Doney. I heard that he later admitted that Old Doney had something he didn't know anything about, and he was pretty downcast over the whole thing.

As in every big outfit, cowboys came and went. We drew one prize package when "Spike" came to the Vs. The Super, Tom Cavness, was an old cowman and we never figured out how he came to hire

Spike. He was a Dutchman just out of the bowels of Texas, where he had been raised on a goat ranch down in the sand hill country. I don't think he'd ever seen a cow before. He had an old nickel horn, Sears Roebuck saddle, and a cheap pair of sharp-rowelled spurs. I don't recall his name, but Demus immediately dubbed him "Spike" because his head came to a sort of a point. Demus cut him a short string of horses, one of which was named Juicy Fruit. He was gentle, but a crazy, nervous head slinger, and all he knew was to run. Held down, he could prance and run sideways and worry himself into a sweaty lather. His rider had to mount on the fly because the minute a foot was in the stirrup he was off like a rocket. Demus used to claim he would be just the thing to work a herd of antelope on.

We were all mounted and waiting for Spike. He couldn't even get his saddle on Juicy Fruit. John Driver finally dismounted and helped him. When he started to mount he looked just like a man climbing up a step ladder. He jabbed his big foot into the stirrup as far as it would go and, with the horn in one hand and the cantle in the other, tried to pull himself up astraddle the saddle. Juicy Fruit was a hundred yards away before Spike could get set in the saddle, and then he was in the back seat behind the cantle. He had already lost one rein and his hat, and was hollering "Whoa, Whoa," like he was driving a plow horse. He was just about to fall off when Tom Pearson and Demus ran up alongside and grabbed the loose rein to stop Juicy Fruit. They didn't want to have to run him a mile or two to catch him after he had lost Spike. While the men held the horse the Dutchman wallowed over the cantle and got his feet in the stirrups as I handed him his hat. A quarter of a mile from camp he was finally mounted. From there on he rode all morning with a death grip on the saddle horn. He wouldn't have gotten off to pick up a twenty dollar gold piece.

Spike was a total stranger to any part of working cattle, and Demus tried him out on different things, hoping to find something he *could* do. He was so awkward flanking calves that they would get him down, get a foot in his pocket, kick him, and drag him around. Branding, he would get the iron on upside down most of the time. He was near sighted and wore thick-lensed glasses, but that didn't explain his troubles. He couldn't turn a cow, and to catch a calf he would have to run it until it fainted and fell down so he could get off and lay the loop over its head. He just didn't fit in any place.

Now Demus hated to fire a man if he was trying, and that Dutchman was trying hard. But he just couldn't learn, no matter how many times he was shown or told. So to get rid of him Demus decided to slip him a bad horse, figuring that if he got bucked off right hard he'd roll his bed and quit. That's when we found the one thing he *could* do. Scorpion was a shiny black VII brand horse. He had never been anything but a rough string horse *all* his life, and it took a real bronc rider to stay aboard him. He was hard to mount, and I'd seen him fall over backwards, and buck off good riders aplenty.

It was cloudy and sprinkling rain as we left camp the morning Demus gave Scorpion to Spike to ride. As awkward as a cub bear, Spike began climbing onto his mount. Scorpion's tail was tucked tight, the whites of his eyes showing like those of a mad tom cat. We were all watching, just hoping he wouldn't kill the poor dumb bastard. As Spike straddled his right arm to drop down in the saddle, Scorpion whirled from him and Spike almost fell off the other side. We could see the muscles bunched like steel springs under that black hide, ready to explode in any direction, as Scorpion eyed Spike hanging way off on his side, trying to pull himself back upright. None of our gentle horses would have stood for that, but damned if Scorpion didn't just sort of jump up and down nervously in the same spot until Spike was all set again.

Demus had a habit of leading out from camp at a walk until he was about a hundred yards away, then suddenly hitting a high lope. That usually tapped off any horse that wanted to buck, and sometimes there would be a half dozen horses bucking in every direction. Demus wouldn't look back for a mile. It was up to the riders to catch up when they could. He followed that same routine this morning. Spike was holding a tight rein, and pretty soon everyone was out in the lead of him by quite a distance. When he realized how far behind he was, he jabbed Scorpion with those sharp rowells to make him catch up. For a little while we lost sight of them because of the brush and trees. Then here they came, burning the wind.

Several minutes later a hard shower hit, and we dismounted beneath a big pine tree until it passed. Ten minutes later we mounted up again. This time Spike did go clear over the saddle, and only saved himself from landing on his head by grabbing Scorpion's off front leg. That crazy horse just snorted and pranced while Spike pushed himself back up his foreleg. We just sat there with our mouths hanging open, expecting the slaughter. That performance must have given Demus ideas, because he kept eying Spike with a speculative look for the rest of the day.

Not long afterwards, Demus sent me in charge of the crew to take a bunch of steers to the Sullivan Pasture. He had to go to the Indian camp at the head of Pocomatay Canyon to see if Broncho Anne's sub tribe would fence off a little hidden spring in the Canyon for the Company. He left camp before we had saddled up. And damned if Spike didn't come out mounted on Doney. Now we all knew that old Doney was a horse of many moods — all bad. We were not surprised that he let Spike mount but we knew it would only be for a little while. The steers we were moving had been driven a good deal and were not rollicky, so the herd moved off easily enough. Old Doney just followed the drags along as contented as could be, clear to the Pasture.

After we had shown the cattle the water there and left them drinking we turned back from the Pasture to return to camp. Spike dismounted, opened the outside gate, let us all ride through, then shut it again. Joe Evans and Jim Pearson stayed back to wait for him to mount up again. He got on and came along at a little jog trot, old Doney's favorite gait. Those two stopped to roll a cigarette out of the wind and plan a little devilment. After Spike had ridden ahead a little way, Joe pitched one end of his rope to Jim and at a nod they spurred their horses into a run up behind Spike and Doney. One horse went by him on either side, the rope catching Doney under the tail in a perfect rim fire maneuver. The most foolproof horse in the Vs' remuda would have bucked all over the flat after a trick like that. But old Doney just humped up and almost sat down on the ground until Joe turned loose his end of the rope. I never saw anything like it. They couldn't even *make* that horse buck with Spike. When Demus returned that evening I got him off to one side.

"How come you gave Doney to Spike?" I queried.

"Well," Demus smiled, "I knew if I told him it was old Doney he'd be too scared to ride him, so I told him this horse's name was Old Jitney. What he don't know won't hurt him, and if he can get along with Doney for another few days we're set, because the Super said he'd put him in camp at the Sheep Ranch, where he'll be out of our hair."

Spike did move to the Sheep Ranch and kept Doney as one of his mounts there, and never knew he was the worst outlaw on the Three V Ranch. Old Doney was a lamb, for Spike.

Later we rode in to the Sheep Ranch early one morning, to find Spike trotting around the water lot leading a big unbranded calf on a slack rope. He had trapped some cattle on water, and roped the calf to brand. The trouble was he didn't know how to get it down. He had dragged it around for an hour or so trying to choke it down, but instead had broken it to lead.

"Dese olt, big cafs is sure hell to choke down," he explained to Demus.

We just watered our horses and rode on. Out of earshot Demus said: "I've always heard the Lord has his arms around babies and damned fools, and Spike sure ain't no infant. He ain't got brains enough to get hurt."

Spike stayed on at the Sheep Ranch to feed bulls in the winter. The Super came by one day and found several of the weaker bulls dead. The stronger ones had fought them off the feed troughs and Spike was too dumb to separate them. So the Super did what Doney wouldn't. He put the skids under Spike, who went back to the bowels of Texas. Doney returned to the remuda, where he went right on shelling cowboys like peas out of a pod.

Abe Caufman, former owner of Rose Wells, had built up a good ranch before he sold out to the Sanford Cattle Company. He had been paid seven-hundred thousand dollars for his holdings. That was a lot

of money in those days. Abe loved to hunt, and after selling Rose Wells he took advantage of his leisure to go on big game hunts all over the world. He finally grew homesick for his old stomping grounds and returned to start another little ranch at the head of Pocomatay Canyon. He was doing so well with it that the Sanford Cattle Company bought him out again, to get him off the middle of their range. Once more he began big game hunting. Somewhere in his travels he met and married a wealthy woman. Between the two they had more money than Carter had liver pills, so they could do anything they wished.

Now Abe was a regular old cowman who liked to associate with cowboys a lot better than society folk. His wife had never seen a real live cowboy. I guess Abe told her a lot of big windies about his country and the Indians until he finally convinced her that she should see it. Anyhow, returning from a safari in Africa he joined her in Paris and brought her along to his old XI Ranch at the head of Pocomatay. He brought along an old cow camp cook who used to work for him, and a colored chauffeur. His wife had just outfitted herself in Paris with a lot of highfalutin clothes, and she had trunks full of them when they reached camp.

Young Beecher's sub tribe of Hualapais had settled at the old XI Ranch a few years back, so when the Caufmans arrived they found they were right in the middle of an Indian camp. Young Beecher was pretty well off for a Hualapai, with a lot of cattle and horses in his own individual 34 Bar brand. But his squaw, "Broncho Anne", was the *real* boss of the camp. She was a lot older than Young Beecher, and a typical Mohave Apache. Her forehead was tatooed with a butter-fly, and there were three vertical stripes running down her chin, plus a dot on each cheek bone. She wore the long-flounced Apache dresses and moccasins, with her long hair hanging down her back. I never saw her smile. Young Beecher and his oldest boy Frank always rode with us when we camped in their part of the Reservation. "Broncho Anne" herself always turned up the evening we butchered a beef, to get the guts.

Once established at the XI camp, Abe hired an Indian to guide and began hunting mountain lions. That part of the country was thick with lions and he had good hunting. He had brought along two little Irish terrier dogs and one old coon hound. When they found a fresh track he would put the terriers on it and they would be off like a shot in the brush and canyons after the lion. But they were silent trailers and would soon outdistance Abe and the guide. Then he would turn the old coon hound loose to trail up the terriers and follow his baying voice. Seldom a day passed that he didn't return with one or two lion scalps.

In the meantime his wife was left in camp with only the Indians for company. "Broncho Anne" could speak some English and swear eloquently in that language. She and Mrs. Caufman got along fine, and before the Caufmans moved back to civilization Mrs. Caufman gave Broncho Anne two evening gowns she had brought from Paris: one a red-velvet, the other a black-lace. Both were practically backless, and were cut real low in the brisket, with long trains dragging behind.

Broncho Anne was delighted with her gifts. The red-velvet gown she stashed away to be buried in. The black-lace one she wore only on state occasions, such as coming to the V wagon to get the beef guts. Her first appearance in it really knocked our eyes out. Just about dusk at Pine Springs she drove up in her old black Model A Ford. She was in all her glory, with two of her kids and her husband riding in the back where they couldn't detract from her grand entry. Braking to a stop in a cloud of dust, she climbed out and gave us the Grand Duchess treatment, Indian-style.

"Mister-Cavness-tell-me-I-can-have-the-guts-and-hide-when-you-kill-a-beef," she stated in the slow monotone with which Indians speak. Demus was so flabbergasted at her get-up he could only nod. Waving her bare, wrinkled arm imperiously she shouted over towards her Ford:

"Beecher! You-no-good-son-of-a-bitch-come-here!"

He and the kids piled out and followed her dragging train over to where we had butchered out the beef. They spread the hide out on the ground and began filling it with Indian tidbits. When they had it loaded, Beecher and his kids bunched the legs of the hide and dragged the lot to their car, while Broncho Anne came along toting the head, hardly the vision of loveliness nor the beautiful Indian maiden we read about in story books. After they had chugged off into the pine timber, Demus said:

"That's the prettiest sight I've seen since all them sheep died from eating loco weed in the Double A pasture that time!"

Owen Susonatomie always had a few Company horses in his string, but most of his mounts were his own. He was always riding two or three broncs to gentle them a little. Like most Indian-broke horses, his were wild-eyed and crazy, and only an Indian could get along with them. I often watched how Owen handled them. He would sneak up to catch one like a border collie on a sheep. One of his horses, a light red roan, was a good looking horse, but wild as a deer. Owen mounted him one morning at Long Point against a fence where the roan couldn't get away. Once he was in the saddle, his mount began to run. Owen just kept him headed out into the open country, never even lifting the bridle reins. We all sat there watching that horse eat up the miles until he grew so small in the distance he was just a speck. Finally horse and rider disappeared entirely, perhaps in a draw. In about thirty minutes we sighted them again way off to the north, still burning the wind. Then they were circling back our way, and after a while came in to camp still on a run. The horse had worked up a good lather and was blowing bubbles from his nostrils, but just now simmered down enough to start out on the drive with the rest of us.

A couple of hours later Owen and I threw our cattle together coming down a draw toward the holdup ground.

"That horse of yours is a running fool," I told him. "You must have made a fifteen mile circle on him the *first* time."

"Honiga Ve-eola" — (good horse) — Owen answered in Hualapai, grinning. Then he explained that the horse would fall at the lightest

touch of the reins when he was fresh. So every time he got him up from a month or two of rest he first had to make one of those Marathon rides. From then on the horse was all right. Every one of his horses was hell to shoe, too, but he could always get them plated.

One day on a big trail drive of cows and calves to the railroad, he and I were chousing a large group of calves in the drags. They were trying to run back the way we had come. In the cedars, they had lost sight of their mothers and every now and then about twenty in a bunch would try to go back. We would fall in after them to turn them back and whip their little tails back into the drive again. The men on point couldn't see what was going on back where we were, so they hadn't stopped the leaders to let the drags catch up. And we couldn't quit those calves long enough to ride up front. We were spurring hellity-toot to head off a flock of those runaway calves when Owen's horse stepped in a prairie dog hole and piled right up on top of him. I saw his horse get up and limp off a few steps, and I saw Owen lying flat on his face, out cold. I had my hands more than full whipping the calves back to catch up with the drive, and keeping them there until the boys up front finally held up the herd. As soon as I could, I went back. Owen was still out cold, so I turned him onto his back and began feeling him over to see if he had broken any bones. He looked as though he might be dead. I couldn't locate any breaks and his neck felt O.K. so I loosened his belt and pumped his arms for a little while. Pretty soon he opened his eyes, sat up, and spit some dirt out of his mouth.

"Damn horse fall down," he said.

With that he got up, caught his horse and rode on to the drive as though nothing had happened. He was a tough Indian.

The majority of the Hualapai cattle ran on the west side of the Reservation, and each spring the Indians held their own roundup for about a month, starting their wagon out from the Agency at Valentine. The Vs always sent Owen to that works to gather any stray company cattle and shove them back. The Indian roundups never lasted long because once they got under way whole families of Hualapais would descend on the chuck wagon and eat up all the grub inside of a week. After the wagon had returned to Valentine to be re-stocked on groceries a couple of times, the agent got wise and called the whole thing off. Also the cowboys spent more time running horse races and roping the calves for fun than they did working.

It was rather sad to see the way they treated their real old people. Women or men, once they were too old, or blind or crippled, to share in the camp duties would be rocked out of camp. From then on they were at the mercy of the elements and had to beg or steal food as best they could. Many died out in the brush somewhere. Old starving Indians often came into our camps to beg food. We always fed them, but when we moved away they were to infirm to follow far. Their mortality rate must have been high.

Three Indian cowboys trapped cattle with me at the Park for five days one summer. The wagon was at Pine Spring, four miles south, and the cook always gave us some cold steaks and biscuits to take along for a lunch at noon. We seldom could eat all he gave us, and threw the rest away. The next day we would return to the Park to find every scrap gone. We would find footprints of some of those old outcasts who had slipped in and retrieved every crumb of food we had left. There were a number of big old moss horned steers watering at the Park which we had never been able to catch. While we lay hidden behind a fallen pine tree they would venture a few steps down the hillside, stop, look and listen for ten or fifteen minutes, then take another few steps and stop again. They would stand so still they could hear the least sound. And all the time they would be testing every scent on the air. Sometimes they would be within thirty feet of the gate, then suddenly turn and climb back up the hill into the brush. At night we closed the gates, and the same thing would happen again the next day. Four days those old steers refused to venture into the water lot, although we could see they were gaunt from lack of water. The last morning about ten o'clock they finally came in. We tied the gates and returned to camp to get men enough to move them down to Pine Springs. Right after noon several of us returned to the Park. Those nine big old steers, grouped together, watched our approach warily. They realized they were trapped and were plenty worried. Their old foreheads were wrinkled just like a meeting of Supreme Court Judges on a big case.

We knew we could never hope to drive them loose to Pine Springs. The only thing to do was neck them together. We cinched our saddles tight, got our ropes ready, and made a futile try at corralling them. They were not going to be corralled. Nothing was left but to head and heel them, one at a time. That was no picnic, because no sooner was one caught by the horns than he'd charge. If the heeler missed his throw, the man tied to that steer had to do some fancy maneuvering to dodge those long wicked horns until someone scooped up his hind feet in his loop. Once the steer was down, it was no amateur's job to tie him. We tried to get the steers as close to each other as possible before jerking them down so we wouldn't have far to drag them to tie two together. We'd brought lots of tie ropes with which to link them. As soon as we had one pair necked we let them up and caught another pair.

Bob Scott roped one salty old steer on a little chunky brown horse called Conejo. He never got a chance to tighten his rope, for that old ox chased him the full length of the water lot with blood in his eye. Conejo could barely keep ahead of those horns, and Bob was hollering for someone to get another line on him quick. On their second heat across the lot I made a lucky throw and speared both of the steer's hind feet, stretching him out. Bob wiped his brow and blew off a big sigh of relief.

"If that steer was broke to ride, he'd take the money at Churchill Downs," he swore.

Once we had the four pairs necked, we still had the odd one left. The country was too brushy for him to travel side-lined, so we corded him with a tie-down, pulled tight over his gambel cord, above the hock. We spent another half hour working the steers around the water lot, trying to accustom them to being handled before starting for Pine Springs.

It started to rain just as we left the Park. The steers were so busy fighting the ropes that we got along pretty well for a while. One pair forked an oak tree and broke the rope, so we had to catch those two and re-neck them. The rain wet and stretched the ropes, and for a time it appeared we would lose some of our captives. But the ropes held. At Pine Springs we left the steers in a tight corral over night, then drove on to the Pipe Line Pasture next morning, where we cut them loose. It had been a pretty good haul. Some of those steers were eight or nine years old, and had gotten away every year the crew had worked their part of the range.

Later we returned to the Park and trapped almost ninety head of cattle. We had a lot of mavericks; two to four-year-old bulls, cows with a yearling and a younger calf; in all, three generations unbranded. We spent all one morning branding the mavericks. The yearlings we worked into one separate group, and just as soon as we let them out the gate the race was on. We did manage to keep them fairly well bunched for about two hundred yards before they began breaking for the timber in groups of a dozen or so. Soon there were bunches of them running in all directions, with cowboys riding breakneck trying to haze them back together, over rocks and down timber and stumps.

I was mounted on a big grey horse called Ribbon. He had a lot of action and was fast. We were mortally flying to turn a bunch of yearlings, when his forefoot hit the burned-out shell of a stump and we turned over. Ribbon's head and left shoulder hit the ground first. Just before he landed on top of me I remember seeing the whole rear part of him coming on over in a cartwheel. He struggled to get up, and did part way, then fell back on my leg.

Demus rode back to see where I was, and got Ribbon off me. He helped me up and I took a few steps before falling down again, like a big tumblebug. Millions of sparks were shooting in front of my eyes, but they gradually cleared away. My left spur was bent into a pretzel and I had lost some hide off my hip bone and wrist. Otherwise I was all right. But poor old Ribbon was bunged up pretty badly. A big flap of skin was torn loose on his forehead and hung down over his eyes, and his left kneecap and shoulder were dislocated. Both the browband on the bridle and my breast collar were burned in two where he had slid on them in the gravel. I unsaddled him and rode double with Demus to camp where I got another horse and rode back after my saddle. I also brought back a morral full of barley and a couple of flakes of hay for Ribbon. I had to leave him where he was overnight.

Before I left him, I sewed his forehead back up with a buckskin string so the poor old fellow could at least see. It took me most of the next day to lead him back to the Pine Springs pasture, a few steps at a time. He was awfully lame. We doctored him the best we could and brought feed to him every day. A year later he was still in the pasture able to get around, but his cow-working days were over forever. He was a good horse and I sure *hated* having crippled him. It still bothers me, thirty years later.

Jim Pearson had a worse experience with the top horse of his string, Coal Oil Jonny. As they were crossing a dry wash at a fast trot, a round rock rolled out from beneath Coal Oil Jonny's hind foot, and the bone of his leg snapped about half way between ankle and hock. It broke at an angle, and the sharp end shot out about a foot through the flesh and skin. Jim carried food and water to old Jonny for four days before he got up enough courage to shoot him and put him out of his misery. I think Jim would almost as soon have shot one of his own kids. He left the wagon not long afterwards and never punched cows again. The last time I saw him he was driving a road grader for the highway department out of Seligman.

Along about then we had another spell of cook troubles. One of the best we ever had, George O'Brian, quit to take a job with the government. We sure hated to see him leave, for he was the only cook we ever had who could cook a *first class* "Son-of-a-Bitch" or a "Bastard in a Sack." For the uninitiated, a Son-of-a-Bitch is a sort of cowboy stew made of about everything contained inside a beef, cooked slowly and carefully to just the right consistency. Made right, it is a delightful feast. A Bastard in a Sack is a suet pudding, cooked in a sack. It, too, is "mighty fine chewing and swallowing" as the old cowboy said, if put together by a cook with the right savvy. But George left us, and the Super had to prevail on old Ed Byers to wrangle the pots again until he could locate another cook. He hired a family man from New Mexico to stay at Frazier Wells in Ed's place. This old boy was a Morman preacher and we all called him Deacon Jones. I think Demus was the one who started the name. He had one boy, Jonny, a lively little button about eight years old. Living there, they seldom got to see anyone except a few Indians going by, or us cowboys when we were camped at the Well.

Just to contrary Demus, old Ed would get up and have breakfast an hour or more earlier than he needed to. Unless it was raining too hard, he was sure to yell chuck not later than four a.m. After we left camp he would do up his dishes, get his noon meal all ready to start, and then take a long nap under a tree until just before we were due back. It sure made our day long. Demus thought up a plan to give us that extra hour in bed we were missing. He and I had a pow-wow about it.

While Deacon Jones was off working on the pipe line, Jonny grew pretty bored with no one to talk to. And Jonny just loved to talk. At every chance he'd slip off from the house and come over to camp to talk to the cowboys. He'd really tamp them full of conversation, for he had a good imagination. Demus and I got to him down by the corrals, away from old Ed, and told him that the cook was a great admirer of his and just *loved* Jonny's stories.

"Sometimes he pretends to be sleepy and not listening," Demus explained, "but don't let him fool you. He hears everything you say and he never gets tired of you talking to him. Now after we leave camp, you go over and keep him company *every* morning, and just talk to him. We will give you three nickels apiece for every morning you do."

Jonny's eyes lighted up like a Christmas tree at the idea of six extra nickels a day for something he liked to do so well anyhow. Right off he began earning his money. He'd go over to where Ed was bedded down on an old soogan under a tree, and *talk*. He would tell Ed what Papa said to Mama and what she said to him, and everything he'd ever heard of and some he hadn't. Old Ed would nod and grunt and hope he would run down after awhile and go home, but Jonny wasn't half out of conversation yet.

After the second morning of keeping Ed awake on his bed ground we got results. The first pink wisp of cloud on the eastern horizon, which the Indians call the "Dawn Feather", had come and gone and it was broad daylight before Ed had our breakfast ready.

"I must have overslept," he apologized to Demus. Demus appeared to be digesting that some before he grinned and said:

"Well, we aren't in too big a rush now, so don't let it worry you."

The next morning it happened again. And this time Ed thought he had to alibi, so he told Demus,

"That danged kid of Jones' came over and pestered me so I couldn't get anything done. I tried to send him home but he stuck like a leech."

"Seems to me that's between you and Jonny," Demus answered. "Every son of a bitch has his troubles, you know."

One of Ed's specialties was bread pudding. The pudding's main ingredient consisted of all the uneaten cold biscuits saved in a can until he had enough to make one with. Sometimes he saved the biscuits too long and many were mildewed before he had enough. Demus called them "Old Ed's Grindstone Puds." At Kesaha Camp Demus had a bad appendix attack and had to quit to go to Prescott for an operation. I took over the wagon for him until he returned to us at Rose Wells. Ed, who was as nosey as a ring-tailed coon, could hardly wait for Demus to set up his tepee before he began asking where he'd been and what they had done to him at the hospital.

"Well, they operated on me right away and found one of your Grindstone Puds that never dissolved," Demus replied. "Once they chiseled that out, I was all right but they aren't safe to feed the crew, so give 'em to the Indians from now on."

We never had another of Ed's Puds. Finally the Super sent out a new cook and Ed returned happily to Frazier Wells.

An old boy named Oliver Kingston came up from the Agua Fria country to work with the wagon awhile. He had seen hard times I guess, because he didn't have much of an outfit when he reached us. He had stiffened the brim of his old black hat with sugar water to keep it from flopping in his eyes. One spur, a few old ragged coats, and an old Sam Stag tree saddle with the rigging wired together and the cinches tied with string completed his outfit. Demus reserved opinion on him until he could see what sort of hand he was. After two or three horses had bucked him off and he had been set afoot by a few others which got away from him while he was trying to get on them, Demus gave him the gentlest mount we had. We were at Black Tanks at the time.

Our horses had all been ridden hard and we expected to gather a fresh remuda when we reached the S.P. Pasture. We still had a few old outlaws along that were taking life easy, and a couple of the boys asked to take them on in place of their leg-weary mounts. One of them was Brown Hog, a tough, mean old rough string horse. He was a real booger to shoe, so we gave Bill Chestnut all the help he wanted to do the job. Brown Hog knew what was about to happen the minute a rope was tied around his shoulders and he wasn't having any, by a jug full. He charged, biting the air and pawing with both front feet at anyone in reach. He scattered cowboys like a whirlwind in a cocklebur patch. Finally, roped by one front foot, and with one hind foot partly jacked up, he broke loose and, kicking and fighting, took to the group again. With ropes dragging all around, he singled out Oliver for his attention. Before Oliver could get out of his way, Hog's teeth snapped together on the shoulder of the boy's old ragged coat, tearing the whole sleeve out. It was a nip and tuck race, with Oliver just barely ahead, when they reached the big square rock-walled water tank. This was no time to hesitate, and Oliver sailed over the wall and into about four feet of water like a bird on the wing. With one down and more to go, Brown Hog turned to see who he wanted to match next. By then a couple of boys had gotten on their horses. They roped old Hog and choked him down until the ground men could tie him hard and fast. He fought the whole bunch with everything he had and it took over an hour to get him shod, even though tied down. From then on Demus named our new man "Oliver the duck."

One cold windy morning Demus sent Oliver and me into a far fence corner to look up a few dogie calves that couldn't find their way out to water. We were riding along, heads down against the biting wind when Oliver's horse almost stepped on a baby antelope hidden in a clump of tall grass. It jumped out under his horse's nose with a squeal and started to run. Spooked, this old grey horse whirled back so quickly that Oliver fell off over his shoulder. The leather string holding his chaps legs together slipped over the saddle horn, leaving Oliver hanging head down on his horse's shoulder. The two or three old ragged coats he had on fell down over his head, sort of blind-folding him, and the grey went to whirling around trying to get away from all that scarecrow stuff on his side. Oliver was hollering "Whoa" at the top of his voice. But that old horse didn't know "whoa" from "get up", never having been a work horse. Finally the string broke and Oliver went soaring off. I think he was glad to get loose.

When we got to camp he said he thought he would go back to the Agua Fria where the weather fit his clothes better. And he did. In his place we got a Texas raised cowboy who had been working for John Neal over on the Big Sandy Wash near Kingman. We were camped at the Sheep Ranch by then.

The company had a big tanking crew on the job, making new dams and repairing old ones all over the ranch at the time. The crew was badly in need of more work teams, and the outfit had four such teams in a seven section pasture on the east edge of Seligman. These had been running loose for a year or more. Demus cut the new hand a mount of horses, among them a long-legged brown called Sailor. He had been one of Charley Hiler's horses when he ran the wagon, but he hadn't been ridden in a long while. Demus told me to take this new man and bring those eight work horses to the Sheep Ranch. I roped out a big bay Box K horse of my own named Mandy, and this new man saddled Sailor.

Old Mandy always warmed up by bucking for a hundred yards when he was first mounted. He was a high jumping bucker, but he went straight away and wasn't too hard to set if the rider got away with him "even steven." Sailor was a great one to run a whizzer on any cowboy he could bluff. Sometimes he would buck too, but he wasn't any great shakes to ride if he did. I mounted up first, and as usual Mandy took off pitching and bawling down through the cedars. That out of his system, I rode him back to where this old boy was still turning Sailor around and around, making no attempt to mount up.

"This horse sure acts like he wants to pitch," Texas said.

"Well, the only way to find out is to try him out," I replied.

Sailor *was* putting on a good act. The rollers in his nose were rattling like a snare drum, and he was walling the whites of his eyes, moving around stiff-legged like a mad coyote. I could see with half an eye that Texan was scared to death of him. He would put his toe in the stirrup, raise off the ground a foot or so, then step down again. He kept doing that, trying to get up nerve enough to hit the saddle.

"I don't know what's the matter with me, but every time I get on a horse that acts like this I just tremble like a fool," he stated.

"Well, we have to get started sometime," I said. "I'll haze him out of the cedars if he *does* buck."

Finally he eased up into the saddle and, holding a tight rein, gently turned old Sailor around and let him take a few steps. Nothing happened. After walking our horses a quarter of a mile, Sailor loosened up and went along like any old gentle plug. But that old Texas boy sure didn't trust him, for he had a strangle hold on the horn which guaranteed either a one-armed man or a muley saddle if the horse did buck.

We found the work teams on a malapai hill at the back side of the pasture, and corralled them near town. There we roped and necked them together in pairs before heading them back to the sheep ranch, driving the teams ahead of us. Everything went fine until we came to a gate in a fence about four miles from town. I rode around and opened it so that we could drive the horses through. One pair forked a gate post and broke loose, one horse going on through the gate, the other running down the wrong side of the fence. Texas took out after that one, while I had a horse race with the seven on my side of the fence before I could get them together and held up in a bunch. I waited for Texas to bring his horse on up, but he never came. After about thirty minutes I decided it best to take mine on, figuring that he should be able to haze just one work horse into the ranch alone.

By mid afternoon, when Texas still hadn't shown up, Demus sent me back to find him. I met him walking and leading Sailor about four miles from camp. He had lost his hat, and was real upset. He had a tall tale of woe to relate. After he had chased his work horse around and around, he finally got him back to the gate but he couldn't put him through it. After two tries he attempted to rope the horse. The wind blew the loop under Sailor's tail, and old Sailor clamped down on it and stampeded. That's when he lost his hat. He finally got Sailor stopped, got off to get the rope out from under his tail, and was kicked in the belly. Sailor then jerked loose and ran off. That was near a fence corner where Texas eventually eased close enough to catch a rein.

Then, he claimed, Sailor wouldn't let him get on again. So he had led him all the way afoot. Sailor sure had his number. I let him have Mandy and I rode Sailor on back to camp. As we rode along he expounded on having been postmaster at some little wide place in the road down in Texas.

"I've always hankered to be a railway mail clerk," he told me. "I just believe I'll go down to Phoenix and see if I can be postmaster there and then work my way up to a mail clerk on the railroad."

Boy! He was as nutty as a pinon tree.

"That's a *hell* of a good idea," I agreed.

He left us on the next truck going to town and I never heard of him again. I sure hope he handled Uncle Sam's mail better than he did old Sailor.

Texas must have had a lot of good cowboys, but the ones that came to us from there sure weren't. There were two exceptions: Tom Vest and John Driver. They were plenty good hands in anybody's country. Old Tom had run the Hat Ranch down in Bonita Canyon for a long time. John Driver had also worked a lot in Arizona before he came to the Vs. They were each sixty-five or so, and didn't need any wet nurse. John got drunk on some poison bootleg in Seligman and died in bed one night. The company failed to find any trace of relatives, so buried him in the little rocky cemetery south of town. Old Tom got bucked off a sorrel horse called Banjo and broke his hip. His wife moved to Seligman and took in washing while he was laid up. The spring he was able to work again another horse threw him and broke a flock of his ribs and one arm. He never recovered from that fall.

Septer Shelton was the windiest Texan we ever had. To hear him tell it, he had run a lot of the biggest outfits in the Lone Star State. One or two down on the Brazos were so big it took a four-horse team and wagon just to haul the knives and forks for the chuck wagon. Demus dubbed him "Shep" right off, and the name stuck as long as he did. He delighted to ride alongside someone and tamp those big windies into them at every opportunity. Soon any of the boys who saw him riding towards them would lope off ahead. One real windy morning he trotted up alongside Bill Chestnut, who had his hat pulled down low over his eyes, and began one of his tales. Bill never looked around to see who it was.

"You sound just as windy as that lying son-of-a-bitch, Shep Shelton," he snorted.

Shep took the hint and dropped back. Pretty soon I caught up with Bill, who was still pretty grouchy.

"You know," he said, "it takes every kind of a son-of-a-bitch to make a world. And they're *all* working for the Three Vs."

Yaqui Ordunus was the only man in the outfit who would listen to Shep's tales of cutting horses he had owned which would pen a rooster in a cracker box without even a bridle on, or the little bunch of "caves" (as Shep called calves) he'd "carried" up to the Panhandle country. "Just nine thousand in that little bunch."

Out in the flats he got around all right, but just as soon as we hit the rocks he was lost. When we reached the pine timber he was a total loss. The first time Demus dropped him off on a drive in the timber, he hadn't gone half a mile before he got lost. Demus had to send two Indians back to trail him up. They found him and brought him out.

The next day the same thing happened. While we were at breakfast on the third day, Demus went out and put a big cow bell on Shep's horse. When we went to mount up Shep started to take the bell off.

"Leave it on," Demus told him. "We want to be able to find you without working the whole country clear to the Grand Canyon."

All morning we kept track of Shep by the clanging of his cow bell. He had had enough. That night in camp he confided in Yaqui he was going down to the Sulphur Springs Valley, south of Willcox, and file a claim on a homestead where he had found a little yellow jacket seep one time, and be a farmer. He should have made a good one, for he certainly would never have been a cowboy. He is still down there, married to a school teacher, telling bigger lies than ever, I hear.

Neither Demus nor I had shaved in months and we sported a pair of beards fine for owls' nests by the time we hit town again. There were two barber shops in Seligman; one on the street facing the railroad tracks, the other one across the street. We headed for the one along the tracks but the two barbers there locked the door and pulled down the window blinds pronto when they saw us coming. We knew those bastards were inside but they wouldn't answer us, so we had to go to the other shop. We surprised them, and got in. First they sheared us with the clippers, like two burros, then shaved us with the razors. There was enough hair on the floor to make a hair rope when they were finished. In the mirror we sure looked funny without our hair.

Rumor had it in Seligman that the Three Vs were on a deal to sell out to the Waggoner interest of Texas. By this time there were only about five-thousand head of cattle left on the ranch, and the Indian Service had refused to renew leases on the Reservation. Instead, the Service began building a fence to enclose the entire Reservation. The Indians were to build the fence on contract. The posts and wire were furnished by the company. Honga and his sub tribe had a ten-mile stretch to build from Rose Wells northeast; Young Beecher and his group, several miles east and west of Frazier Well; Dr. Tommy and his people, farther west; and Prescott Jim and his sub tribe, over the top of the Aubrey cliffs and mesas eastward to Rose Wells. Other little bands were fencing along the boundary at different spots.

We began moving stock out of the Indian country. The Super sold off a lot of range horses and bought about twenty-five of the best and gentlest of the old V cow horses for his own ranch in Yavapai county. His foreman, Deane Curry, and a Pima Indian came to Seligman and trailed them through to his Fifty-one Ranch near Bloody Basin.

One afternoon Demus and I were sitting against a water tank out of the wind, trapping horses at the Pipe Line corrals.

"Looks to me like this outfit's about done for," I said. "If Waggoners do buy this spread, it won't be long until it's fenced up in little bitty pastures, and all a cowboy will need is a pair of wire plyers to fix fences and one stirrup to get off and on with, opening gates."

"Yeah, the shrinkage will be bad," Demus agreed. "I think I'll go over and work for Roy Wolf at the Circles when the Vs quit." Not long afterward, while we were camped at Thornton Tank, we awoke to a heavy frost. Winter was on its way, and so was I. Demus gave me his hand in warm friendship as I threw my outfit on the truck.

"Come up next spring and throw in with me at the Circles," he said. "I'll see that you get a good mount of horses, and I'll even stock up on arnica."

"Honiga Ka-tooch (good,—fine)" I replied.

We waved our last goodby just before the truck drove into the trees, never to meet again. That winter Demus turned a car over on himself while on a spree and died in the Prescott hospital. As he had said: "Every son-of-a-bitch has his troubles." His were over.

I'll never forget that old red-whiskered cowboy.

Twelve   Desert Mesas, Mountain Slopes

Young men (and some older ones) never seem to know when they're well off. When they are single and have a pocketful of money, they can't wait to spend it. Improvident is the word, but a young fellow doesn't know the meaning of the word, and cares less. When I came into Phoenix on the old Pickwick Stage from Miami in the winter of 1924, it was cold. The town was full of men who were out of work and who had little or no money. The country had gone through a long drought and cattle ranchers were hard hit. The banks were already carrying so much of their paper they didn't want any more, and money was tight. I hung around town for a couple of months, hoping that things would change for the better and I could get out on a ranch again. I fed a lot of old boys who were down on their luck and worse off than I was. Although Phoenix was the State capital and also the largest town in Arizona, it still wasn't much more than the same small desert farming and ranching center it had been for the past twenty-five years.

Several months after my arrival I ran across a fellow I had known on the Tonto. He had moved to Phoenix with his family the year before and was headed out to the north side of town to pick grapefruit. I went along. We soon got lost, driving around and trying to locate the grove which he was supposed to work. As we drove I noticed an old fellow across a fence in a field of stubble. He was driving eight or ten Hereford calves along ahead of his horse into a corner. I saw him rope one by both hind feet, pull it down and begin taking a fence yoke off its neck. The way he handled his horse and rope told me he was an old cowman. Clarence stopped to ask directions, and we talked a while. I had on a good suit of clothes, but was itching to get hold of a calf again, so I offered to help this old fellow.

It felt good to flank a calf once more, and the man commented on the way I downed and held them. He told me that he owned a ranch about thirty miles north of Phoenix and he needed a cowboy all right, but couldn't pay much in the way of wages right then. I told him high wages weren't as important to me as getting out of town, so we made a deal.

The next morning he picked me up at Joe Strinker's Pool Hall on South Central Avenue. He had a load of baled alfalfa hay on his old Franklin truck and told me that he had been hauling hay so steadily that he had pretty nearly worn the truck out. His name was Logue Morris, he said, and his son Elmer ran the ranch at Cave Creek.

We chugged along out North Seventh Street until we crossed the

Arizona Canal, where the pavement ended. Now we were in the desert from here on. The road skirted some small black desert mountains a couple of miles to our left, then we were out in a wide expanse of desert called Paradise Valley. To the east were the McDowell mountains. Westward were several scattered smaller mountains. The road was narrow and sandy, crossing many washes through thick palo verde and ironwood trees, greasewood and cactus. We saw several bands of wild horses running off away from the noise of the truck. Logue pointed out the Cave Creek Flood Control Dam to the west as we passed.

This desert looked barren yet beautiful to me. We crossed the remains of an old irrigation canal Logue called the Verde. He said it had been built about fifty years before to irrigate a lot of this Paradise Valley land but had never carried water, as the eastern end was too high for water to flow through from the Verde River. It had been abandoned, then the Salt River Water Users had gone to court to prevent its completion.

As we neared the little settlement and Post Office of Cave Creek Logue pointed out old mine dumps on two or three different hills, with names once hopeful, now almost forgotten; names such as Happy Jack, The Maricopa Girl, Black Beauty, and Little Opal.

We stopped to pick up the mail from old man Howard, then took the side road to the ranch a couple of miles beyond. Logue's son Elmer helped us unload and stack the hay in the barn and then we went to the house where I met Elmer's wife, Nell. This part of the ranch was called "Grapevine" because of the many wild grapevines growing in the canyon by the spring just above the corrals. Elmer was a heavy, good natured fellow, and Nell slender and pleasant. I felt I was going to like working here on the Quarter Circle One Ranch.

That afternoon the sky began to grow overcast, and by night it was drizzling rain. At daylight we awoke to a slow steady winter rain which lasted for two days and nights. By the time it quit the weather had turned quite cold. The clouds were still down almost to ground level, blotting out the mountains around us. Logue, Elmer and I saddled three horses to ride north up the Cave Creek Canyon to see how the cattle had survived the storm. Logue called me Boy. In fact, he called every man Boy, be he twenty or eighty.

"Boy," he drawled, "look sharp now for dead cows. This storm hitting when there were so many weak ones, we're bound to have lost some. I'd like to get a count on what dead ones we find today."

By the time we had ridden five miles up the creek the clouds had receded higher up the mountains and we could see the snow line below them. We had counted eighteen dead cows so far. Just before we turned back I spotted one more, lying on top of a bluff.

"There is another," I pointed.

"By God, Boy, let's look for some *live* ones," Logue said. "We've seen too many dead ones already."

That storm took a heavy toll, and the Grapevine Pasture was full of poor weak cows which we had to feed daily.

Before the drought, Logue had been offered ninety thousand dollars for the ranch and cattle. By Spring of this year he owed about fifty thousand to the bank. The bank was pressing him pretty hard to sell enough cattle to pay off some of the interest on its loans and a former partner, Jim Gibson, was also clamoring for five thousand still due him, too.

Two nephews, Perley and Little Logue, promised to come help through the roundup in May. Alex Don, a cowboy from Scottsdale, and old John Lewis, owner of the 6L Ranch joining the Quarter Circle One up Cave Creek, would also ride with us. Then Cartwrights would have a couple of their Mexican cowboys ride Bronco Mountain, Skull Mesa and Skunk Ridge when we worked that part of the range; and E. E. Brown (Brownie) always sent two or three riders to work the Camp Creek Divide and the desert country to the east. Jose Cline would swap work with them on the Deer Valley, Black Canyon and New River Mesa parts of the roundup.

By the time we were ready to gather the horses from the pasture atop Skull Mesa, I had been pretty well over most of the mountain country and some of the desert. With our horses in off the high mesa country, we began shoeing on the third day of May. Elmer was a good blacksmith, and I was a pretty good horse shoer. Between us we made a fast team on that job. Perley and Little Logue were top hands, and shod their own. In three days we had our horses all shod and were ready to start riding. Old John Lewis came down from his ranch with his bed and three horses, to start with us on the mountain.

Most of the cattle running in the higher country were wild and hard to gather, but we had a pretty good crew of brush hands. On Big Brushy and Bronco mountains we made a pretty good gathering. We got a second chance at some of the wild ones that did get away on Continental Mountain and the Broncho Ledge lower down. By the time we were off the high places we had a couple of pastures full of cattle.

We moved camp over to the old Phoenix Mine Ranch on the west bank of Cave Creek. From here we worked New River Mesa, and the rugged canyon of Cave Creek north to Gray's Gulch. By this time we had plenty of cattle in the big pasture on the steep slopes of Skull Mesa to convince the bank that the outfit *still* owned enough stock to be a good risk.

Elmer had been in conference with the bank before roundup and had asked for a further loan. The officers had promised to send a man up to tally the cattle whenever we were ready for him. Now, with the pasture full of cattle, Elmer decided to drive in to Phoenix, stay overnight, and return early the next morning with the bank's appraiser. After he left, Perley saddled a mule and rode off up the Canyon. About an hour later he returned with a gallon jug of uncolored moonshine whiskey. We all took a pull at it, but one was about enough. It hadn't been cut and was about a hundred and eighty proof.

The next morning we got up earlier than usual, knowing it would be a big day's job working that Skull Mesa Pasture. To fortify ourselves we began hitting Perley's jug, and by the time we had breakfast cooked some of us were feeling pretty happy, especially Old Logue. We finished eating, and now we had nothing to do except wait for Elmer and the appraiser. Old Logue, with a happy jag on, was singing and making a lot of noise. Finally we heard Elmer's car drive in. The fellow from the bank happened to be a teetotaler, and since he himself didn't drink he didn't much approve of anyone who did. His name was John Kleinman. Elmer introduced him around and finally came to old Logue who was sitting on the bed.

"Mr. Kleinman, this is my father, Logue Morris," he began.

Old Logue cast a bleary eye his way, then shook hands.

"You any kin to Old Dan Kleinman?" he asked.

"Yes! I'm a brother of his," the gent replied.

"Well by God, Boy," old Logue exclaimed. "I've known Dan Kleinman for forty years and I've never known anything good about the son-of-a-bitch yet. If you're as big a horse's ass as he is, you're sure in the right business."

Now this was old Logue's way of being friendly, but Elmer was fit to pop a gasket. He wanted to make a good impression, hoping to get that loan from the bank, and here was his dad, drunk and piling insults on thick and fast. Kleinman didn't look a bit happy, and as quickly as he could Elmer rescued him by getting him outside and on the horse we had saddled for him. Old Logue tried to follow them out the door, but his feet got sort of tangled and he fell down between the wood box and the stove. He was in no shape to ride, so Elmer told the rest of us to leave him there to sleep it off. We worked the pasture, tallied out the cattle, and the bank did come through with the loan. Elmer was sore at Perley for a week for bringing that jug to camp.

On the last day we worked that country my horse fell while running full tilt around a mountain side, spraining my left wrist badly and banging my kneecap on a rock. At first I thought my knee was broken, but within a week it was about well, while the sprain hurt me for over a year.

When the roundup was over, we drove the steers to Tolleson, west of Phoenix, where we loaded them for shipment to Denver, Colorado. I went along. In Denver I stayed only long enough to turn the cattle over to Louis Wolf, the buyer, then took a train to Cheyenne, Wyoming. By easy stages I hit Laramie, Medicine Bow Lodge, and Kemmerer, just looking around. A fellow who owned some shallow oil wells inland offered me a ride to Daniel, a wide place on the road to Jackson Hole and Yellowstone Park. I took him up on the offer. We left Kemmerer late on a rainy afternoon, reaching Daniel about eleven that night. There was a dance in progress at the Lodge, a great rambling, three-story log building catering to summer tourists and fishermen. I checked in there for a three-day stay, during which time I met a Mr. Ball, President of a bank at the town of Green River. He was an old cattleman as well as a banker, and we had much in common to talk about. When he found that I was looking for a riding job, he phoned the boss of the Pinedale Cattle Association, fifty miles north. The Association had just taken on two new men and needed no more, so Mr. Ball then called the Big Piney Association and landed me a job with it.

The roundup wagon was camped on the outskirts of the little cow town of Big Piney when I found it after catching a ride downriver with a fur buyer. The camp was on a little alkali flat, with no one but the cook present. The crew rode in early in the afternoon. The boss was George Hereford and the crew consisted of about twenty cowboys. One dark-complexioned cowboy looked very familiar, and turned out to be the fellow I had known at Lemon, South Dakota, years before, the one who had shot out the lights of the hotel.

All the ranchers along the west side of Green River belonged to the Association. The wagon boss was chosen by vote, and given carte blanche to hire and fire his crew, and to have full say as to how and where the men worked from the time the cattle left their home ranches until the beef was shipped in the fall and the remaining cattle returned to their owners for the winter. This was high country with short summers and severe winters. Just the crew now was throwing the cattle out of the winter pastures along the river in preparation for driving to summer range on the forest.

For a week longer we worked the river ranches, moving southward until we had reached the end of our range. Then we began picking up the cattle on the return trip. With a thousand or more gathered, we headed them into South Horse Creek, camping behind them each night until we reached the gate in the forest fence, where they were counted in. Then we returned to Green River to gather to the next canyon—North Horse Creek. This procedure was followed all the way along. We threw cattle up both the Horse Creeks, then the two Cottonwood Creeks, Red Creek, Beaver Creek, North and South Piney Creeks, Fall River, Boulder Creek, and several others. Eventually we had the bulk of the cattle on the forest. Then we began drifting the remaining cattle up the different canyons, on where grass was stirrup-high and there was shade and clear, cold water everywhere. Salt was scattered on salt grounds, and a couple of men left to camp for the summer to look after the cattle in their particular canyons. Roundups were thrown together and all the calves branded before the crew moved on.

Great snowbanks on the north slopes, that never entirely melted, fed the streams full of trout. Deer, elk and moose were to be seen every day. Bear, too, were plentiful. Once I surprised some mountain sheep on a high windy ridge and, on that same day, an old grizzly bear. Every now and then we ran across huge buffalo skulls, remnants of the old plains herds which had been driven from their open country into the mountains.

By September, cattle had begun drifting down from the high places and we opened the forest gates to allow them to work towards the river. Then we rode the mountain, bringing off the stock, now fat and slow-moving. On the sagebrush flats we threw great roundups together. There owners came to cut out the beef cattle they wanted to send to market. Sometimes there would be six or seven pairs of ranchers cutting from the herd at one time. Up there two men cut together, walking the fat cattle out of the herd, one on either side. We helped each rancher drive his cut home where the cattle were left in a pasture until later.

When the last roundup was made, we began our drive to the railroad shipping point at Opal. As we moved down Green River, we picked up the beef from each rancher's pasture to throw into the drive. Crossing the river at the old Oregon Trail crossing, we went on to Opal. There the cars were loaded and the cattle on their way to Omaha, the great buyer's center for the Northwest.

First snow had fallen in the mountains by the time we returned from Opal. Now we moved to the high ranges to make one final search for any cattle left up there before they would be trapped, to die of winter kill. We hurried our last small remnants out just ahead of a storm that lasted three days. The counts over, the roundup crew was disbanded until the following spring. Most of the men would soon be feeding hay through the long cold winter months from great stacks on the various ranches along the river. I had several offers of such a job, but with temperatures seldom higher than twenty below that country had no appeal for me in winter. I drew my pay, caught a ride to the railroad and caught a train for Salt Lake City, Utah. A week of old settlers' reunion days was in progress there. I stayed through that show, then went on to Las Vegas, Nevada, and eventually on back to Phoenix, where the weather was more to my liking. I'd had a good few months but I was glad to get back to the desert once more. I had never found people friendlier in all my travels, nor a better place to work, in summer.

Logue and Elmer wanted me to come back to the Quarter Circle One at Cave Creek to range brand calves on the desert. This suited me fine. They had traded for some unbroken colts from the Valley and a couple of old badly-spoiled horses, some of which they wanted me to ride. With one old spoiled horse, two colts and three gentle horses, I moved down below the old Verde canal in Paradise Valley and set up camp at Vondracek's Well.

Dromier Vondracek was a widower, with two sons about thirteen and fifteen. He had homesteaded in Paradise Valley years before. He had the only well in the valley, a deep one of over four-hundred feet. For years he had depended on the water and on his big adobe corrals for most of his livelihood. He sold corral room and water to the cattle herds moving down to the Valley from the back country each Spring and Fall; outfits like the Coburn ranch in Bloody Basin, the JM on the Verde, the 51, Cartwright's CC, Morris' Quarter Circle One, the Horse Shoes, Brown's EC Ranch, Moore & Asher's Box Bar, Pink Cole's Whiteheads, Cline's Flying Y, and many more.

By pumping night and day for a week he managed to store up enough water to take care of the many big herds that corralled there for the night while on the trail. He was happy to have me camp by him, as he was lonesome with his boys away at school during the day.

I rode the wide expanse of Paradise Valley from the McDowell Mountains to the east, clear to the Agua Fria River on the west, and from Cave Creek on the north to the Arizona Canal at the edge of the Salt River Valley. I learned that big desert country like the palm of my hand that winter. Now and then I ran across an old Mexican with a team of burros and a light spring wagon. He scoured the desert for Bisnagas (Barrel Cactus) and made a living selling them to old man Donofrio in Phoenix. Donofrio operated a small candy store there and used them to make cactus candy to sell to the tourists.

There were a few old abandoned houses scattered over the desert, all that remained of a flurry of homesteading by veterans of World War One. With no water, they became discouraged after a year or so and moved away. The bands of wild horses running over the country had torn down the fences, and wood haulers had carried away the houses piece by piece until little was left but the foundations. It was sort of sad to ride around the old places and see an old rusty kid's wagon or a part of some little girl's doll, and picture the little family who had lived there, their first high hopes growing dimmer as it became apparent with time that, without water, they would have to give up their homes and move again. Now only the wild horses and coyotes trotted over the land they once expected to make into green fields of growing things.

The following fall, after a summer at the Vs, I went back to work for the Quarter Circle One. By that time, on the Agua Fria side of the Valley, some of the ranchers had begun to miss cattle often enough to point to rustlers. One afternoon over in their part of the desert, I spotted something from a distance lying under a Palo Verde tree. It didn't look natural, so I rode over to get a closer look.

There was something there all right, covered with canvas. Carefully I opened it to find three quarters of a freshly-killed beef. Covering it again, I brushed out my tracks back to the horse, mounted and cut a wide circle for sign. One set of tire tracks led in and out. Little pieces of the cow hide were scattered all around. Two sets of men's footprints, one larger than the other, were easy to read. I rode back to the Black Canyon highway, then an old dirt road, which I had crossed earlier, and along it to the only house that had a phone. I called old Logue's house in the Valley and explained my find, advising him to call the Phoenix Livestock Inspector, Walter Card, and to bring him out to meet me on the road so I could guide them to the place. I felt sure that someone would return for the rest of the beef that evening and wanted to have a reception committee to greet whoever it was.

Just before sundown Logue and the inspector met me in the inspector's old Ford, and I led the way on my horse, avoiding the desert rat towns and the sandy washes, where they were likely to get stuck. I was perhaps a couple of hundred yards in front of them when I got within sight of the tree. There was a car already there and I put spurs to my horse to reach the tree before it could get away. Just before I got to it, I glanced back to discover that the inspector's Ford had stopped.

Two men were trying to get their car started as I set my horse up on his hind feet alongside the driver. I had my short 30-30 rifle barrel stuck right in his ear before he got over the surprise of my sudden appearance. Leaning over from the saddle, I switched off the ignition and removed the key, ordering the two men to slide out on my side of the car. They did, and only then did the inspector get his car going and drive on up to us. These two men had already loaded the beef in their car and had been ready to leave when I reached them.

The men were taken to the county jail in Phoenix. I attended their hearing, at which they plead guilty, but left before I learned what sentence they were given. Walter Card made such a to-do about how he got stuck crossing a wash, and kept on alibiing so strong that I couldn't resist telling him that I felt sure that all the sand bothering him was the sand that ran out of his craw when he saw that car at the tree. He wasn't about to come up that day until he made sure there would be no shooting. He was a perennial candidate for sheriff but never got more than a half dozen votes on Election Day, including his wife's.

Cattle were still being rustled, so old Logue and some of the other ranchers went to the sheriff and the Livestock Sanitary Board, asking that I be appointed a range detective and deputy sheriff and given any help I needed to catch the rustlers.

I began my new job by high pointing that part of the country, moving around where the bulk of the cattle watered at various tanks and corrals. It wasn't long until I picked up the trail of two riders on shod horses. These men had evidently been riding the country pretty closely, looking over the cattle. I kept out of sight of them, but followed them around wherever they went. They came from a house on the east bank of the Agua Fria, and by inquiring around I learned who they were. They came from a large family and, except for a couple of milk cows, owned no cattle, although they did have a number of horses running on the desert.

One afternoon from a vantage point among some rocks on a little desert mountain, I spotted some cattle moving a couple of miles to the northwest. Through my glasses I watched two riders easing about ten head along, staying way off to the side so that their horse tracks wouldn't look as though they were driving the cattle. The desert here was pretty open, mostly greasewood, brush, and only an occasional ironwood or palo verde tree. I knew that if they saw me they would leave the cattle, so I let them have a good lead before cutting across and following one set of the horse tracks. Their tracks were going too far north to be in line with their ranch, and I wondered just where they were heading.

Just before sundown, nearing the banks of the Agua Fria, they suddenly changed course and turned south toward their place. Now they were going through some mesquite thickets alongside the river, and I almost ran into them before I saw them. They had stopped the cattle in a small open space in the mesquites. Ducking back, I watched for their next move. About dusk I heard bells, and a third rider came driving a couple of milk cows ahead of him. The three talked a minute, then drove the whole bunch on downriver. Following them to their place, I could not venture close because in the still night air the least sound carries for great distances. I knew they might hear my horse walking, or he might step on a dry stick in the dark. When the bells were quiet I knew they had corraled. I stayed out there in the brush for at least an hour listening for activity, yet nothing out of the ordinary seemed to happen.

Chill air began to rise from the river bed and soon I was too cold to sit still. Figuring all the angles, I couldn't see just what I could gain from staying here any longer if they did come out to butcher during the night. I knew there were four men in the family, and walking in on them with their stolen cattle might not be very "sanitary", as the Mexican said. By morning, if I could secure a search warrant, plus a witness or two, we might catch them with evidence enough to go to court. But how? There was no town nearby, and no phone. I had only my horse for transportation, and no one for a witness. It looked as though the best thing to do was back off tonight and come back better prepared.

My camp at Vondracek's was miles away and it was late when I reached it. Dead tired, I went right to bed and didn't awaken until sunup. When Von's boys started to school in their old stripped down Ford I rode along with them to the post office at Cactus just outside the Valley. There I phoned the sheriff and asked to have a search warrant drawn up as soon as the justice office opened, and for a couple of deputies to pick me up at Cactus. Then I called Jose Cline at his ranch on New River, bringing him up to date and telling him where we would meet at the rustlers' ranch.

When we drove into their place, everything was serene; no sign of cattle in the corral, no tracks, no blood or indication of any butchering — nothing. After searching the house, sheds and barn, with still no sign of anything wrong, the deputies began looking at me as though they thought I'd had a nightmare and dreamed up the whole thing. But they changed their idea when I led them on a circle of the place and pointed out the tracks of the cattle leading into the flat before the corrals and not a single track leading out again. The only answer was that these smart hombres had carefully brushed out not only the tracks in the corral but even on the flat, clear back to the mesquites. But where in hell were the beef and hides?

We pretended to be satisfied that we were on a bum steer, and got in the cars and drove away. Out of sight of the house we stopped and waited in a thicket. Pretty soon an old car took off from the place, racing across the river bed toward the main highway leading to Phoenix. We had searched that car too, so we knew that there was no beef in it.

Driving back to the house, we began another search. The men had all left, and only a couple of young girls were there alone. We talked to each one separately. The oldest, a girl of about fourteen, was very nervous and finally she broke down and cried. She said she didn't know that her father and brothers had stolen the cattle, but she did know that they had been working around the corrals during the night. She told us she had seen them burying some old hides once before, out in a little field, but never thought anything about it. We asked her to show us the place, and she did. Getting some shovels from the shed, we began digging and soon came upon not only fresh hides, but a mess of older rotten ones beneath. Every one of them had had the brand cut out before they were buried. These fellows were no amateurs. They evidently knew enough about the law to destroy the brands. Thus, if the hides were ever found, there would be no legal proof of ownership for evidence. One of the fresh hides was from a steer with a few brindle stripes along the shoulders and neck.

"That brindle steer was mine all right," Jose Cline said. "I bought him from Florian at Rock Springs last January. His wife had had another baby and he was hard up for money, so I gave him thirty dollars for that steer. It was out of his milk cow and a Hereford bull. I'd know that hide anywhere."

But it too had the brand cut neatly out.

"Wait a minute," Jose said. "Florian had his brand on that steer before I bought it, and here it is."

He pointed out a small brand, real low behind the left shoulder.

"They sure missed seeing that one, and that's where they slipped up," one of the deputies said.

We dumped all the green hides in the car trunk and headed for Phoenix. There we left the hides in a freezer locker and Jose swore out a warrant for the arrest of the four men for grand theft; to-wit, one two-year-old steer bearing such and such brand, and so on. About sundown that night the arrest was made, and four surprised rustlers were booked into the county jail. All plead not guilty. Since they couldn't raise bond money, they were remanded to the sheriff for a sojourn in the steel chateau. Their trial was short and *very* unsatisfactory to them. Guilty as charged was the verdict. Six to seven years in the state penitentiary the sentence, and that was that.

Once that case was cracked, investigation by the sanitary board found a number of Phoenix stores which had been buying beef from the rustlers, among them some of the large chain stores. But one thing still bothered me. That was a set of horse tracks north of the Arizona Canal which I had been seeing often when I rode that section. As yet they were unaccounted for. They didn't match any of the horses those rustlers had ridden, and I kept seeing them *after* the men had been salted away in the state penitentiary at Florence.

One morning I cut sign on these tracks again—this time accompanied by tracks of another horse. They weren't over an hour old when I crossed them, so I decided to try to find out who had made them. About noon I spotted two riders in the act of roping a fair-sized calf from a little band of cattle near the foot of a small, black malapai hill. Watching from a palo verde tree, I saw them turn the calf loose again pretty soon and ride on. The men were looking through each bunch of cattle they came to as though searching for one fat enough for beef. By late afternoon they had made a big circle and were nearing the canal bank. I watched them ride into an old abandoned sheep-shearing camp, unsaddle, and go inside an old tar-paper shack. An old wreck of a truck and a black Ford touring car stood nearby. Smoke was coming from a stovepipe in the shack, so someone else was evidently inside. The camp didn't look to belong to any cowboys, so I figured that it would definitely bear watching.

From a hill I watched the same two men ride out again the very next day. Again they looked through every bunch of cattle they came across, but returned to their camp by noon. Unless they had some tie-in with the men we had previously caught, I doubted that they would have any idea of who I was. Anyway I thought it worth the chance to ride over and see who they were.

Before sundown I rode in to their camp to find out what sort of yarn they offered for being there. Just in case, I had cooked up a little story of my own. As I suspected, there were three men; one about twenty-two; the second a rough looking, sawed-off man of about forty; and the third a slim, sandy-haired jasper who appeared to be nearing thirty. They were a ragged, dirty, shiftless-looking trio all right. The two horses they had in the old sheep pens were skinny old Indian ponies; nothing a cowboy would ride, certainly. The short older fellow looked vaguely familiar, but I couldn't remember where I had seen him before. All the time we were talking I could see they were sizing me up and looking my horse over pretty closely, so I figured I might as well go into my spiel right then. We had just been talking about the bad times and the scarcity of jobs around this country. They claimed they were just waiting for the sheep-shearing to begin so that they could get in a couple of weeks' work on that. That gave me an opening. I told them that I had never done any shearing, but had to get work of some sort and I wasn't particular what kind. I had been working for a cow ranch on New River and the boss had fired me after I'd knocked him down for cussing me out. Then he wouldn't pay me my month's wages, claiming I had nothing coming because I had only been working for my board. I didn't know how, but I sure aimed on getting even with that dirty bastard some way, if it took me from now on. Wouldn't have been so bad if he were hard up himself, but he owned the whole country from New River clear to here, and all the cattle on the desert belonged to him. *Hell* of a way to treat a poor boy!

Before I had finished my spiel they were nodding their heads in sympathy at the injustice of the rich, and I saw their suspicion was allayed.

"Might as well stay here tonight, since you have no place to go. Maybe we can help you out some on getting back at that skunk you was working for," Old Short and Ugly said. "We're short on chuck but we got plenty of hay for the horses. Me and Jess here hijacked eight bales of good alfalfa from a farmer's stack across the canal last night."

While we were cooking supper, I gathered from their conversation that all three were kinfolk. The two youngest were cousins, and Old Short and Ugly a brother-in-law. They called home some place in the Animas Valley in New Mexico just east of the Arizona line.

After supper "Grandpa" drove into the yard. He was a tall, skinny old codger, maybe sixty-five. I gathered that he lived west a few miles in the Valley, and that Short and Ugly's wife and kids stayed with him there. He was a typical old yarn-socker, working on a big cud of chewing tobacco.

"Yew boys havin' any luck?" he asked.

"Nary a bit, Grandpa! We ain't found a thing worth speakin' about," answered Sandy Hair.

"Well, I was hoping yew might have somethin' to take back to Ada and the kids by now. We ain't had a piece of fresh meat in the house fer three weeks. I tried pickin' some cotton over by Marinette but I had such a misery in my back I had to quit," says Grandpa.

"You come back day after tomorrow about this time and we'll have something for sure," Sandy told him.

Listening, I had just about decided that these jaspers were only stealing a beef once in a while to feed themselves and their family, until I heard Grandpa say, just as he was leaving:

"Now don't yew sell it all this time, cause we're gettin' powerful hongry fer meat."

"Don't fret none Grandpa. We'll fix you up day after tomorrow," was Sandy Hair's parting remark.

After Grandpa left we went to bed. Short and Ugly slept alone, and the cousins and I piled up together with me in the middle. They didn't have bedding enough to wad a shotgun with, and we all slept in our clothes.

Before riding into their camp I had stuck my six shooter in my belt, under my shirt. So far they didn't know I was armed, and it was hard sleeping between two men with that big old Colt Frontier on, without them feeling it as they rolled over trying to keep warm. My hip bone and ribs were sore by daylight. While we were eating the salt pork, cold light bread, fried potatoes and flour gravy breakfast, Short and Ugly began airing the thought I'd seen back of his eyes last evening.

"I've got to go get up a jag of wood, and Jess can help me today. While we're gone, why don't you and D.V. (Sandy Hair) see if you can find a cow or something fat enough to kill? If you find one, don't bring it in to camp, though, till after dark. We'll give Grandpa a quarter for him and Ada and the kids, and we'll keep one to eat, and sell the rest to the Chinaman's store down on Northern Avenue. I know where we can sell some more too. You can stay here with us and by shearing time you should be *even* with that fellow, and *then some*. O.K.?"

"Sounds fine to me," I replied.

D.V. and I jogged around out in the desert, but didn't see anything very good for beef. My horse got a cholla cactus in his hind leg and I got off to take it out. With a couple of dry sticks, I pulled it loose, and my old "baldy horse" flinched and kicked. Awkwardly I got back on him, holding my shoulder like it was hurting bad.

"What's the matter?" asked D.V.

"Damned horse kicked me on the shoulder just now," I explained.

Riding along I kept complaining and bellyaching about my shoulder. Circling toward camp we found some cattle in a brushy draw about two miles from the Canal. D.V. rode in to look them over and re-appeared chasing a big heifer, with his rope swinging for a catch. He caught her down the draw about fifty yards and pulled his horse to a stop.

"Help me tie her down here," he said as I rode up.

"Hell, fellow. I can't raise this arm even," I told him.

I could tell right away he wasn't much shakes as a cowboy, but he did manage to get her tangled in his rope until she fell down. After a lot of puffing and cussing he tied her and got back on his horse.

"Man, she'll make *fine* eating," he grinned. "Let's go on back to camp."

On the way, I was planning on just how I could get away from these rascals long enough to do what I had in mind without arousing their suspicions. Jess and Short and Ugly had returned with a sort of rat's nest pile of sticks for wood before we got back. D.V. told them the good news. They wanted to look at my shoulder to see how bad that kick was, and I had to fast-talk them out of the idea by telling them I was going down to Miller's farm below the canal to get some liniment to rub on it.

"While you're gone, we'll go butcher. Then after dark we'll bring her in. We'll have a good feed tonight!" Short and Ugly promised.

"My shoulder hurts so I'll have to travel slow," I told them. "But I'll be back as soon as I can."

Two or three times I almost gave myself away by starting to use that arm, then I'd remember and groan, and hold my shoulder.

Jess stayed in camp as I rode slowly towards the bridge across the canal, and the other two headed for the heifer tied in that draw. Once out of sight I loped on to Miller's hay farm. Using the farm phone, I called the sheriff's office and alerted the deputies. To be on the safe side, I suggested they get a search warrant for the camp.

"Then have two deputies come to Miller's and wait until about dark. With their car hidden, one deputy could watch the bridge from each end, from the weeds. I'll do the rest."

I took up my stand in the brush about a mile from the canal, and waited. Not long after dark I heard Short and Ugly and D.V. coming on their horses. I moved around just enough to let them pass near me. There was no moon, but the stars gave enough light to make out each man packing a whole quarter of beef on his lap, with one tied behind each saddle. They were moving slowly, with such an awkward load to carry. After they had passed by I fell in behind them, timing my gait to theirs. I guess they felt pretty sure they had the desert all to themselves, for I could hear them talking as they rode along in the dark. As they neared the canal I eased my horse up a little closer until I was almost on their heels. And still they didn't hear me.

"Gents, you are under arrest! Hang on to that beef and head your horses toward the bridge," I ordered.

Their heads swiveled around like those of two barn owls. I couldn't see their faces, but I knew from the silence their jaws were hanging open.

"*Who* in hell are you?" Old Short and Ugly asked.

"Just your old partner, 'the ranger'," I replied. "And this here pistol I'm pointing at you says I am the caliope behind this parade, and the parade is headed for the bridge where the spectators are waiting to see the elephants. Now get going, and remember Old Betsy here has a hair trigger."

I think they were too surprised to say anything, because they followed orders fine until we were almost to the bridge. Then all of a sudden they stopped. I cocked Old Betsy, and the click was loud on the night air.

"Now wait a minute. Let's talk this over," Short and Ugly began.

"Nothing to talk over, boys. Save that for the judge. Just move on across the bridge."

"But hell, fellow, can't we make some sort of a deal?" he ventured.

"No deal, just move on to the bridge."

Just as they rode out on the plank flooring of the bridge Sandy Hair (D.V.) said:

"Let's throw the damned stuff off in the canal and let him swim for it."

Suddenly in front and behind them two strong flashlights sprang to life as the two deputies appeared. That changed their notion real sudden. Across the bridge, one deputy left to bring up the car. After the beef was loaded in the trunk, both men were handcuffed together, searched, and put in the back seat. Then one deputy removed the spurs from D.V.'s boots and snapped leg irons on each man. From D.V.'s hip pocket they removed a circle of hide bearing the brand of the beef they had butchered.

"I'll take their horses back to camp and see you boys at the office in the morning," I told the deputies. "Take good care of our customers and see they have a warm place to sleep tonight."

"Be seeing you. Good night."

And they were off toward Phoenix.

Leading their horses, I rode to the camp. Jess heard me taking the saddles off in the sheep pen and came out.

"What's going on? And where is D.V. and Charley?"

"They changed their plans and went across the canal. You feed the horses good and I'll go back and see how they are doing. You'll probably be hearing from them pretty soon, so don't worry. Just wait," I said.

Returning to Miller's farm I put my horse in the corral, fed him, and hit the bunk house for some much needed sleep. After breakfast with the Millers next morning, I called Sheriff Jerry Sullivan for a ride to the court house. The morning was taken up with the county attorney, justice court, and the livestock board. As usual, a not guilty plea was made by my boys, and a trial date set for about a month later. Bonds were set pretty high and they couldn't raise enough money to get out so remained in jail. Then I returned to my camp at Von's Well.

Someone had reported an odd character camped in a mesquite thicket near the canal, east of the Seventh Street bridge. A ditch rider for the Water Users' Association reported that he first noticed the camp about a week previously, and some kids playing along the canal bank said a big tall man chased them away with a stick and threatened to throw them in the canal if they ever came back. Some folks living on the valley side across from the camp also reported a tall man prowling around their barn just about dark one night.

Since the ditch rider had told of seeing horses around the camp, I figured to investigate. Riding down the draw in which his camp was located, I came upon it about noon time. No one was about so I looked it over carefully. Reading the signs, I realized this was no ordinary cowboy's camp. First it was so well hidden that anyone could have passed within thirty feet without seeing it. Only from the elevation of the canal bank could it be seen at all. Second, his small cooking fires were carefully screened so the firelight at night would only be visible from straight above. Third, his entrances and exits were all made over the exact same trail, leading from the weedy ditch under the canal bank. Once before in the Tonto country I had run across just such camps when three of us were trailing four horse thieves as they went through the Matazals on their way from Utah into Mexico. Whoever used this camp was an old hand at the game of hideout. He knew all the tricks.

Following his horse tracks westward under the canal bank I trailed him to the Cave Creek Road where he had crossed over the wooden bridge into the Salt River Valley side. He had been riding one horse and leading two. From their tracks, size, depth, length of stride and shape, I saw they were good-sized horses (probably around a thousand pounds) and from mountain country. Not big-footed valley or desert stock. That night I intended to watch his camp from the opposite side of the canal.

After dark, leaving my horse tied out far enough away so that he wouldn't be heard if he snorted, I took up a position, lying in some grass on the canal bank where I could see the approach to the camp. By ten o'clock, cold and stiff from lying in one position so long, I began to think he wasn't going to show up. Then suddenly I heard a snap and ping, followed quickly by two more, quite close behind me and off to my left. Then silence, except for some fool rooster crowing off in the valley somewhere. There was no mistaking that sound. Someone had cut three wires on a tightly strung fence nearby. I lay there listening for some time before I heard anything else. Then I hear the swish, swish of someone walking through tall barley or alfalfa, away from the fence.

Carefully feeling my way down off the canal bank to the fence, I followed it along, feeling the wires until I came to the place that had been cut. Hearing the faint creak of saddle leather farther along, I was almost at arm's length before I saw the dim outlines of two horses tied there. One was saddled, the other not. Trying to hurry, yet make as little noise as possible, I returned to where I had left my horse. It didn't seem as though I could have left him so far away, and once I thought I must have passed by the place in the dark. Then I heard him move right in front of me. Hastily jerking the cinch tight, I mounted and trailed him up and over the steep canal bank into the water that was flowing silently through it. I knew there was about seven feet of water, so let my horse take his own time easing into it. Once out and over the far bank, I put spurs to him and raced for the Cave Creek bridge, which I felt sure my night rider would cross pretty soon. Again I took up a stand with nothing to do but wait, and I was glad for the warm Mackinaw coat I was wearing. In the left pocket was my strong flashlight and Old Betsy, my six shooter, resting easily in the spring clip shoulder holster under my left arm. I was as ready as I'd ever be.

About a half an hour later I heard my quarry coming toward the south approach to the bridge. When he had ridden up onto it I turned my flashlight full into his face, holding it way off to my left. That way, if he threw a snap shot at it, I wouldn't be right behind the light. Both he and his horse were temporarily blinded by the strong white light, and stopped suddenly.

"This is a state officer. Keep both hands up where I can see them, and don't move." I ordered.

Now he was leading *five* horses, each tied to the tail of the one in front of it.

"Who are you? And where are you going with all those horses," I asked.

He sat silent a minute, trying to think up a good lie I guessed.

"Me? Aw, I am just a horse trader. Live over at Glendale. Just going home with some horses I traded for today."

"Seems to me you're traveling a little late. Must be getting close to midnight now, and if you're going to Glendale how come you're on the wrong side of the canal, mister?" I questioned.

"Well, what do ya know about that?" (His speech suddenly became blurred). "Thought I was on the wrong side awhile ago. Guess I jest had a little bit too much to drink. Whoever you're looking for *can't* be me. Cause I'm jest a drunk old hoss trader. So how about letting me go on home?"

"Where did you trade for these horses?"

"Aw, away down in the Valley. Maybe six or eight miles from here. "They don't lead very good, that's why I'm so late," he offered.

Not more than an hour earlier, I'd felt over his saddle and the rawhide string braided around his saddle horn. He was a fast liar all right. And he wasn't even a little drunk, either.

I had seen this jasper a couple of times before; once at Rock Creek, and once at Scottsdale. His name was Jack Wolf, or Jake Wolf, I had forgotten which. And his reputation was plenty shady. He had served time in Arizona for horse stealing at least once. I sure wasn't letting him go until I checked back on that fence cutting and those extra horses he was leading.

"Keep your hands where I can see them because I'll be right alongside you. Turn around and ride straight down the road until I tell you where to turn. Let's go."

"Am I under arrest?" he asked.

"No! Not yet, but if you give me any trouble you will be," I told him.

Keeping my light in my left hand along with my reins, I sided him along the road to the first house which was set back some distance from the road in a grove of young citrus trees.

"Hello the house!" I called loudly a couple of times.

Finally a light sprang into life in a side window, and after a few moments a man's voice from the dark doorway asked who was there. I identified myself as an officer and asked him to call the Sheriff's office and have them send me a deputy or two.

The deputies made a fast run and were there shortly. Only then did I let Wolf dismount. He was disarmed of an almost new 45-caliber army-type automatic, and a long-bladed knife. Leaving one deputy to guard him, the other and I took the car and drove down a side road, trying to locate the house adjoining the field where the fence had been cut. After arousing several grumpy householders with negative results we called it a night. I told the deputies to book Wolf into jail on suspicion of grand theft. I promised to come in within the time limit either to sign a complaint or release him, depending on what I found out.

Leading his horses, I reached Von's Well in the wee hours of early morning, dog tired. Seemed as though all my work lately had been done during the nighttime. In the morning I borrowed Von's car and located the house we had looked for last night. It belonged to a man, who had made quite a reputation for raising good, well-blooded horses in the valley. When I asked if he had missed any horses he said not that he knew of. He had taken his wife and kids to visit relatives in Mesa the past evening and they hadn't returned home until after midnight. They had only been up for about fifteen minutes when I arrived on the scene. When I told him a little of the night's happenings, he perked up quickly and went to the barn and stables to check up. He was back in a hurry, before I had time to drink the coffee his wife poured for me.

"By George! Three of my quarter horses are gone," he exclaimed. "They couldn't have gotten out of the box stalls alone. Let me look in the fields a minute. Maybe they are there."

Now I was sure. He wouldn't find them in the fields, I knew. Back he came, pretty worried now.

"You'll find them in Vondracek's adobe corral, over in Paradise Valley," I told him. "They were stolen last night, and your fence is cut. I have to go in to the Court House now. When you get home with your horses, come on to the Sheriff's office and help us put this gent where the dogs won't bite him awhile."

"I'll sure do that. And thanks a million. I thought the days of horse thieves were over," he said.

"Not quite, while there are guys like this Wolf left running loose," I said.

By the time I got to the court house the I.D. boys had come up with a record on Wolf a yard long. Among other things he had done and was wanted for was shooting a town marshal in Searchlight, Nevada. The marshal recovered, minus one kidney, and Searchlight had put out a flyer on Wolf in several of the southwestern states. Later, officers had even traced the horse he was riding that night as having been stolen from a Mormon rancher near Pine, Arizona, months before.

The rancher made such a to-do about my getting his horses and the thief, before he even knew they were stolen, that the newspapers got in the act some way and hunted me up for the story. That was the last thing I wanted on the job I was doing, so I wouldn't tell them anything. But they did print a lot of stuff I had hoped they wouldn't. Publicity would scare off some of the people I most wanted to meet up with.

When trial date rolled around for the boys I had caught with the beef, they had retained about the best lawyer on livestock cases in the country: R. E. L. Shepherd. I had run up against him in court before and knew him for a pretty slick customer, and a slimy one, too.

Challenging during the selection of a jury, he managed to have excused every member of the panel who knew anything whatever about livestock. Through four days he ranted and raved about the rich cattle barons and the poor, misguided, starving boys who were being persecuted by hired minions of the law, trying to railroad them into the dark dungeons of the penitentiary just because they had killed one little animal to feed their starving families, and on and on and on. His tears and pleas were to no avail, however, when the prosecution proved that these same poor boys had sold stolen beef before.

In the time which had elapsed before the trial I had remembered where I'd seen old Short and Ugly. One evening I had ridden up on him after he had taken the roof from a house on the Black Canyon Road and was loading it onto a truck. I had made him leave it and had called the owner, a lady who lived in town. She had had it put back on the house. I was surprised that he hadn't remembered *me*.

When the prosecutor injected that phase into the trial, old R. E. L. Shepherd popped up like a bee had stung him, to shout "objection, immaterial, irrelevant, nothing to do with *this* case," and so on. Of course that testimony was stricken from the record, as I had known it would be, but not from the minds of the jurors.

When the jury retired and stayed out too long, I was afraid that these ribbon clerks and merchants and such were going to come up with a not guilty verdict, but they didn't. Old R.E.L.'s crocodile tears had *some* effect, however. Short and Ugly got a five-to-seven-year sentence, the cousins a flat five, with recommendation of a suspended sentence. Judge Phelps gave them a choice of leaving the State of Arizona, not to return, or doing the five years, and of course they left pronto. Later when Wolf was convicted, he drew a ten-year rap, knowing that Nevada would be waiting at the gate to welcome him at the end of his stay. So much newspaper publicity resulted from all this that I only stayed on my job a short while longer.

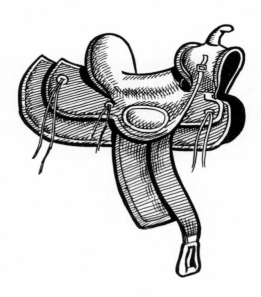

In those days of long cattle drives, when great herds were on the trail from the ranches to the shipping pens for many days at a time, the cattle were kept together on their bed grounds at night by several shifts of cowboys working the night guard. One shift of two or three men usually took over just before dark, the second shift about eleven, and the third shift, known as the cock tail guard, would be roused out about three a.m. to ride around the herd until daylight. This last guard drew its name, in all probability, from the crow of the rooster at the first gleam of daylight at dawn of the new day. I guess none of us realized it at the time I rejoined the Quarter Circle One after the windup of my range detective job, but the cattle people were on sort of a cock tail guard of their own. The end of an era was fast approaching. Several old ranches began breaking up around the country. Jose Cline sold out to Laird & Evans his old Flying Y Ranch on New River and the Black Canyon. I repped with him that last Spring, and he was pretty pleased. Said he received fifty dollars straight for every cow with a calf by her side. Next, the old Coburn Ranch in Bloody Basin began trailing out to Cordes, their nearest shipping point. When they had gathered all the cattle they could from their huge, rough country they moved a couple of thousand head to Old Mexico and sold the remnant to Ryan Brothers of Globe. Then the Horse Shoe Ranch began trailing cattle to Phoenix in herds of six to eight hundred at a time. Then the old JM Ranch on the Verde sold their range to the Francis Campbell Sheep Company of Ash Fork, retaining the cattle. It took almost a year to gather and ship from Phoenix. Old Chico Jaques, their foreman for eighteen years, borrowed two thousand dollars to buy the remnant. Six months later he sold over ten thousand dollars worth of cattle from that same remnant. And still there were cattle left on the range for a couple of years afterward. The Cartwright brothers at Seven Springs retained their ranch, but Elmer, the middle brother, sold his interest to Manford, the eldest.

Things were changing fast. New people began coming in to file for homesteads wherever there was water, or to buy up any little piece of patented land available. The old-timers who had used the range lands for most of a lifetime were dismayed to find many of their water holes fenced off, with No Trespass signs nailed to nearby trees. Too late, they woke up to the fact that they should have secured their water years before.

Then in the early thirties, the national forest service began sending out their young college graduate range management experts to tell the old-time cattle men how to operate their ranches. In Albuquerque and Washington, the service had drawn up a batch of new ideas for the cattle men. Some of them were little dandies, too. Salt grounds near water must be discontinued. Cattle hadn't been going far enough back, away from water, to feed. Young men were sent out to show the cattle men where the new salt grounds were to be located, on top of almost inaccessible rocky peaks, miles from water. To make sure the cattle knew where to go, they had wooden signs painted to nail to trees or posts saying in plain letters, "Salt ground number 1 — 2 — 3 — 4" and so on, according to the number of places used. The cattlemen's arguments that their cattle weren't educated to read yet were to no avail. A few deer were all that ever salted on the new grounds. I often later found salt that had lain there for two years or more until rains and weather finally disintegrated it.

Next, the forest service insisted that running creeks be fenced along both banks, with openings about three miles apart fenced into the stream so that cattle could go in to drink, then return the same way. This was to prevent erosion of the banks where cattle came down to water and protect the young willows and plant shoots growing near the water's edge. Of course the experts didn't take into consideration that steady use of the water gaps by the cattle in the few places that *would* be left open to them would wear the banks down much worse than letting them come in scattered along as they had been doing for years; also that several times each year the sections of fence in the water would wash away in floods and have to be rebuilt each time. The boys with the sharp pencils hadn't figured very well. With the threat of having their grazing permits cut there was nothing the cattle men could do but accede, and grumble.

In the forest, it had always been the policy of the ranchers to build and maintain trails for use of the rangers traveling from place to place on their job. Our local ranger, Joe Hand, had been hiring some old prospectors who needed the work to clean and repair the trails each year. With their burros and camp equipment and tools, they just worked along from place to place moving their camps as they needed to. Joe was about as disgusted as the cattle men when he received orders that all trail work and repairs would have to be done by college graduates from now on. That first summer he had a hell of a time rounding up the necessary graduates to do the work. They didn't figure that pick and shovel work was what they went to college for.

Finally he recruited a few and started them out. It didn't work out worth a hoot. They got lost; they didn't do the work; they quit and went back to town. Soon the trails were filled with rocks, washed out in places, grown up in brush, and ruined. But still the boys with the lead pencils wouldn't admit they were wrong.

A general shift in rangers was ordered. Good men who had been located at their stations eight to ten years or longer were sent to other ranger stations. It had taken them years to learn the country, the people, and the problems of their districts. Now they had to begin from scratch again. Not many of them took kindly to the new order. Rangers who knew the forestry business like the back of their hands were transferred down to the cactus areas where there wasn't a pine or juniper tree in fifty miles. Those who knew the brush country and grazing business best went to the tall timber of the Mogollon Plateau, a foreign world to them. Then, to put the icing on the cake, came an order for the new rangers to count all the cattle in their districts. Afraid that the ranchers would purposely leave out cattle on roundups, these rangers insisted on riding with the cowboys as they gathered. What time they weren't trying to get out of brush thickets they had gotten hung up in, or trying to figure out what had become of the cowboys and cattle that were in sight just a minute ago, was spent in being hopelessly lost. The ranchers didn't like it either, having to hold up their drives two or three times a day while their cowboys were searching for lost rangers. It would take at least two years before the new men could learn the country and the drives well enough to make the rounds.

There were many instances of growing friction between the Forest Service and the grazing permittees. Then another change began to appear. Members of the American Hereford Association began to put on a concerted drive to sell *their* idea of the ideal beef type cattle for the Arizona ranges. Prior to now, the majority of the mountain cattle were of Roan Durham or Red Durham stock. The desert country cattle were in most cases Mexican cattle, well equipped to survive the heat and frequent droughts, but not very uniform to look at, being all colors and combinations of pintos, roans, brindles, and what not. Cattle were not yet being sold by weight; just for so much per head, according to class. And very few buyers could be found for steers under two years of age. Now, wherever cattle men got together the conversation soon got around to Herefords. White face bulls began finding their way to Arizona ranges from Texas, New Mexico, and Colorado, but good Hereford bulls alone were not enough to show any overnight degree of change in their offspring. It took years of selective breeding to the *best* of the ranchers' young she stock to eliminate the old strains of Durham and Mexican blood.

Then the pendulum swung too far the other way. Once the whole country had changed over to Herefords, the herds began to suffer from what I called "Hereforditis." Cattle became too finely bred. Offspring began to grow smaller and finer boned and lighter in weight. Some of the old-timers had savvy enough to revert to the old Durham strain of bulls for a few crosses; but the Hereford Association had sold most ranchers so strongly on the breed they kept on using registered white face bulls without change.

Then, when buyers began to pay for cattle by weight, they griped about the horns, offering to pay a few cents more per pound on calves and yearlings that had been de-horned. Their argument was that de-horned stock shipped better and fed better in the feed lots because, without horns, the danger of bruising one another was greatly reduced. Another reason was that they were paying by weight, and on a hundred head they were buying two hundred horns. Of course they didn't explain *that*. Many old-timers refused to go along with the de-horning trend. If the Good Lord hadn't intended cattle to have horns he wouldn't have had them grow any was their thought on the subject. Also, many of the mountain cattle were still so wild they had to be roped and tied, and horns were made to fit in the loop of a cowboy's rope, "by Ned!"

Next, a few enterprising trucking firms tried their luck at short hauls. They built stock racks on some of their trucks and brought cattle into Phoenix from nearby ranches in areas where the roads weren't too difficult to negotiate. Of course, the ranchers had first to build corrals and loading chutes. As roads improved and were extended farther into the back country, more and more ranchers took advantage of the trucking. The days of cattle drives to market were becoming a thing of the past. Barbed wire fences divided the ranches into holding pastures, and trucks hauled the cattle to market. Day herds and night guards, long grueling drives to the railroad shipping points, with stampedes, rivers to swim and all the things that kept life interesting for the cowboys were fast disappearing.

With the disappearance of the old tough, wild breeds of cattle came *new* problems. Ticks, flys, grubs, septicemia, lump jaw, pink eye, wooden tongue, plus a whole series of fresh diseases we'd never heard of before plagued the Hereford. With the increases in price for the breed came also medical and veterinarian bills to keep the cattle healthy. The Hereford Growers' Association's claims to the contrary, this was not a good breed for the desert country, especially in the summer. Unless fed expensive feed supplements, the cattle laid down and died during drought years. Their stamina was poor, and they were not up to traveling miles to water like the old desert cattle they had replaced.

Desert ranchers then began looking around for a hardier type. The Brahma seemed to be their best bet. This breed had been successfully raised in the Texas country and was mostly immune to ticks, eye trouble, and most of the diseases that plagued the Herefords in the hot country. Brahmas were good rustlers, and hardy. The cows were good mothers, not bothered by heat or far distances to travel to water. Because of their conformation they brought a few cents less per pound as beef, but more than equalized the difference in price in other ways. Mountain ranchers found them too nervous and hard to handle in rough, brushy country. The Herefords did well enough there, especially in the higher elevations where it was cooler and feed more plentiful.

During the next thirty years ranchers were to experiment with many different beef breeds, searching for the perfect type. They tried about all the known breeds, plus combinations of crossbreeds, such as Angus, Santa Gertrudis, Charolais, Brangus, Brayfords, Barzone, Charbray, and many more, but most eventually stayed with or returned to the Hereford and the Brahma.

No one has *asked* for my opinion as to the type of cattle they should stock on their ranges. If they ever should, I still would claim that there never was a better breed of cattle on the mountain ranges than the old Durham they had in the first place. However, I agree that the Brahma is better on the desert country than the old Mexican breeds of years ago; not tougher, and certainly no better able to survive heat and scarcity of water; just a better money-maker. Years ago we build finger traps at many of the desert water holes. Where there was permanent water and corrals, we trapped the cattle when they came in at night to water. Even in June, when the desert was dry and hot, we often caught old cows who had stayed out as long as five days between drinks. When they did come in for water they would stand around, drink, then lick salt for a while, then go back and drink again several times until they were so full of water they could barely waddle away. They knew how to survive in the desert.

I used to watch those old "sisters," and I learned a lot about them that is not in books. Riding the desert in early spring, I often came across as many as a dozen small calves lying around not far apart. One old cow was acting as nursemaid for the bunch, while the other mothers were drinking at some water hole. When they returned, then she would leave her own calf with them, to go water out, herself. No matter how long the cows were gone, those little calves would never leave the nursemaid until the mamas came back to them. In the mountains, wherever we developed a new spring or water hole in a canyon, it wouldn't be long before the cows had laid out a trail for themselves from the water to the higher country where better feed was to be found. An engineer with a transit couldn't have figured out a better grade than those old Nellies did. Invariably, the best trails were the old cattle trails.

On a hot day I've watched old cows start up the trail after filling up on water. They would climb for a while, then stop and rest, climb again and rest. Sometimes it would take them an hour or more to reach the top of a ridge, but they would make it without any great loss of energy, while carrying enough water to founder a camel. One or two ranches I worked on made some trails for their cattle in some of the rougher parts of their range. Usually it wasn't long until the cattle had made changes in them to suit themselves, and *always* for the better.

Home to a cow is the particular part of a range on which she locates, and where her first calf is born. Take her away, no matter how far, and she will try to return; if not right away, certainly in time for her next calf to be born there. Her sense of direction is better than a compass and, unless fenced off, she will travel across any sort of country, any distance, to go home. Horses, too, have that trait or instinct.

All these little asides are "old hat" to most any old-time rancher. But many people do not know about them unless they have been raised in the business. The old saying "as dumb as an ox" doesn't have much to recommend it as far as I'm concerned. True, cattle can *act* dumb when they want to. But I've seen old mossy-horned steers out-smart good and experienced cowboys on many and many a roundup. Old Pete Leterette used to tell his cowboys to "charge 'em, boys. Don't give 'em time to stop and think, or they will out-fox us for sure." I have also seen some button kid come home disgusted, after trying to drive three or four old cows and baby calves when they didn't *want* to drive. They would start off fine. Then pretty soon one old cow would go one way, her calf another. While the kid was getting them back together, another pair would split up, and so on. Pretty soon the kid would have his horse run down, and the cows and calves would all take off in separate directions. After he had quit and ridden off, the cows and calves would get back together to laugh up their sleeves at how dumb humans were.

Range cattle and horses can trail by scent almost as well as a good hound. I've watched them do it many times. How *old* a trail they can follow I have never figured out, but I do know that they can trail up other stock by following the scent made the same day. Wild burros have the same faculty, plus the keenest hearing of all.

The Quarter Circle One at Cave Creek lost a good deal of its desert range in the changing times, and many of the old water holes were gobbled up by new people. One more severe drought in the early thirties left the ranch in pretty bad shape, just at the time the whole nation was undergoing the worst depression it had seen in half a century.

While the desert was hardest hit by drought, the mountain country wasn't far behind. Even the oak brush and kindred brouse, always the ranchers' hole card in times of drought, turned black and died that year. Springs that had never failed before dried up. Cattle were dying everywhere, and the government began *paying* ranchers to kill their own cattle. The W.P.A. works project offered a weak stop-gap to keep men off the soup lines in town. Formerly well-to-do cattle ranchers found themselves unable to hire the help they needed, for lack of money.

Rather than lean on a shovel handle for the W.P.A. and bewail the hard times, I gathered about fifty steel traps and took to the mountains to trap furs. Manford Cartwright was happy to have me trap around his place at Seven Springs, where the foxes and coyotes were playing havoc with his chickens, turkeys, guineas, and several pairs of prized pea fowl. From his ranch I moved to Tom Cavness' 51 outfit, just south of Bloody Basin. From there I went to the TT Ranch on the head of New River, then eventually back to Cartwright's. Wherever I camped, the ranchers were happy to grubstake me and furnish me a horse or two in return for the range branding I did for them while riding my trap lines. Three or four times during the winter I made shipments of furs to a Salt Lake City fur company, and a couple more to St. Louis, Missouri. Fur prices were remarkably high that winter and I had had real good luck with my catches. Before spring I figured up my earnings and found that I had made a lot more money trapping than I ever had in better times riding for wages. But now it was too late to trap any longer. Furs would be too light, now that spring was so near. I couldn't see myself lying around Phoenix hunting odd jobs in competition with a town full of other men looking for work. I knew that I could survive much better here in the mountains where I only needed enough chuck and horse feed to get by on until things loosened up, no matter how long it took.

The Cartwrights had an old cabin in Lime Creek, a tributary canyon that emptied into the Verde River on the eastern edge of their range. I had camped there often when riding roundups for them, and knew the country well. The cabin set beneath a high bluff where there was a waterfall of clear cold water, just a few steps south of the house. The pasture back on top of the bluffs was an ideal place for my horses. The steep slippery trail up the bluffs to the pasture had long been a source of worry to the ranch, as several horses had been crippled when crowded over the edge by others as the wranglers drove them in from the pasture to the corrals below. Once ten head of cattle had fallen to their death the same way. Manford and I made a deal. For my chuck and horse feed, I would make a good trail up the bluff. He was to furnish me the tools and dynamite, caps and fuse which I needed for the job.

With my bed and belongings on a pack horse, and a pack mule loaded with tools and dynamite, I made the ten miles of steep rugged trail across the mountains from the Seven Springs Ranch into Lime Creek. The old cabin was infested with mice and I had to put most of my food stuff in tin cans to save it from the hungry little cusses. With pick, shovel and drill steel, I began building a good trail up the bluff. It was hard, rough work, but I enjoyed it. My muscles grew hard as iron from swinging a four-pound single jack hammer and drilling eighteen to twenty-inch holes in the hard quartz and layers of glassy rock all day. Between the thumb and forefinger of my left hand, thick horn-like callouses formed from the continual twisting of the drill steel.

Along in late March the days were warm and sunny, as I was nearing the end of my job, not far from the top. While I still had plenty of dynamite, my fuse roll was about exhausted. Rather than use up a whole day making the round trip across the mountain to get more, I decided I could just about finish the job with the little I had left if I cut each fuse real short and wasted none.

One morning as I climbed my new trail to work I spotted a shallow overhanging rock in a small canyon beside the trail. The overhang was just what I needed for protection from the blast and rock fall when I fired my holes with their short fuses. With three deep holes loaded and tamped with forty percent dynamite I was ready to light those short fuses and race for cover under the overhang just down the trail. To prevent any lost motion in case a match blew out before the fuse caught, I placed several matches in my teeth where I could grab them quickly. Lighting the fuse of the highest hole, I ran down the trail to the next one, quickly lit it, then ran to the third just below. I waited just long enough to see the first sputter as the last fuse caught, then leaping like a mountain goat I raced for my sanctuary under the overhanging rock. I dived in just as the first blast shook the bluff and sent rocks flying overhead like schrapnel.

To my dismay, I found my shallow hole inhabited by a big rattle-snake, on the fight the second I jumped in with him. His first strike barely missed my ankle. Before he could recover his coil for another, I kicked him across the hole to the far wall. With his rattles buzzing his war cry, here he came, determined to dispute my right to share his warm niche in the rocks. Twice more I kicked him away, but he came slithering swiftly back during the rock fall from the second blast. Rocks, some as large as my hat, were still falling around us. With one more (the closer) blast yet to come, I was between the devil and the deep blue sea. To stay, or not to stay—ah! that *was* the question.

I took my chances with the blast.

Just outside of our hole was a skimpy cedar tree about eight feet tall. Scrambling up the bank where it grew, I crouched behind it, although it offered about as much protection as a toothpick. Ka-blam, the last blast came. Rocks whizzed by me and over me, one peeling bark from the cedar tree within inches of my head. That was a close shave; too close for comfort.

"Mr. Snake, your time has come." I was mad.

When I looked back into the hole, he had found a crevice along the floor where he had stretched himself out full length. Outside of the hole, I found a dry stick and tried to rake him out of the crevice so that I could kill him, but he was pressed so tightly against the rocks that all I could do was make him rattle. Finally I picked up a short piece of fuse which I had dropped earlier in the week. Cutting a quarter stick of dynamite, I capped the fuse, stuck it into the dynamite, placed the whole in the split end of the stick, and shoved it, lit, up against the snake, then ducked out. When the smoke had settled, I looked in to find my snake still very much alive, but stunned. I finished him off pronto with the stick, glad to see the last of him.

The trail completed, I made a trip over to the ranch to return the tools and bring back a load of groceries. When Mrs. Cartwright learned of the trouble I was having with mice at the cabin she gave me a kitten. I put him in a cardboard box on the very top of my pack for the return trip. After we had crossed the mountain pass and begun the steep descent on the switchback trail into Lime Creek, the pack mule's stiff-legged gait made the pack swing from side to side like the deck of a ship in heavy seas. The kitten had one arm stuck out of an air hole in the box and was waving it like mad and yowling his protests at the rough ride. I think he was mighty glad when we reached camp and he was back on terra firma once more. He was in seventh heaven with a wonderful supply of mice to work on, and soon grew fat and happy.

In a rincon near the head of a side canyon a few miles to the north, I had discovered the ruins of a prehistoric Indian village. With nothing to do, I decided to dig and explore it. Each morning, taking a lunch, I rode to the village and spent the day digging, returning home at dusk. My kitten seemed to know about when to expect me, and on the way home I would meet him coming up the canyon, sometimes a mile from the camp. I would pick him up and let him ride back on my horse and he would purr all the way like a miniature motor boat.

Digging from the outer edge of the ruins, I cleaned out seven rooms and part of an eighth before I left the canyon. This village had been three stories high at the center, then graduated down to two for a depth of three or four rooms. Below those, there were one-story rooms, seven deep, all the way around the village. From its size, it probably had been home to three or four hundred people back in twelve or fourteen hundred A.D. Fire had destroyed the upright timbers, and eventually the walls had fallen in. Later they had been covered by the centuries of rains, storms, dust and debris, until now there was just a huge mound of rocks and earth, with trees and brush growing over it.

I uncovered countless artifacts of those early people. Many were unique and very interesting to me, for I had long been an amateur archaeologist and had absorbed all I could learn about ancient civilizations at museums, from other archaeologists, and from libraries. I found a few things which were quite different from any I had ever seen or read about. In one long narrow outer room, evidently used as a storage place, was a row of great brown pottery ollas. They were about three feet tall and four across the middle, each with a flat round limestone lid, roughly hewn and about an inch thick. They were badly cracked from the great weight of the earth that had lain on them through the centuries. After I had carefully removed the overburden and the air reached them, large slabs and pieces fell away from them, leaving a shaped form of earth inside. Curious to see what they had contained, I began removing the earth. About an inch or so in I encountered a second olla, identical with the first. A few of those were intact and I finally had them standing, cleaned of dirt and whole. Their necks were about eighteen inches across, the whole vessels exact duplicates of the outer ones. They were far too large around the middle to have been placed inside the outer ones. This meant that these had been made *first,* and the outer ones formed around them by some method of retaining an inch of space between. Later each pair must have been fired, but I was unable to see *how* the whole process had been accomplished. These inner ollas also were full of black earth, which must at one time have been corn, grain, or perhaps acorns or some solid. Who knows? Possibly they may have been water storage vessels.

Another oddity was a baked yellow clay form, grooved around the outside for a cord and divided in the center like a pie shell cut through with one stroke. Tied together, the two halves probably made a form which could be smeared inside with a quarter inch of clay, smoothed evenly. When the cord was loosened and the halves removed, a perfect clay bowl remained, to be fired later.

A child's burial beneath a hard-packed floor had a rough mescal-fiber string leading from the child's head which had been covered with a beautifully made inverted bowl. The string came through a hole drilled in the bottom of the bowl up through the floor to the room above. Prehistoric mothers used these strings, I had read, to keep their dead children from being lonesome and feeling lost from their parents. When the mother pulled on the string, the child knew the parent was near, and she would talk to it and comfort it so that it would not be unhappy. One day I dug up a tiny clay replica of a three-legged matate, or meal grinding stone used by the ancients to make flour or mast. Some mother had made it for her little girl, just as later mothers made rag dolls, I guess. Seldom did I find a bowl or pot intact, but the few I did recover I placed in a cave near the camp, where they would remain dry and protected. I carefully catalogued every find down to the last mano and arrow point.

I would have liked nothing better than to have been able to uncover the whole village. But the time soon came when I had to leave the rough, lonesome canyons where I had spent such an interesting few months, to return to civilization and the work-a-day world. Some day I hoped once again to return to Lime Creek, that wild, beautiful "Shangri-la" of varicolored mountains and canyons; to watch the black-tailed deer romp and play around the salt grounds, and the coyotes making a concerted drive on rabbits, strung out abreast about a hundred yards apart like cowboys working the brush for wild cattle. On my way out I stopped at the top of the divide and,

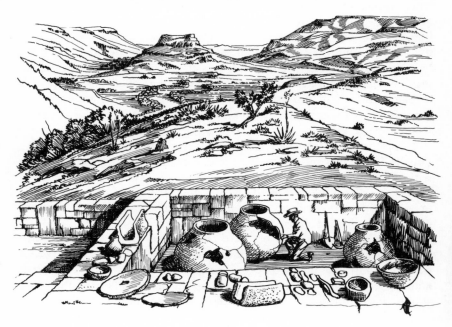

looking back, I said, "Goodbye, Old Lime Creek. I hope to see you another day."

But I never did.

The Porter boys, sons of N. Porter, an old-time saddle and harness maker who had a saddle shop in Phoenix, decided to change an operation they had at Snowflake in the northeast part of the state. For years they had run a sheep ranch on Mingus Mountain, near Prescott. Later they leased seventy sections of land from the old Aztec Cattle Company (former owners of the Hash Knife Ranch) and moved their sheep there. In the fall the sheep would hit the long trail to the Salt River Valley, where they wintered each year. Then after shearing in spring, they took the trail back to the Snowflake ranch where they spent the summer.

On the west side of the range was a natural boundary, formed by the two-hundred foot perpendicular cliffs of Silver Creek. The east side was bounded by the fence of the Bill Bourdon Ranch, but the north and south ends were wide open, with nothing to keep out the herds of Mormon cattle that grazed the country. So from fall to spring while the sheep were gone, these herds of cattle used the Porter range, keeping it grazed off pretty close. The boys figured they might as well get the benefit of all that grass themselves, so they planned to go into the cattle business also. Casting around for a good man to run the spread they picked Deane Curry. They couldn't have made a better choice. Deane was so pleased with the working interest they offered him he could hardly wait to get started. He'd been a bachelor all his life, and now at forty-three suddenly got a yen to marry and settle down. A dude girl from Indiana who had been around the Cave Creek country for a couple of winters was charmed by Deane's weather-beaten face and bow legs, I guess, because she married him real pronto, and early in 1935, they moved to the Porter Ranch at Snowflake.

Deane Curry was a cowboy with ambition. If fate hadn't stacked the deck against him he would have been pretty well off by the time he was forty years old. When I first knew him he was working for Ed Cavness on the Verde River, in some of the wildest, roughest country of Arizona. Ed's ranch practically stood on end, and he always claimed that if it was rolled out flat it would be as large as the State of Texas. It was a long day's ride to the ranch from the nearest road and, as everything had to be packed in, Deane spent a lot of his time between Cordes on the old Black Canyon Road and the ranch, worrying with a string of ornery pack jacks. Ed finally sold that ranch and bought another one farther down the river at Ister Flat so that he would have a place where his horses and chickens could lie down and roll without falling off into the river (or so he claimed). Deane didn't make the move with him, hiring out instead to Ed's brother, Tom, on the old 51 Ranch, just south of Bloody Basin. After a few years there he threw in with another fellow and the two of them started a little ranch of their own over on Burro Creek, west of Bagdad. Two straight years of drought cleaned them out, and Deane returned to the 51 to work for wages, while his partner went to the Yolo's as a cook. After the ED Ranch on the Verde, Tom's 51 seemed positively suburban to Deane. He only had to pack in twelve miles here from the end of the road.

Besides Deane, Tom kept one other steady man on the 51, Louis Manuel, a Pima Indian. Louis was a good reliable Indian and a hard worker. If he hadn't been, he could never have gotten along with Deane because, bar none, Deane was the hardest worker of *any* cowboy I ever knew. His only fault was doing everything the hardest possible way. Winter or summer, no matter what the weather, Deane was up and dressed by four o'clock in the morning. On days so stormy nothing could be done outside he would pace the house like a caged tiger, looking out first one window and then another. Finally the fidgets would get the best of him and he would plow through the mud or snow to the barn, find an old piece of a broken riata and bring it to the house where he would unbraid and then braid it back again for the rest of the day, jumping up every once in a while to look outside at the sky again. He was plumb nervous.

Louis and I had a lot in common. We could prop our feet up by the fire and enjoy the storm without a worry. Deane nursed that ranch along for several years just as though it belonged to him instead of Tom, and I'm sure he worked harder to make it pay than Tom ever did himself. He always came up with a high percentage calf crop every year, and his death loss was practically nil. At long last, another chance presented itself for him to get into the cattle business for himself with the working interest offered him by the Porter boys.

About a month after he moved to the Porter Ranch, Deane wrote and asked me to come up and give him a hand starting the cattle end of the outfit. He had several horses of his own at the 51 which he was going to need, so I gathered them up and hit the trail for Snowflake.

It was a four-day ride across rough country, but I made it with all the horses arriving in good shape.

I spent the last night on the trail at the little Mormon town of Heber and talked with a couple of brothers who had once run cattle on the piece of range now owned by the Porters for a couple of years. Their experience there hadn't been good. Loco weed had put them out of business, and they said that it had grown worse since. When I mentioned that hazard to Deane he just hooted. There had been loco on the ED Ranch and even on the 51 and it hadn't bothered the stock much.

"But that was rattle-weed, a milder form of true loco," I explained. "This variety up here looks like the *pure quill* to me, Deane."

He refused to be discouraged by a little thing like that, so we let the subject drop. I couldn't blame him for being as enthusiastic as an Apache squaw with a hundred feet of beef guts; for, after all, with his pretty young wife and rosy prospects ahead, Deane felt himself sitting high in the saddle. He had more plans than a politician and we sat up late into the night going over what had to be done to ready things before he brought in his first herd of cattle.

First we surveyed each end of the range for fence lines, and gave the fencing contracts to some Mormon families in town. While the fences were being erected we had a driller move his rig in from Holbrook and start punching down a deeper hole in an old, shallow, weak well. Around the last part of May Deane went south to the Willcox country to buy some cattle, while I stayed on the ranch, hurriedly finishing up a lot of work to prepare for his return. When he wired me the date his cattle would arrive in Holbrook, I gathered a crew of men and was camped at the stockyards waiting for him when he unloaded four hundred head of cows and calves one night.

At daylight we crossed the herd over the boggy quicksand of the Little Colorado River and headed them for Washboard Canyon, where we planned our first night's camp. Just before dark we reached a water hole where we expected to water the thirsty cattle, only to find it dried up to a tubful of slimy, muddy water, scarcely enough for our horses.

"Guess we will have to sing to 'em tonight and hope for the best," I told Deane. "They are too tired to go on, and too dry to stay put."

We put out the night guards for the first three hours, and crawled into our beds with all our clothes on. Deane and a few of the men took the second guard, and when he awoke me to take my men out to stand cock tail guard he told me that the cattle were almost impossible to hold, but to do the best I could.

When we reached the herd the three men left there had their horses in a high lope, chousing the thirsty, crazy cattle back into the bunch. The dust hanging in the still night air made everything so obscure we couldn't tell a cedar bush from a calf, except that it wasn't trying to run away to hunt water. Our horses were in a lather in less than an hour, for no sooner had we whipped one string of cattle back into the bunch than we could dimly make out a dust of another bunch leaving farther around the side. One big ornery old calf must have been run back a hundred times. When he broke out, he left with a jar, running full tilt, and we had a horse race to overtake him. Along about three o'clock, according to the handle of the Big Dipper in the northern sky, I ran him back in for the last time. Pretending to go on around the herd, I was ready for him when he popped out like a grapefruit seed, and headed for the tall uncut. The cow horse I was riding bored a hole in the ground with both hind feet when I threw my loop, and bedded that calf down hard. I had him tied down before he even got his breath back, and right there he stayed for the rest of the night, bawling his displeasure.

By daylight we drifted on without even eating breakfast. There was no time for that. We had to find water. In the middle of Jim Flake's range we at last reached a tank with plenty of water for the herd. We had to watch the calves closely to keep them from being trampled underfoot and drowned by the cows, they were so crazy from thirst. From there on into the ranch the drive was a breeze. Our only trouble was keeping the local range cattle from mixing with our herd.

As soon as we arrived, Deane turned back to take a train to Willcox to receive another herd while I put the crew to branding out this bunch in the Porter iron. Once branded and turned loose, the cattle had to be located. Right away, as the nature of a cow directs, they headed straight for Holbrook where they had been unloaded. We drifted them back, then the next morning overtook the leaders once again, six or seven miles on their way.

When Deane wired, I left a couple of men on the ranch to throw back the cattle and the rest of us went to Holbrook to meet him and another four hundred head. This time we took a different route home, on which there were no dry night stands.

Shortly after that the fences were up and we were able to have a breathing spell. I stayed until August, when Deane felt we had things well enough under control that he could handle the outfit alone. The Porters had shipped their buck herd up from the Salt River Valley by train, and their ewe and lamb herds had arrived over the sheep trail, driven by the Basque herders and their dogs. Everywhere one looked there were sheep. I was ready to move on.

I went up the Rio Puerco River to the Navajo Indian reservation near Crown Point, New Mexico, to help an old jasper gather out some cattle he was moving off Indian land. The Indian department in Washington was just about to move all leasees from reservations all over the country, and this old jasper was beating them to the punch a bit. When I wound up my little ball of yarn with him and was once more at loose ends, I decided to pack my wardrobe (two pairs of clean socks and a union suit) and drift down into the White Mountain country around Springerville. There it was cool among the tall pines.

I had only been there a couple of days when I ran across Mr. T. T. Swift, then assistant-supervisor of the Tonto National Forest. Seemed the Forest Service was *still* trying to get a count on a few outfits their rangers had never been able to tally. But *this* time they were going to use real cowboys to do the job. The pay was good, and the work as easy as licking butter off a knife, for a cowboy, so I told him that I would take a fall at it. One crew was working the Bar T Bar ranch near Payson at the time. The next ranch on the agenda was the one belonging to Bill Lee and Harry Shute along the Salt River and Coon Creek junction, under the Sierra Ancha Mountains. That's where I was sent.

Bill Lee's ranch on Coon Creek was as pretty a setting for a cow ranch as I have ever seen. It was tucked away beneath the towering cliffs of the Sierra Anchas, honeycombed with little cliff dwellings of the ancient peoples who had called this home thousands of years before. The crystal creek ran right by his doorway on its way to join Salt River, a mile below. Irrigating some barley fields just south of his house, he had a plentiful supply of water the year around, a real prize in Arizona. Growing in his back yard were two of the largest black fig trees in the world. They were a sight to behold, being sixty feet tall, with branches spreading their shade over a great area of ground. During the summers the whole family practically lived under those two trees.

Bill knew that the forest service was going to count his cattle, but he wasn't peeved. To the contrary, he was glad to get the extra help the cowboys would give him. He and Shute were dividing their cattle and they would have been short-handed without us. When all of us had finally drifted in, there were five cowboys and one Forest Service man in our group.

Shorty Carroway, an old waddy from the Apache country, was one of those who had been counting the Bar T Bar cattle. His own horses had been pretty well ridden down from that works, and he was slightly afoot when he reached Coon Creek. Bill Lee had a lot of fresh horses, among them a sleek, slim brown one belonging to one of his twin daughters. This horse had been spoiled in the process of breaking. He was a straight-legged old pony and was as pretty as a picture to look at from one side. On the other he had the wildest eye I ever saw on a horse. None of Bill Lee's cowboys wanted any part of him, knowing that he was treacherous and mean, and had thrown a lot of good riders. But old Shorty was a pretty wild hand himself with a bronc and he jumped at Bill's offer to stake him to that horse for the roundup.

Our first day's work was to be on the south side of Salt River, on Shute's range. The cattle were as wild as antelope, and the country rough and fairly brushy. At about eleven o'clock, while we were spread out driving some ridges, we could see Shorty on another ridge. All of a sudden his horse tapped off in a bucking match. Shorty put up a good ride for a while, then suddenly he did a parabola from the horse's back and didn't get up. His horse bucked on a little farther, then stopped when his bridle reins caught on a Spanish dagger cactus.

When a couple of us reached him, Shorty was sitting sort of humped over, holding one spur in his hand, the strap broken. He couldn't answer us when we asked if he was hurt, but one look convinced us that he was, and pretty badly too. Catching his horse and knocking a bunch of bald cholla cactus from his belly and legs, I changed saddles and we lifted Shorty into the saddle on my horse. It was about six miles over the top of the backbone main ridge to Mark Hicks' Ranch at Wheatfield, the closest road 'o us. With me leading his horse and another cowboy holding him on, 'horty humped forward, hanging on to the saddle horn for dear life. He groaned at every move of his horse during that entire six mile ride. At Wheatfield, Mark called an ambulance from Globe and at long last Shorty was on his way to a doctor and the hospital. For days we had no report on his condition until Mark Hicks rode across the mountain to relay the news that Shorty had bled so much inside that the X-rays couldn't show what was broken and what wasn't. The doctors *did* know that many of his ribs had been broken away from the back-bone when he had landed on his back on a sharp edge of granite rock. It was a cinch that he wouldn't be back to complete *this* roundup, if he ever came out of it at all, and Bill Lee was pretty upset at having furnished the horse that had boogered him up so badly.

In those days I still had less sense than the law allows, so I offered to take that horse in my string during the rest of the works. Bill told me not to spare the spurs if he threw any fits with me.

"Just take to him like he belonged to you, and if you kill him in the process he's paid for. Just don't let him hurt *you,* that's all."

I did have a few interesting sessions with him. The first was when he tried to pull a whizzer one early morning not far from camp. I took to him so strong he thought I was a wildcat. That go-around discouraged him for a week. I roped a runaway steer in the brushy draw on him another day and he tried me out again. And lost. When the works were over and we were driving to Globe to ship, he picked up a few chollas in his flank and began bucking and kicking the stir-rups some. But by then he had sort of grown leery of the after-effects, and didn't turn on strong.

The day I cut my string of horses to leave Coon Creek, Bill Lee offered him to me for fifty dollars.

"You're the only man I ever had ride him that didn't get hurt or bucked off. He's no good to me, and my daughter *sure* don't want him."

"I don't want him either," I told him, "but if you'll take thirty-five, I'll lead him off."

Bill sat down in the kitchen and wrote me out a bill of sale, and I had myself another horse. I stayed at George Cline's ranch on the Tonto the next night, and he tried to trade me an old owl-headed pelican for him. By then I had grown sort of fond of that wild-eyed cayuse and wouldn't trade.

I wound up back at the Cartwright Ranch on Cave Creek for a few days, shoing up for their works. Then Bernard Gillespie came along and hired me for a watchman at the Red Rover silver mine nearby.

The Cartwright Ranch was on its last big roundup. From around three-thousand head of cattle, the Forest Service had cut Manford's permit to seven hundred. Charley, his brother, had his permit cut from one thousand to three hundred. Laird and Evans on New River had sold out. Logue Morris on Cave Creek was down to a handful of cattle, and later Tom Cavness died of a brain tumor and his widow sold the ranch.

This was the end of an era. The old days of big outfits and wild cattle, with even wilder cowboys to work them, were at an end; no more night guards, singing to a herd of nervous cattle to keep them from stampeding; no more long trail drives to the railroad shipping pens; no more rough string horses to uncork on cold, frosty mornings. This was the cock tail guard for the old-time cattle men; the *last* before the dawn of a new era.

Today, the old cattle-drive trails are grown over or plowed under. Barbed wire fences criss-cross the great sweeps of once open range country. Docile muley cattle stare curiously at tourists speeding by on super-highways where once wild, sharp-horned cattle made life real interesting for the cowboys, and vice versa.

A way of life has now passed into history. As the cowboys have grown fewer in number with the passing years, the garb which once distinguished them alone has become fashionable with people who have never even seen a herd of cattle, except perhaps on television. When the present-day tourist's little boy spots a man in boots and a big hat and asks, "Mommy, is that a cowboy?", Mommy can only answer, "I guess so," adding under her breath, "Or maybe he's just a barber. Who knows!"

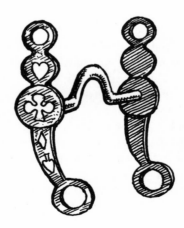

Epilogue   Thirty Years Later

A fellow once remarked: "Old cowboys never die; they just smell that-a-way." But I am not too sure about the truth of that statement, at least the part about never dying; for, some thirty years later, I find myself one of only a small remnant of the old boys I knew and worked with in the saddle days. The long end of them have cashed in their chips by now or are retired to pasture like an old cow horse.

I am still in a pretty good spot to see and hear what is going on in the cow business of modern day Arizona because, since 1951, I have been brand inspector for the Live Stock Sanitary Board of Arizona in the Tucson district. Then too, the Arizona Cattle Growers Association, covering the activities of ranchers statewide, kindly sends me its Weekly Market Report and Newsletter. In it I may read a letter from a rancher telling of the rain last week down around St. David, for instance, usually with the writer's familiar comment:

"One more good rain needed to keep our feed growing, to carry us through into shipping season. Our calves are going to be pretty light this year as we only had a few scattered showers in September on most of our range, and only two of our tanks caught any water. Our son Jack is in college this year at Tempe, where he is taking a course in business administration. We would sure like to attend the November meeting of the Cattle Growers, but guess we'll have to postpone that pleasure on account of we will be on Roundup about that time. If you hear of, or see, a good cowboy that looks like he might be able to turn a cow and that wants a job, send him down, — but not a family man with school age children, for we are fourteen miles from a school and not on the school bus route. The last man we hired couldn't shoe his own horses and sure didn't know much about working cattle. Quit us right in the middle of spring roundup with the excuse that the hours were too long and the pay too little. We were paying him $150 per month and his board. Even had to furnish him a saddle and bedroll."

Or I may read another letter which states:

"We contracted our cattle to a California buyer early, for 34c for steers and 32c for heifers straight across—delivered at Globe—no shrink, just a twelve-hour stand in the corrals overnight. We've sold to this man before, and he is mighty fine to do business with. He made all the arrangements for the trucks, and says the calves he bought from us last time made fine gains in his feed pens. When is it going to rain again?"

On another page of the Newsletter is a list of the Auction Markets, the number of cattle sold at each, plus prices at Phoenix, Yuma, Casa Grande, and Tucson. These chatty, informal bits of news from all corners of our State give a pretty good picture of the cattle people of today in contrast to those of the days long gone – when everything was done the hard way.

Of course there are a few outfits still left which haven't gone modern to any great degree, but even they aren't nearly as primitive as they were in my day. Roads have made the greatest difference, I believe. Bulldozers and road machinery can scrape out a road just about anywhere now, and have. Some of them couldn't quite be classed as boulevards yet, but they are passable. After driving for miles up some rocky, crooked canyon to reach an isolated ranch, it still amazes me to find a neat, modern frame house equipped with hot and cold running water, electric lights and all the modern conveniences enjoyed in town, all furnished by a Kohler plant and butane tanks.

With refrigeration, television sets, and, quite often, telephones, ranchers never had it so good; but with the blessings of access to hard-to-reach ranches also come a few headaches. The cities and towns of Arizona, which is becoming one of the fastest growing Western states, have increased populationwise by leaps and bounds. As a result the city folk, on warm, sunny weekends or holidays, will load up the old station wagon with a picnic lunch, the kids, the dog, and whatever else they can think of, and head for the countryside. Most of 'em have no destination in view when they leave home.

"We'll just drive until we see a nice place to eat our lunch, then camp," a typical family will agree.

So they take the first road that looks like it may lead into country new to them, and merrily they roll along. The farther they go, the worse the road becomes, and Mama starts to worry.

"John, I think we should have turned off on that other road back there."

But John, with adventure in his blood and lots of horses under the hood of his station wagon, is not to be deferred until he sees where the road leads to. Along about 11:30 they may come to a cattle guard in a fence across the road, with a sign reading: IX Ranch. No Hunting. A mile or so further along, John looks at his wrist watch and says:

"Keep an eye out for a good camping place and we'll stop."

"There's one, there's one!" Mama and the kids all shout at once, pointing to some shady oak trees and a windmill off to the left about a quarter of a mile.

A dim, little-used road leads them down to a corral, the windmill and a 6,000 gallon galvanized storage tank. John parks the car near the gate to the corral, and Mama and the kids and Skippy, the dog, all pile out and head for the brush on a pretended exploration mission.

"Jimmy, you stay with Daddy," Mama orders. "Judy and I will be right back."

Skippy, yelping his head off is already in hot pursuit of a chipmunk along the dry creek bed, and 11-year-old Jimmy isn't far behind.

By the time they have all straggled back to the car, John has decided to build a fire for Mama to cook some hamburgers and coffee on. The trouble is there doesn't seem to be any dry wood available; but the old pioneer spirit of making do with what one has prevails, and John begins pulling good dry oak and mesquite pieces out of the corral fence for his fire. After two or three abortive attempts to get a blaze started, John has another brilliant idea. The tank sets on a platform of boards, and he manages to break off a couple of feet of one to use as kindling. His penknife doesn't cut shavings very well, but after a while he has a few, plus a cut finger which doesn't help his temper very much. There is a slight breeze which Mama complains will blow the smoke at them, so John places his wood close to the corral fence to shelter his fire.

While the liliput army unloads the table cloth, food and what not, Skippy sets up another clamor, down the creek this time.

"Gee, Dad, you think maybe Skip has a bear treed?" asks Jimmy.

"No, Son, I hardly think so. But why don't you get your .22 out of the car and we'll go see what he *does* have."

So the two mighty nimrods go on safari while Mama and Judy stay in camp to prepare the feast. Skippy is furiously digging a hole straight down to China when they reach him, determined to avenge the insulting remarks that long-snouted rock squirrel made just before he dived into his hole. Finally all three give up on ever getting to the squirrel and seek new fields of entertainment. John finds an old, empty condensed milk can, remnant of some past camp or roundup, and brings it back to the tank where he places it on the platform as a target. He and Jimmy take turns shooting at it with no great degree of accuracy—except that they do manage to puncture the lower past of the tank in three places.

"Look, Dad, there's water coming out," Jimmy exclaims.

"By George, there *is* a little bit. Funny they would make tanks so thin. Anyway their water doesn't cost anything out here, as it does us in town. The windmill does all the work!"

About then Mama sounds the car horn to call the men in for lunch.

"Boy, this is the life," John expounds as he picks his teeth. "Good fresh air, swell scenery, and no one looking down your collar to tell you what to do or not to do."

After a while Judy and Mama wander off searching for pretty rocks and whatever else they might find to take home as mementos of their picnic. John and Jimmy walk through the corral on their way to the top of a nearby hill to scout buffalo, Indians, outlaws or whatever else may inhabit this wilderness. The back side of the corral opens into a holding pasture, but the gate isn't too hard to open.

"Might as well leave it open, Jimmy, because we'll be coming back through it in a little while," John tells his son.

Shortly after they all leave camp, a vagrant little breeze moseys down the draw and scatters the still-burning campfire into the bottom of the dry corral fence. Little by little a few, wind-encouraged flames lick at the dry bark of some cedar poles near the ground. Faster now it licks its way to the dry wood above it, finally to race with crackling speed to more and more tinderdry pieces. John and Jimmy are the first to become aware that all is not well when Jimmy, from his vantage point atop a rock, notices the smoke and sounds the alarm. He and John race back down the hill, climb over the fence and run around the corral toward where the car is parked, only to come to a sudden halt when confronted by a big old gentle Hereford bull that had been on his way to water when they burst upon him from a corner of the corral. The old bull, as surprised by them as they are by him, whirls about to face them.

"My God, the car, Jimmy, the car!" John shouts. "It will burn up if we don't move it quick. Give me the gun and stay way back. This bull is vicious, but I've *got* to get to our car."

Taking quick aim, he pumps a shot at the bull's head. Stung by the first shot, the old bull turns half way around, only to receive the second shot in the stomach as he trots off. John races to the car, all thumbs in his excitement, as he clambers behind the wheel and roars away from the burning corrai, rocks and dust flying from the rear wheels. Once far enough from the burning corral, he begins riding the horn button to summon the girls. No piper calling the clans together from the misty glens of the Highlands ever created more of a raucous tocsin. Mama and Judy, skirts flying, reach the car all out of breath.

"What happened?"

"How did the fence get on fire?"

"What were you shooting at?"

"What? What? What?"

"I think we had better head toward home," John decides. "You know, we damn near lost our car."

So they all get into the station wagon and drive back toward town; the end of an exciting day in the country.

Of course the rancher cannot seem to find much humor in the situation when he finds his corral burned down and all of his storage water gone — especially since the well is weak, and it takes a lot of pumping to recover 6,000 gallons of lost water. Nor is he overjoyed when he finds all of his cattle out of the pasture because the gate was left open; about two weeks of hard riding wasted. One day, weeks later, he spots buzzards circling on a hillside and reins his horse over that way to have a looksee. There lie the remains of his bull, martyr to the city man's carelessness and ignorance.

No wonder he curses the day that road was built. It's a tossup, however, for without the road his life would be ever so much harder. With it, each week he can truck into the auction yards any undesirable stock he has, and realize the best possible market price by delivering the cattle in good shape, and fast.

There is no doubt about it, there have been many changes in the ranching and marketing phases of the cattle business in the past three decades. Almost every ranch now has its own corral and loading chute, plus a truck with a stock rack which enables the rancher to haul a few horses by road to whatever part of the range he wants to get to before he unloads and rides into the rougher places. Or he can haul cattle to the home place for doctoring, then put them in a pasture where he can keep an eye on them until they are well enough to turn out onto the range once more. A truck is almost a must to the rancher in these times. Nowadays, trucking firms with whole fleets of stock trucks go to the ranches and haul out any number of cattle to almost any destination desired, in jig time.

Feeding pens are another new wrinkle since my day in Arizona.

There are any number of well-planned and operated feed yards where cattle are fed scientifically balanced rations on gain-per-day (sixty or ninety-day basis) charges. Experts in these fields are continually searching for new and better formulas, and the Animal Science departments of our Universities and State Colleges are constantly experimenting on new feeds and new ideas.

Slaughter and packing houses have undergone tremendous changes from the old fly-specked, unsanitary places where meat was processed in years past. Modern packing houses must be built to exact specifications, fly and vermin-free — with overhead rails where beef never touches the floor from the time the carcasses roll through the kill door until they reach the freezing rooms; skinned, dressed and ready to be delivered as whole carcasses or in any form desired. Each packing house now has its own Lay Veterinary Meat Inspectors, assigned by the Chief Veterinary Meat Inspector of the State. These men conduct ante-mortem and post-mortem inspections and enforce sanitary requirements in the most stringent way.

"Meanwhile, back at the ranch," as they say in the Western movies.

Eastern people began to grow really interested in the Southwest with the introduction of air conditioning and refrigerated cooling into buildings and homes. Many of those coming into this part of the country had already made their pile in various businesses, from textile mills to kingpin of the numbers racket — or what have you. Some had to move West because their doctors advised it for health reasons.

The appeal of being a big rancher in Arizona has sent many hurrying to seek an agent to find them the sort of place they could see in their mind's eye; thousands of acres of rolling grassland dotted with herds of fat, white-faced cattle and a big, rambling ranch house with lots of guest rooms where they could entertain their visiting eastern friends. Why, with a foreman to do the work, it couldn't miss fire. All one had to do was round up the cattle twice a year, brand the calves and watch the money roll in. Hadn't they seen it all done on television?

Usually the agent, who wasn't behind the door when the brains were passed out, likes to take these prospective customers out to see the ranch in early spring after the rains have brought up the grass, so it will look all green and pretty. In speaking of the acreage he may remark:

"Let's see now—there is a section and a half in the Black Jack Pasture, isn't there? And the Windmill Pasture has over a section in it."

Before he stops talking the prospect gets the impression that if he buys this ranch he will be the owner of three or four counties at least. He is not yet used to the vastness of the Western scene. He is usually very well impressed with what he has seen so far, and pretty sure he will close the deal, but there are still some things he wants to look into before he signs on the dotted line. So he has his agent look up the recorded deeds and titles of the owned land, the leases on what State land is included, and how much Forest land belonging to his Uncle Sam he will be using. His good wife is often the one who puts the clincher on the deal. She has already picked out the site for their house "on that darling little hill with the lovely view."

Let us for awhile follow the fortunes of one such pair of new ranch owners. The first three months after the purchase have passed with a flurry of activity. The dream house is now a reality. There are gleaming white new corrals, and paddocks for the horses. Tack rooms and various other improvements are in place on the flat below the house. Everything is complete now except for the stock. The cattle that were on the ranch before the purchase were definitely not what the new owners had had in mind, so they have decided to sell those off right away and replace them with others more to their liking. Fred's good friend and business partner, now in public relations in California, has sent them a foreman with the highest of recommendations, "Nev" Hughes by name. The "Nev" (short for Nevada) is a nickname acquired while he was manager of a combination guest and cattle ranch a few miles out of Reno, Nevada. He is a very personable young man; tall, goodlooking, and handsomely dressed in black gambler striped riding trousers, a forty dollar pearl gray Stetson hat, expensive red boots with white inlays in the tops, and a fringed leather jacket. A six-inch square silver belt buckle immediately captures one's attention, with its raised letters N. E. V. in turquoise diagonally across its face.

A year after Nev's arrival, Mr. Ranch Owner begins to wonder if he has made a wise choice in foremen. There seem to be a good many flies in the ointment. His C. P. A. informs him that he has paid out an unreasonable price per cow unit for his choice Herefords and received practically nothing for the ones he sold off. The rancher recalls that the first roundup had been a terrible fiasco. Seems the cattle just couldn't be found, especially those in the rough mountainous part of the ranch. Nev had hired most of his crew through an employment office in town, but he did pick up two local cowboys he had met at a bar.

Nev's experience on the small Reno ranch, where the little herd of cattle kept was only dressing for the dude trade, hadn't prepared him for these mountains too steep to climb, nor this brush too thick to ride through. The wranglers he had had under his orders at Reno had called him Mr. Hughes, and never, never questioned his orders. These two local cowboys just seemed to ignore his presence once they got back into the rough country. True, they brought in cattle from impossible places, where he couldn't even see any, but that was no excuse for them to act like he wasn't even along. One day when he had lost his bearings and started hollering at his crew to turn the cattle in the opposite direction, they had just kept on driving ahead, so he had hastened up to read them the riot act. They had just looked at him in a sort of dumb way and pretended they hadn't even heard him, which ruffled his feathers even worse than if they had talked back. A sort of helpless feeling had hit Nev as they topped a rise from which he could see the ranch directly dead ahead. No one likes to admit he is wrong, and Nev least of all at this point, so he had just puffed up like a pouter pigeon and began making an ass of himself, chousing the drags along so lively that the whole bunch of cattle had soon scattered out all over the landscape. At that point these two hayseed cowboys had just moved away from the herd, dismounted and squatted down to smoke a cigarette, while Nev's other green hands had dashed around in a high lope *behind* the cattle, swinging their new ropes and yelling as loud as they could.

Soon cattle were running in all directions at once, with riders in hot pursuit, each apparently trying to reach a different destination than the ranch corrals. Nev, with a quick glance over his shoulder, had seen the two cowhands watching the race from their grandstand seats atop the hill. By that time he was so mad he could have swallowed a horned toad backward. Imagine those louts deserting the drive right when he needed them most. It was time someone taught that pair a lesson, and he was just the Bucko to do the job. His palomino was wringing wet with sweat and slinging flecks of foam from his mouth as Nev sat him up with a flourish near the closest man. Dismounting, he had strode over to the squatting cowboy, stiff legged as a mad ostrich.

"On your feet, fellow. We are going to have this out right now, and afterward you may draw your pay and get off of this ranch, both of you!"

Nev weighed about two hundred and was twenty years younger than the slender cowboy he was challenging, but he wasn't thinking of that right now. All he wanted was to get the bile out of his craw. When the cowboy, still squatting, had looked up at Nev from beneath his hat brim and grinned, Nev had lost all his remaining control. His right boot had drawn back to kick this infuriating peasant clear down the hillside, but the boot had never landed. Instead, two surprisingly strong hands had grabbed his ankle as the cowboy sprang erect like a jack-in-the-box, and Nev had hit the ground flat on his back, sliding a few feet down the hillside among the rocks. Before he could even sit up, the wiry cowboy had been right in the middle of him, slamming away with both fists at Nev's nose, eyes, and belly. His nose spurting blood like a soda fountain, Nev had tried to roll out from beneath his assailant, but the cowboy wasn't to be dislodged. Years of flanking, and holding big husky calves by the branding fire had made him tough as nails, with reflexes like a cougar. Nev had taken the worst beating of his life on that hillside, with the added disgrace of tearing the whole seat out of his fancy gamblers pants. Holding his handkerchief to his still streaming nose, he had managed to get on his horse and ride back to the ranch.

News gets around via the grapevine in the country as well as it does anywhere else, and in no time at all this new rancher had been pegged as no good to work for among all the local cowboys, all on account of his foreman. Of course Nev had shaded the story to his own advantage, claiming both of the cowboys had ganged up on him, and jumped him when he wasn't looking. If the rancher had known what really happened he might have made a change in foremen because he was a fair man, even if he did not know much about ranching yet. As a result of that little fracas, Nev was never able to hire a local cowboy again, and neighboring ranchers didn't bother to go out of their way to offer any help to the new rancher.

Nev's ignorance of the mechanics of a working ranch had kept the ranch operation books continually in the red ink. Transfusions from the owner's banking account still didn't get it in the black, so the owner had begun taking a new look at the situation, trying to figure out what was wrong. He had talked about his troubles to his local banker, his C.P.A., and a few ranchers who belonged to his lodge in town. The banker had been of the opinion that he was over-extended and should sell part of the ranch that was least desirable. The C.P.A.'s idea had been to write off his losses as a tax deduction, and the ranchers had given him a number of good pointers about where he had gone wrong. But one thing they had all agreed on was that he must get rid of Nev.

Nev had created quite a scene when his boss broke the news to him, and the owner's wife had almost had hysterics.

"Nev is *so* helpful with our guests, and such a gentleman," she argued. "I just think you're mean. Plain mean."

The ranch now has a new foreman, a good one, who knows the business and has the respect of both the owner and everyone in the country around him. He draws a good salary and has a working partnership which gives him a percentage of any profit the ranch makes above expenses. The owner has taken his C.P.A.'s advice and written off in tax deductions part of the losses the ranch incurred under Nev's management. And he has sold off a part of the range that wasn't particularly useful to him. Now everybody is happy except the owner's wife. She still insists that *no one* can mix a cocktail to compare with those that Nev whipped up.

Later down the line land speculators from the East came into the deserts and mountains looking for land to buy, or to tie up in long term leases. They had sniffed out an influx of people and businesses which would be moving into the Southwest in the near future. They haunted the recorders' offices of county seats, scanning the land plats and maps to find out who owned old homesteads or any deeded land, no matter what the location. Old timers, who couldn't have sold their ranches for three dollars an acre on unimproved land a few years before, were confronted with offers of from one to three hundred dollars an acre, by smooth talking gents with a ready pen and money to back up the offers. Some of the old ranchers, plagued by drought or pressure from the banks to pay off some of the paper the banks had been carrying on their spreads, sold out, lock, stock, and barrel. Others kept their back country and sold off land that lay alongside highways or easily accessible places.

Within a couple of years just about all the available land within a radius of fifty miles of the larger towns had been bought up. Then a building boom began to take place. Almost over night, it seemed, tract houses sprang from the ground. First close in to the cities, then farther and farther out; all kinds of houses. Some were small, with one or two bedrooms and a carport. Others quite large and fancy, with walled patios, swimming pools, and elaborate landscaping. In normally dry country where lack of water had long been the reason no one lived on the land, water had been developed and pumped, even to high elevations. Hilltops had been leveled, and great rambling homes built on them, with superb views in any direction. Country clubs and golf courses grew like toad stools, watered by pipelines and sprinkler systems, complete with sand traps and water hazards. New dams were built on any stream that furnished enough water to create a lake. Motor boat sales began to boom, and on weekends and holidays the highways were crowded with cars and trucks pulling boat trailers, headed for one lake or another. Forty years ago if some oldtimer had met such an outfit on the road he would have been sure he shouldn't have stopped at that last "thirst parlor."

At night near the towns the whole sky was soon lighted up by neon signs and electric lights, the streets and roads lined with cafes, supper clubs, stores, night clubs, bowling lanes, drive-ins and any other number of businesses. Fire, police, and ambulance sirens combined with the roar of heavy traffic on paved streets that a few years back were dusty roads where sidewinder snakes and coyotes roamed at night. Progress had come to the range lands in a big way.

The higher and higher land prices soon resulted in increased tax rates, making it a losing game to hold on to land just to have a place to graze a few head of cattle. So more ranchers sold, just because they couldn't afford to pay such taxes. Some of the Johnny-come-latelys, with plenty of money at their disposal, have bought up much of this choice rangeland throughout the State. Tax deductions have afforded them a convenient loophole to make up for any losses suffered through ignorance, mismanagement, or any other causes. Many of these men still conduct businesses back where they came from, and if those businesses show too large a profit in any one year, they deduct a whopping ranch loss to even up the score so they won't have to pay Uncle Sam much of a tax on the business gain. Some of them only bought ranches with that idea in mind in the first place. To these people the ranch is just a plaything, not a money-making business nor their only means of livelihood as it is to the oldtime rancher. With a benevolent government trying to buy good will and business by giving away huge sums of money all over the world, I guess they figure that they may as well get their nose in the feed trough too.

It is fortunate that this stripe of cow rancher is in the minority, and that there are still many ranchers whose primary concern is making a go of their business. *Real* ranch people have long been a rugged, individual breed, they have stood on their own two feet and battled, through their legislatures and Congress to control and operate their own business in their own way without any more interference than is absolutely necessary. They have never asked many favors of their county, state or federal governments. During the Second World War, under Franklin Roosevelt's presidency and his alphabetical gravy train, very few of them signed up to receive federal aid in any form. They preferred to go it alone, with no help or hindrance from the government. And, except for a scattered few, they still do.

With all the so-called "modern improvements," cattle ranching seems to have lost much of the color and romance of former days; the romance which enticed boys to run away from home and become cowboys and, once they had gotten a taste of the life, *kept* them in its magic grasp forever after. Only those of us old timers who have lived that life can recall the thrills and excitement of topping off some old hammerheaded bronc on a frosty morning, along about sunup. Or of seeing our loop fit around the wide horns of some old renegade steer after a breakneck race around a brushy, rough mountainside and suddenly realizing we'd latched onto an old bushwhacker which had outsmarted and outrun a lot of older and better cowboys than we ever hoped to be.

Once the steer was caught, it was up to us to get him to the herd or pasture or corral from which he would later be shipped. We asked no odds. Whatever we started, it was up to us to finish. Sometimes, if the going got too rough, another cowboy might offer to help. Mostly though, the other men figured that, if you didn't expect to lead him in,.you shouldn't have roped him in the first place.

Sometimes the leading was a lot harder than getting our twine on him to start with. Maybe a half a day later, when we finally got him to pasture and let him go, we knew we had made a hand: the highest honor a cowboy ever hoped to attain. We might come in scratched by stiff brush and with a badly rope-burned hand and torn clothes. Our shins, where old Mossy's horns had beaten our legs, might be so sore we could hardly stand; and with blood from both of us on our chaps and saddle, we might sort of look like we had tangled with a den of bobcats. Yet we wouldn't have traded places with the governor of the State. We had caught and led in this old renegade ox which had been the subject of many a yarn around campfires of this and other roundups, and we had done it *alone*. Tomorrow we might have to catch and lead in another, but if so, it was all in the day's work.

I guess that one of the things that kept life interesting was *not* knowing what would happen next. When three or four of us crawled out of our soogans, mounted our night horses and rode out to the bed ground to relieve the previous guards, we never knew, as we rode around the herd, whether or not we might have a stampede before the handle of the Big Dipper in the northern sky had moved our four hours worth. Sometimes we did, and at those times we were lucky if we even made it back to camp by noon the next day.

Cowboys who bellyached about the weather, we called sunshine cowboys.

When we had a lot of big husky fall calves to brand, we would pair off in three or four sets of flankers. A couple of good head ropers would ride into the herd and, with a flip of their rope, cast a neat overhand loop around the neck of a three to four-hundred pound calf. With a quick jerk on the rope to take up the slack in the loop, they would head for the branding fire at a lope with a mad and surprised calf bucking and bawling at the end of about thirty feet of manila hemp. One flanker would step in from the side, grab hold of the rope and let it slide through his hands until the calf was alongside him. Reaching over the calf's shoulder with his right hand, he would catch its brisket while his left came over its back and grasped its right flank. With the calf bucking and nearing the fire, just as all its feet were off the ground at once, the flanker would give a quick jerk toward himself. The jerk would turn the calf on its side in the air. It would hit the ground on its right side as the flanker's left hand slid down the flank to the foreleg, just above the dewclaws, his left knee on its neck and his right hand twisting its nose up so that only the back of its head touched the ground. His partner would grab the left hind leg just before the calf hit the ground, slide to a sitting position behind the calf, his left boot heel fitted just above the hock of the calf's right hind leg, pushing the leg ahead as far as it could go. Its left hind leg would be tucked under his armpit while he held it by the gamble cord with his left hand. With his right hand he held the small part of the leg. Once the calf was in that position, no matter how he struggled, the flankers could hold him firmly while he was being branded, castrated, and earmarked.

Sounds easy. 'Taint though. Takes a heap of practice and speed and perfect timing on the part of the flankers. With one man branding and one marking and the sour smell of burning hair on the air, there were only a couple of surprised bellows from the calf before he was released to trot back into the herd and rejoin his worried mammy in just about the length of time it takes to count off sixty seconds.

The flankers would alternate on downing the calves because that is the hardest part of the job. One split timing mishap, or the loss of a hand hold and one of those big, husky calves was apt to kick the flanker down, step on his face, or get away from him entirely. It sure would make the roper mad when that happened, and he had to drag a calf by the flankers for a second time. Sometimes he would try to jerk the calf right over the top of them, if he was riled up enough. After flanking some seventy-five to one hundred head of those big calves in one after-noon, those cowboys sure didn't need any setting-up exercises to work up an appetite for the next meal.

Nowadays you are apt to find cowboys working calves into a squeeze chute which catches them by the neck, tilts over like a table and eliminates all the heavy work, while they are being branded with irons heated by a butane burner. New wrinkles such as band castra-tors are in use on many ranches. These have special rubber bands which are applied to the scrotum, to continually constrict until it dries up and drops off for want of blood supply. Some use a pinching tool called Burdizzo for the same purpose. We old timers tried those methods thirty years ago, and abandoned them when we found that they were a long way from fool proof and often left a percentage of staggy steers on the range. A good sharp knife and a cowboy who knows how to use it *is* fool proof.

Every outfit used to have from one to a half dozen cutting horses, depending on the size of the ranch. It was a pleasure to watch a man ride into a herd on one of these and to see the team work between man and horse as they smoothly worked the animal wanted out to the edge of the herd and, with a quick little movement at the right minute, cut it out and send it on its way to the cut herd. Try as the calf might to dodge back into the main herd, that old pony had it blocked at every turn, and after a few tries there wasn't any place to go *except* to the cut. It was fast and tiring work for the horse, and in big herds I've seen a cowboy change cutting horses as many as three times before he had the herd clean. He couldn't afford to work one horse beyond his endurance, or until he got so hot he might bow up and lose interest. While the other horses made it on grass, or a little hay now and then, the cutting horse was a privileged character. He received his morral of grain twice a day, along with the chuck wagon team, and he was only used to cut cattle. There were no circle drives nor dragging calves to the fire for him. He was a specialist in his field, and worked only at his specialty.

I've seen cutting horses so good they could cut fly specks from a can of black pepper on many ranches. If there are any left now, they are few and far between. The only ones I have seen for years are performing at rodeos and cutting horse contests, where they are crowd pleasers and sell to enthusiasts of the sport for enough money to drill an oil well in Texas. And there's a heap of difference between their work on a smooth rodeo field and the actual ranch work of former days. On the rodeo field, the calves are bunched into a fence corner, then cut out of the little herd while another rider tries to haze them back in and the cutting horse tries to keep them cut out. There are no rocks or prairie dog holes underfoot, no dust to obscure the horse's vision, and usually only two open sides to block his calf in instead of the whole outdoors. Four or five calves are about all he is expected to work out before he has a good rest.

Nowadays most ranchers cut through lanes and gates. Some use what is called a dodge gate at the end of a narrow lane to turn the cattle either to the right or to the left. Others have a series of four or five gates set in a circle in the center of the lane. Filled, it will hold perhaps six to eight head of stock. With one man working each gate from the outside, one man gets into the ring with the cattle, afoot. As the cattle rotate around, the men working the gates try to open their gate in time to let one head slip through and hold the others back, to be let through another one of the gates into the different corrals. The system works pretty well with gentle cattle although it isn't long before they tear up the gates or jump on top of them and mash them down. I have seen the first couple of drafts of cattle entirely destroy such a cutting arrangement in less than twenty minutes.

The general run of cowboys ranchers are able to hire these days couldn't ride a cutting horse when he began to duck and dart, even if he had a stranglehold on the saddle horn with both hands. It isn't that the boys growing up now are less active or less willing than they were in my day. There simply isn't enough work to do for them to become adept at it. Any old button of a boy used to have his rope in his hand most of the time. If he was driving the drags behind the herd, he was always practicing roping the cattles' hind legs. He learned to forefoot cattle or horses. He tried every throw known, and he got pretty dang good at it too. Just about any old waddie was a fine roper, afoot or horseback.

Most cattle now are so gentle they seldom break into a trot, and unless it's an occasional crossbred Brahma or Santa Gertrudis, there is seldom a determined bunch quitter in a herd. Once in a while a little calf will get scared, curl his tail over his back and head for the horizon. The chances are if he does, and some cowboy builds a loop in his rope and gives chase, he'll probably have to run the calf until it faints and falls down before he can catch it. In my day, if a cowboy chasing such a calf came back without catching it, the boss would have given him a cold stare and commented:

"Some cowboy! You a-horseback and him afoot, and you couldn't catch him? Reckon you can ride the bed wagon without falling off?"

No doubt about it, roping *is* hard on cattle. There is a right and a wrong way to do anything. When an animal cannot be turned back into the bunch inside of a hundred yards or so, the right way is to rope him right then; not to wait until he has built up such a lead that the cowboy has to chase him for a mile or more before he can even get close enough for a throw. Under those circumstances, even if he is caught, the animal is so far from the herd that he is going to be mighty hard to bring back. He's hot, tired, mad and sullen. Won't lead, or drive either. The herd has to be held up until the cowboy wallows him back, usually skinned up, rope-burned and exhausted. With a fast catch and quick return no harm is done. The weight loss on a long run, plus the rough treatment in getting him back, raises havoc with the rancher's margin of profit in these days of selling cattle by weight instead of by the head, as was the custom in earlier years.

It's a rare thing to see a steer three years old or over on a ranch today. That is the only kind a rancher could sell once. Now, veal calves and some yearlings are of marketable age, very few older than that. So, aside from rodeo cowboys who are steer ropers, most ranch hands do not even see such stock on the range any more. Where once we handled herds of those big steers for days, weeks, or even months at a time, on occasion driving them hundreds of miles to shipping points, with night herding and often bad stampedes, today's cowboys will never experience the thrill of working the point, swing or flank of a trail drive of big wide-horned steers, strung out for a mile or more, heads up and travelling along almost like saddle horses. Or at night of sleeping with their clothes on and with one eye open, expecting to hear at any moment the awesome noise of hundreds of steers as they all leap to their feet at once, and with a roar of pounding hooves, horns popping together, dash madly and blindly over anything in their way, in a wild stampede.

Riding at breakneck speed through the dark of night over unfamiliar ground to overtake the leaders and try to turn them into a circle is not recommended, either for the best of health or longevity. Many cowboys have done it and survived. Others have not. I'm one of the lucky ones, but I can recall a few times when my chances looked so slim I would have traded places with a steeplejack with a frayed rope. But when the run was over and the steers were going around and around in a huge mill, slowly settling into a walk again, and the boss rode over and said: "Good work, cowboy", we knew the pride of a job well done and that we had made a hand. About the only way a cowboy can get hurt now on the way to the market is to mash a finger in a truck gate or get kicked in the shins tailing some critter up the loading ramp. If a steer acts too rollicky he is put into the squeeze chute and given a tranquilizer shot, and the cowboy's troubles are over.

Even the movie companies are hard pressed to get enough cattle together to simulate a trail drive. The last Western I watched had a herd of perhaps seventy yearlings, and the best stampede they could muster was a slow lope across the picture. I expect they had to use up a quarter of a mile at least to get those gentle little steers out of a trot before they came into camera range. It wasn't very convincing. There were two or three shots of the stampede. Same yearlings each time. I recognized several in the herd by their markings.

Even in the old days there were many more small cattle ranches than there were big spreads. By small, I mean outfits running from three to six or seven hundred head of mother cows. Most of the real big ranches were company owned. In much earlier days, before my time, English capital established huge ranches in Texas and several other Western states; ranches like the XIT at Hereford, Texas whose brand stood for Ten in Texas, indicating that the ranch owned most of the land in ten counties of the Panhandle. It was so vast that the overhead was too great and, combined with a few bad years, only lasted a few years at the original size.

Then there were the Diamond A Ranches, known as the Victoria

Land and Cattle Company, with ranches in New Mexico, South Dakota, Montana, Texas, and South America. The company still has ranches, but these have shrunk to fractions of their former size.

There were Miller and Lux of California, the Aztec Land and Cattle Company of northern Arizona, The L F D of west Texas and eastern New Mexico. I could go on and on with the list of big ranchers which once grazed their cattle over untold thousands of acres across the West. Only a very few survive today, and these are only shadows of their former size.

Except in rare cases where personality quarrels caused bad blood between them, ranchers used to work together quite well. When one outfit set a date for the start of roundup, it sent word to the neighboring ranches inviting them to send a representative to ride on the roundup. That way if the neighbors had any stray stock on the ranch, the "rep" would be on hand to spot them and cut them into the holding herd to take home at the end of the roundup. Also he would see to it that any unbranded calves belonging to his ranch were branded in the proper owner's brand. But if for some reason a neighboring rancher could not send a rep, his cattle were taken care of and branded just as though he were represented, and at the end of roundup were either returned to him or kept in a pasture for him to come after later on.

I've been on many a roundup where reps almost outnumbered the ranch crew. Those days are gone too. Ranchers now seem to resent a neighbor even asking to ride with them when they work their cattle. They seldom even inform a neighbor of the date they plan to begin roundup. Seems they have developed a feudal outlook, not even offering the adjoining ranches a chance to look through their cattle when they get them together, to see whether there might be strays among them.

In the past few years I have driven up to ranches just before a meal and not even been invited to eat. That would never have happened in my time as a cowboy. Anyone, friend or foe, would have been invited to eat and probably to stay overnight, if it was late. If this is progress, you can have my share. I'll take the old days when neighbors were *neighbors* and even a total stranger was made welcome when he came to your door. Don't misunderstand me, there are still ranchers who observe the old customs and openhanded friendliness of the old West, but they are quite far in the minority and about as scarce as upper teeth on a cow.

Today's "new frontier" ranchman doesn't settle differences

man to man as the old timers did. His weapons are lawyers, and lawsuits dragged out for months through already overcrowded courts. In such cases lawyers are often the only financial winners in the long run.

The old timers could, and did, do most everything for themselves. They repaired their own windmills, built their own fences and corrals, and even houses. They raised, broke, shod, and rode their own horses. In other words, they were pretty self-sufficient at anything that had to do with ranch life. That do-it-yourself trait has pretty well vanished into the dim past. I know scores of today's ranchers who couldn't even tooth a cow to tell you how old she is. If something breaks down, the rancher is on the telephone calling a service company in town to come out and fix it for him. He couldn't shoe his own horse if his life depended on it. Somewhere along the way he has lost his self-sufficiency: a trait that built this Western country.

Many of the new innovations are time and labor saving, and I haven't anything against them; but I still contend that, given the same tools to work with, the old timers could, and would, have done a better job than is being done today. The world must keep turning, and progress will continue, but I see no bright future in our Western country for the cowman of modern times. For a few more years he may survive, even make more money, but he has lost something never to be regained: the color, the romance and the satisfaction of making a hand.

Preface to Glossary

Out of ignorant curiosity, a greenhorn may ask a cattle rancher: "How many cattle do you own?" Such a question is rank insult in the range country and almost a sure way to brand the asker as either a dude or a damn fool. It is just like asking a business man how much money he has in the bank.

Before the days of fenced ranches when cattle could, and did, range far and wide from their home ranches, cowmen only had a vague idea of the number of stock carrying their brand. About the only times they even cared to estimate were when they were applying to the banker for a loan or talking to the tax assessor. The figures they gave to the banker were pretty apt to run a trifle high. Of course, when talking to the tax assessor; well, now, that was a different story. Right away their ranch shrank to a little bitty old "greasy sack" outfit, with scarcely enough stock on the range to keep its owners supplied with frijole money. So the number of cattle a ranch actually ran can only be estimated rather roughly. Quien sabe?

The larger ranchers were chiefly located in the grasslands; while the mountain country, mostly situated on one or another of our National Forests, was dotted with many smaller outfits.

Only during the roundup season did even the big ranches work any sizeable number of cowboys. After the roundups were over and the cattle delivered to the shipping points on the railroad, most of the hands were laid off. A bronc rider or two might be kept on to break horses at some line camp where they could also keep up pasture fences, pump water at the wells, look after cattle and brand up calves missed on roundup. Each steady man had to be a jack-of-all-trades. About the only line he drew was when called upon to farm or do any kind of work where he had to be afoot. Batching in a line camp all by himself didn't bother him much as long as he could get into town once in a while to quench his thirst and spend his wages.

Cowboys were fairly plentiful in those days. A cattleman could usually expect to find several lying around town looking for a job most any time he needed one. Many rode the chuck line from ranch to ranch. They knew they were welcome to stay a day or a week at almost any ranch or camp they rode into. If no work was available they would ride on to another. It was not unusual for some of them to ride from Arizona to Colorado in one summer, following the chuck line.

Most of the small mountain outfits were family operations and necessarily ran their ranches as cheaply as they could. About the only times they hired any outside help were during the Spring and Fall roundups. Quite often the wife spent many of her hours astride a horse, working cattle alongside her man, and her children were taught to ride as soon as they could sit on a horse. Naturally, kids brought up on a ranch soon learned to do just about anything that had to be done, and gained a heap of self-reliance in the learning. I have ridden for such outfits where all the members of the family were real "brush poppers". They had to be, working short handed as they usually did.

I guess there are still a few such small enterprises which work just about the same way, but the work isn't nearly as strenuous as it was in those earlier days. Gentle cattle, more pastures and corrals, branding chutes and trucks have changed the picture considerably. Of all these factors, gentle cattle have made the greatest difference. When cattle were wild it took all hands to get together and drive even a handful. Now it's a breeze. It just takes time and patience to work a few old nellies out of the rough places onto a trail and down to the nearest corral. It may be easier on men, horses and cattle, but it sure is plumb downright monotonous. I am glad to have been a cowboy during a more exciting era of the West.

In the early days rodeos were not the big business they are now. When there was one, local cowboys would come from miles around to compete, and about the only professionals would be the clowns and maybe a special event like a Roman Ride, trick riders and ropers or some high school act with horses, contracted for by the local fathers to pep up the show. True, later some of the best cowboys, like Jake McClure, George Cline, Bob Crosby and others of their day, began to follow the shows from place to place as a business.

Where once working cowboys were in plentiful supply and pro-fessional rodeo men were in the minority, now the reverse is true. Real working cowboys who were practically born on a horse are almost non-existent today, while rodeos have gone on to be one of the big drawing cards of show business. The contestants have their own union, the R. C. A. (Rodeo Cowboys Association), once known to the members as the Turtle Association. Most of the members of the R. C. A. were never working cowboys. Some were, among the older men; but the majority are young fellows who wouldn't know which end of a cow watered out of a trough. In the rodeo arena, they go through their paces; competing in calf roping, team tying, bulldogging, bronc riding (saddle and bareback), and Brahma bull riding, and they put on a real good show. But I've worked on the range with some who sure couldn't make a hand at all in the brush and rocks of a mountain country.

As of 1963 the R. C. A. has a membership of almost 3,000. Its headquarters are in Denver, Colorado and Bill Linderman is President. I guess it's like prospecting; once rodeoing gets into a young fellow's blood, he doesn't think he can do anything else. But you'll seldom find rodeo cowboys working on a ranch. The pay is not high enough to suit them, the work is too hard and there are no cheers from the crowds, no bands playing and flags flying when they make a good ride or a good throw with their rope. They need glamour and adoration of the crowds, not a wet seat and a hungry gut.

In modern times, small roping clubs have sprung up like toad-stools all over the country. They can be found almost from coast to coast today. Rodeo enthusiasts, dude wranglers, in fact anyone with enough money to buy a horse and time enough to spare, can be found at one or another of these clubs, trying their hand at calf tying, team tying or barrel racing for a small fee. It's good practice for wouldbe rodeo cowboys, and a great many of them get their start this way. It is the closest thing to a working ranch they will ever encounter, — and that sure isn't very close.

Glossary

Esfaldas — (Spanish) Foothills or skirts of a mountain
Cienega — (Spanish) Boggy or muddy seep
To sleeper — Ear mark cattle without branding
Remuda — (Spanish) String of horses
Soogan — Quilt
Piggin string — Short, light-weight tie-down rope
Chaps — Short for chaparejos. Protective leg coverings
Mavericks — Unbranded cattle
Orejanas — (Spanish) Unbranded cattle
Dogie — Motherless calf
Stag — Ox
Muley cattle — Cattle without horns
Sabino — Roan horse
Lose "coup" — Indian phrase for lose face
Morral — Feed bag
Rincon — Natural amphitheater in a mountain or mesa
Mast — Mixture of nuts.

Some Arizona Ranches and Brands

In the following list are only a few of the Arizona ranches mentioned in this book. To name and describe all of the ones I knew and rode for in the twenties and thirties would take up more room than there is in these pages; in fact such a write-up would make a book all by itself.

The Wagon Rod Ranch

The Boquillas Land & Cattle Company's holdings were in Cochise County at the Southeast corner of Arizona. Most of the holdings along the San Pedro River were on an old Spanish Land Grant, quite extensive in size. Ranch probably ran some 6,500 head of cattle at the time I worked there. Ranch is still in Company's possession, though only a shadow of its former size in acreage and number of cattle in the Wagon Rod brand.

"The Triangles"

Owned by the McKenzie Cattle Company. Headquarters about 2 miles north of San Simon in Northeast Cochise County. "Old General" Ranald McKenzie and his sons brought their original herd from Texas to start the ranch. After son, E. Waller McKenzie, shot neighbor, John Cameron, and was sent to the Penitentiary, "Old General" died and the ranch went out of existence in the middle twenties. Brand no longer used. Ranch ran approximately 3,000 head of cattle in 1921. Overgrazing and erosion have pretty well ruined what was once a good grass country.

The Rail N Cattle Company

Located on North side of San Simon River, extreme Southern part of Graham County. Known as the old Parks Ranch before it was taken over by John Gleeson and his two sons, Ed and Emmett. ⟋ℕ was the Company brand while Ed, the manager, owned the HX Emmett and Hugh Cavitt ran the ☼ and ⌀ brands on a few cattle they owned jointly. The entire outfit once ran about 3,000 head combined. Went into receivership to the Bank of Douglas. Dan Curtin ran it for the bank for a short time, then it was sold to the One Hundred and Eleven Land & Cattle Company of Safford, which still owns most of it.

The MOK Ranch   MOK   JJ   37

Owned by the Monk Brothers, a doctor and a judge. Located near Willcox in Northern Cochise County. Ran a couple of thousand head of cattle. Both brothers are dead. Ranch now only a very small outfit with less than 200 head of cattle.

One Hundred and Eleven Land & Cattle Company   IIIL   LL   MR

Located in Graham County. Range adjoined Rail N Ranch on the West and North of the San Simon River, almost to Solomonville. William Ellsworth, a Mormon Bishop, owned the outfit with Heber Kempton and George Felshaw as partners. Ran a couple of thousand head of cattle. Bought the ranch in 1912, then bought the Rail N Ranch about the middle twenties. Ellsworth died in 1947, and his widow and children still own and operate the ranch. Probably no more than 700 head of cattle on entire ranch now, although the sons have holdings in Colorado and elsewhere.

The Lazy B Ranch   ∞

Owned by H. C. Day. Ranch ran about 1,500 head of cattle along Eastern side of Arizona between Duncan and Steins Pass. Still owned by same family, but now a 500 head outfit. Pastures all fenced in. Horses hauled by truck, with a couple of pickups for saddles, branding irons and equipment. When they work the pastures, cook comes later in another pickup with lunch.

The Johnson and Cook Ranch   o⅛

Located between Bowie and Willcox. H. L. Johnson and J. B. Cook were quite large operators with thousands of head of cattle in as many as 39 brands, including: WGM   VV   ⇔   ⫩   ʊ̄   ⫟

7   7/   ALN   A   B35   ∈I   CEM   ƎC   (+   ᴸᴸA   HF   JWM

◄◇   ϛ℔   UX   W/A   FW   IN   ½   JA   JSL   ⊥   ℔   ℘   TR

Drought broke the partners, and by 1925 they offered fine grade 2-year-old white face heifers at $5.00 per head to anyone who would buy at the ranch. Now under name of Cook Cattle Company, ranch has only two recorded brands. Not many cattle left.

Chiricahua Cattle Company CCC   ✕

"The Cherrys" had lease on the San Carlos Apache Indian Reservation. Mostly rough country. Ran pack outfit for roundups. Had approximately 25,000 head of cattle. When all reservations were closed to white leasees, moved off to two ranches; one at Arivaca, one at Elgin the Empire Ranch. Now rather small operators, though prominent for their fine Hereford cattle.

Cross Seven Ranch   +7

Jointly owned by Frank Criswell of Phoenix and George Felton. Felton was early day bronc rider in Wild West Show that had toured many countries of the world. Felton bought out Criswell, then later bought out Harry Howell, a neighbor to the North. Small, rough range extending from Tonto River to include west slope of Sierra Ancha Mountains. Ran approximately 1,500 head of cattle. After Felton's death in 1936, outfit was sold to George Cline of Lower Tonto Basin who still owns it.

Seventy-Six Ranch   🛅

Owned by Clifford Griffin. Located on Rye Creek. At different times Griffin owned three ranches in Gila County along Salt River before Roosevelt Dam was constructed. Bought Seventy-Six Ranch in 1912. Most of range lay east of Tonto on west slope of Sierra Ancha Mountains. Rough mountain country. Ran over 3,000 head of cattle at one time. All on Tonto National Forest. Cliff died in 1943 and his wife, Laura, about 1960.

Cline Ranches

Lower Tonto Basin. Several Cline brothers were early day settlers along Lower Tonto. All raised families, and many descendants still live there. All good cowboys. George Cline now owns most of the ranches east of Tonto Creek. Among them are J Slash X ✕ , Cross Seven +7 , Vee I Vee >|<, besides his own Butcher Hook ☍ north of Roosevelt Lake. One of the best mountain cowboys I ever knew.

Chilson Ranches   —T— H̲ HI

Gila County. Good grassland and mountain country between the east slopes of the Mazatzal Range and the old Globe-Payson Highway. Headquarter ranch was the Bar T Bar, east of the foot of Ox Bow Hill. Ran approximately 5,000 head of cattle in the combined brands of the ranch. Now operating at Winslow in northern Arizona.

H Four Ranch   H⊢

Owned by France Cooper. Cooper came to Payson in 1883 at 10 years of age in wagon train with his parents. Brought cattle and horses from Missouri. In 1888 helped Tom Graham of Pleasant Valley War fame move part of his cattle to Tempe. Wife, Ella Goswick, sister of Giles Goswick, famous lion hunter. Ran approximately 600 head of cattle on east slope of Mt. Ord in Mazatzal Mountains. Sold out to Richard Taylor and was later Livestock Inspector at Payson.

Doll Baby Ranch   大 NB

Owned by Dick Taylor and Doll Baby Smith. Located on East Fork of Verde River, Southwest from Payson in Gila County. Combined with adjoining NB Ranch. Both mountain ranches. Together they probably did not run over 1,000 head of cattle. George Peters now owns the Doll Baby brand.

The Booths   Y —Y— 大̲ E̲ Æ

Family of early day migrants from Texas. Settled along Tonto River to below settlement of Gisela. The four brothers, Albert, George, Ambrose and Zack were small ranchers. Zack shot and killed two sheep herders who had driven their bands onto his range in the early days. For this he was hanged at Globe, the county seat of Gila County. Before he was taken from Payson to Globe, danced a jig and sang a song for the people of Payson on the porch of the jail.

The Babbitt Brothers Ranches

Located in the Flagstaff area. Five Babbitt brothers were early day business men of Coconino County. Owned stores and ranches. Purchased a trail herd of 1,000 head of cattle from Kansas to start their cattle venture. Formed partnerships with many small ranchers, both in cattle and sheep. At one time had as many as 27 brands, although their main brand was, and still is the 

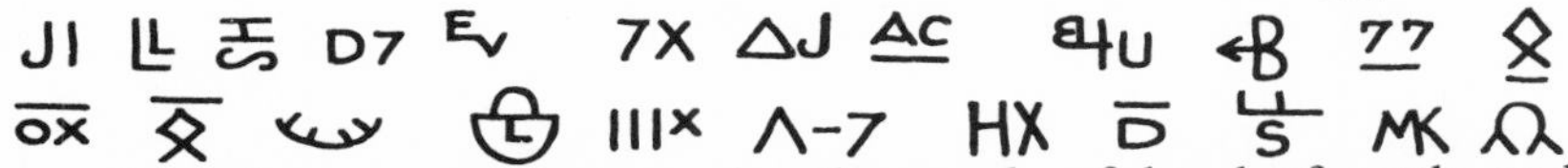

Owned, or were partners in, thousands of head of cattle and sheep in Northern Arizona. Now only run a couple of brands.

Tom Pollock

Coconino County. Originator of many cattle and sheep companies after 1895. These included the Three V Cattle Company and Grand Canyon and Willaha Sheep Companies north of Williams. Others in Chino Valley and White River. Most of these holdings, along with lumber company and saw mills were sold. Sanford Cattle Company bought some of them.

Sanford Cattle Company

Flagstaff area. At one time owned about 20 brands, among them

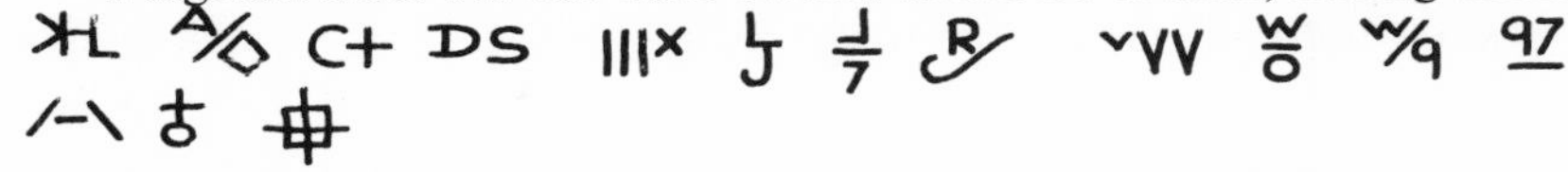

Ran thousands of head of cattle which they subsequently sold to the Pacific Loan Company of California.

Pacific Loan Company of California

Seligman area. Only used the Three V brand  . Had approximately 25,000 head at one time, then sold off all but about 5,000 head over a period of 5 years. In 1930 sold to Waggoner Ranch of Texas with the remaining 5,000 head.

Grapevine Ranch ⌐ᴛ

Located near Cave Creek in Maricopa County, approximately 30 miles north of Phoenix. Owned by Logue and Elmer Morris. Part desert, part mountain range. Drought broke them. Were offered $50,000.00 in 1918 for ranch; by 1926 owed $10,000.00 on ranch. Ran approximately 3,000 head of cattle in ⌐ᴛ and **ND** brands. Ranch has sold several times since the thirties.

DC Ranch **DC**

Ranch located on west slope of Ft. McDowell Mountains and desert of Paradise Valley north of Scottsdale. Owned by E. O. Brown and son, E. E. Brown. E. O. owned most of Scottsdale, which was only a small village in 1925. Ran approximately 4,000 head of cattle in **DC** brand. Ranch still owned by Brown and his sons, though holdings are smaller than in 1925.

6 L Ranch **6L**

Owned by John Lewis. Lay in the rough canyon of Cave Creek. Lewis and Pranty Creek just East of Fish Creek on the Apache Trail was named after John Lewis and Fred Pranty who settled on Fish Creek in the early days. There they ran big steers in the Superstition Mountains and hunted for a livelihood, trading venison for flour and coffee at Mesa and Florence. At the 6 L Ranch, John only ran about 250 head of mother cows on the National Forest. Sold to Cartwright in early 1930's.

Cartwright Cattle Company (family) **CC** **17** **ᴒ**

J. Manford Cartwright, manager, came to Salt River Valley (Phoenix) with parents in wagon from California. Ranch on upper reaches of Cave Creek. Ran approximately 3,000 head of cattle in **CC** brand. Brother Charley ran about 1,000 head in **17** brand on Tonto Forest. Small outfit now with not over 600 head. Son Jack now manages the ranch.

Sears, Kay Cattle Company   JM

Owned by Perry Sears and Harry Kay. Ran thousands of cattle along east side of Verde River. Sold ranch in 1926. Sears, Kay Cattle Company no longer in existence.

Box Bar Ranch   ▱

Owned by Billy Moore and Frank Asher. Located along the west side of Verde River. Mostly desert country below Camp Creek. Ran approximately 2,000 head of cattle. Now out of existence. Moore and Asher both dead.

Coburn Cattle Company   HK ᙆᙠ

Located in Bloody Basin along Verde River, approximately 85 miles north of Phoenix. Montana outfit drove cattle from there into Basin. Company ran thousands of head of cattle under many brands, among them ᗯ ᗡᗡ ᒪ ED ⊥U ‖ JS � Mꟼ OK

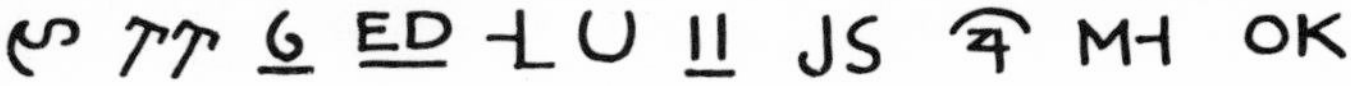

Sold most of their cattle in 1928. Moved some into Mexico.

Fifty-One Ranch   5⌐

Owned by Tom Cavness. Ran about 500 head of cows just South of Bloody Basin. Ranch was established just after Civil War by a Colonel Roundtree. Cavness bought it from Pete Letterette. Ranch was sold after Tom's death in late thirties. Now owned by William T. Cavness, a distant relative.